Watering the Seed

Watering the Seed

With Teachings from His Divine Grace
A.C. Bhaktivedanta Swami Prabhupāda

Revised and Expanded

Giriraj Swami

TorchLight Publishing
shifting the paradigm

Inside drawings by Arcā-vigraha dāsī
Cover design by Jala Keli dāsa and Māyāpriyā dāsī
Text design by Māyāpriyā dāsī

Printed in India
Published simultaneously in the United States of America and Canada by Torchlight Publishing

Library of Congress Cataloging-in-Publication Data

Giriraj, Swami, 1947-
Watering the seed : with teachings from His Divine Grace A.C. Bhaktivedanta Swami Prabhupada / revised and enlarged by Giriraj Swami. -- [2nd ed.].
p. cm.
Previously published: 2000.
Includes bibliographical references and index.
ISBN 978-0-9817273-3-2
1. A.C. Bhaktivedanta Swami Prabhupada, 1896-1977. 2. Spiritual life--International Society for Krishna Consciousness. 3. Vaishnavism. I. A.C. Bhaktivedanta Swami Prabhupada, 1896-1977. II. Title.
BL1285.892.A28G57 2010
294.5'44--dc22

2009054162

Readers interested in the subject matter of this book or wishing to correspond with the author are invited to write to:
Varsabhanavi.GRS@pamho.net or Damodar.GRS@pamho.net

TorchLight Publishing
shifting the paradigm

PO Box 52, Badger CA 93603
Phone: (559) 337-2200 Fax (559) 337-2354
torchlightpublishing@yahoo.com www.torchlight.com

To His Divine Grace A.C. Bhaktivedanta Swami Prabhupāda, who planted the seed of pure devotion in the hearts of his followers, watered it with songs and talks and books about Kṛṣṇa, and even today protects and nourishes it with his divine instructions, the fruits of this book are dedicated with love.

Contents

Foreword

In 1965 His Divine Grace A.C. Bhaktivedanta Swami Prabhupāda embarked upon a mission that would fulfill an ancient, long-awaited prophecy. His spirit of selfless compassion will be imprinted forever upon the pages of religious history. He spread the eternal message of Śrī Caitanya Mahāprabhu throughout the world. By his words and example, Śrīla Prabhupāda established that Kṛṣṇa is the Supreme Personality of Godhead, that all living beings are His eternal servants, and that the ultimate perfection of life is to awaken pure love for Kṛṣṇa through the sublime method of chanting His holy names. With tears in his eyes, Śrīla Prabhupāda would appeal to his followers to assist him in his divine service to humanity. Those illustrious souls who stepped forward to sacrifice their lives to help Śrīla Prabhupāda became the dearmost recipients of his priceless blessings. His Holiness Giriraj Swami Mahārāja is one such shining jewel in the necklace of Śrīla Prabhupāda's beloved followers.

Giriraj Swami is the son of a well-known and respected attorney, judge, philanthropist, and advocate for religious freedom. In fact, to honor his father's contributions to jurisprudence and the community, Cook County, which includes Chicago, dedicated a courtroom in his name.

After graduating from a prestigious university in Boston, Giriraj Swami dedicated his life to the path of pure devotion. Renouncing the pleasures of material opulence and prestige, he became one of the pioneers in Śrīla Prabhupāda's mission in India.

Śrīla Prabhupāda wanted to establish a temple for Śrī Śrī Rādhā and Kṛṣṇa in Bombay. There was no support. Giriraj Swami lived in sub-poverty conditions on a plot of land infested with rats, mosquitoes, and life-threatening diseases. Corrupt government officers and gangs of criminals were creating continuous dangerous disturbances. Still, Giriraj Swami remained faithful, lovingly enduring all obstacles to please his spiritual master.

His father and mother came to India. They offered him a million dollars if he would return home. But Giriraj Swami replied that his service to Śrīla Prabhupāda was a treasure beyond all the wealth in the world.

Śrīla Prabhupāda saw in Giriraj Swami a genuinely surrendered servant and thus invested him with immense responsibility and great trust. Śrīla Prabhupāda offered him the rare gift of being one of his close personal associates.

Watering the Seed is an invaluable offering to all aspirants on the path of devotion. In this book we will find many wonderful personal exchanges between Śrīla Prabhupāda and his dear disciple. Giriraj Swami kindly shares his realizations with the honesty, wisdom, and humility for which he is known and loved. This book will transport us into Śrīla Prabhupāda's intimate association during some of the most historic moments of ISKCON's development. We will be given entrance into his private quarters to see the beautiful human qualities of a world *ācārya* from behind the scenes. We will witness his gentle fatherly love toward his young and sometimes perplexed spiritual child. At the same time, Śrīla Prabhupāda's innocent childlike humor will bring joy to our hearts. We will see how Śrīla Prabhupāda, in his compassion for the fallen, conditioned souls, overcomes all opposition with unrelenting determination and faith. Throughout these pages we will hear his spontaneous philosophical perspectives both in times of crisis and in everyday life. Giriraj Swami recounts how Lord Kṛṣṇa's beloved gardener took such personal care to water the seed of devotion within his heart.

It is my great fortune to have the opportunity to write the foreword to this book, which is the first in a series of publications by my dear godbrother and friend. I pray that all who read

Watering the Seed may be blessed with ever-increasing appreciation for Śrīla Prabhupāda's monumental contribution to our lives.

Radhanath Swami

Preface

In April of 1969, when I heard Śrīla Prabhupāda for the first time, he explained that if we sow the seed of service to God and water it with chanting, God will give us the sunlight to help make it grow. I did not realize it at the time, but Śrīla Prabhupāda had just given me the seed of devotional service.

The process by which the spiritual master gives the seed of devotional service to the disciple is explained in *Śrī Caitanya-caritāmṛta* (*Madhya* 19.151):

> *brahmāṇḍa bhramite kona bhāgyavān jīva*
> *guru-kṛṣṇa-prasāde pāya bhakti-latā-bīja*

"Out of many millions of living entities wandering throughout the universe, one who is very fortunate gets an opportunity to associate with a bona fide spiritual master by the grace of Kṛṣṇa. By the mercy of both Kṛṣṇa and the spiritual master, such a person receives the seed of the creeper of devotional service."

In his purport Śrīla Prabhupāda elaborates: "Kṛṣṇa is situated in everyone's heart, and if one desires something, Kṛṣṇa fulfills one's desire. If the living entity by chance or fortune comes in contact with the Kṛṣṇa consciousness movement and wishes to associate with that movement, Kṛṣṇa, who is situated in everyone's heart, gives him the chance to meet a bona fide spiritual master. . . . Such a person is fortified by both Kṛṣṇa and the spiritual master. He is helped from within by Kṛṣṇa and from without by the spiritual master. . . .

"Everyone has dormant *kṛṣṇa-bhakti*—love for Kṛṣṇa—and in the association of good devotees, that love is revealed. As stated in *Śrī Caitanya-caritāmṛta* (*Madhya* 22.107):

> *nitya-siddha kṛṣṇa-prema 'sādhya' kabhu naya*
> *śravaṇādi-śuddha-citte karaye udaya*

"Dormant devotional service to Kṛṣṇa is within everyone.

Simply by associating with devotees, hearing their good instructions, and chanting the Hare Kṛṣṇa *mantra*, dormant love for Kṛṣṇa is awakened. In this way one acquires the seed of devotional service."

The next verse continues:

> *mālī hañā kare sei bīja āropaṇa*
> *śravaṇa-kīrtana-jale karaye secana*

"When a person receives the seed of devotional service, he should take care of it by becoming a gardener and sowing the seed in his heart. If he waters the seed gradually by the process of hearing and chanting, the seed will begin to sprout." (Cc *Madhya* 19.152)

Here Śrīla Prabhupāda explains, "By the mercy of Kṛṣṇa, one meets the bona fide spiritual master, and by the mercy of the spiritual master, the disciple is fully trained in the devotional service of the Lord.

"*Bhakti-latā-bīja* means 'the seed of devotional service.' Everything has an original cause, or seed. For any idea, program, plan, or device, there is first of all the contemplation of the plan, and that is called *bīja*, or the seed. The methods, rules, and regulations by which one is perfectly trained in devotional service constitute the *bhakti-latā-bīja*, or seed of devotional service. This *bhakti-latā-bīja* is received from the spiritual master by the grace of Kṛṣṇa. . . . The *bhakti-latā-bīja* can be received only through the mercy of the spiritual master. Therefore one has to satisfy the spiritual master to get the *bhakti-latā-bīja* (*yasya prasādād bhagavat-prasādaḥ*). Unless one satisfies the spiritual master, he gets the *bīja*, or root cause, of *karma*, *jñāna*, and *yoga* without the benefit of devotional service. However, one who is faithful to his spiritual master gets the *bhakti-latā-bīja*. . . .

"After receiving the spiritual master's mercy, one must repeat his instructions, and this is called *śravaṇa-kīrtana*—hearing and chanting. . . . One has to water the *bhakti-latā-bīja* after receiving instructions from the spiritual master."

By Śrīla Prabhupāda's mercy we received the seed of devotional service, and since then we have tried to water it by hearing and chanting about Kṛṣṇa.

The present volume is a collection of my efforts to water the original seed Śrīla Prabhupāda gave me when we first met. Several disciples and friends suggested I publish a collection of anecdotes and articles about Śrīla Prabhupāda and Kṛṣṇa consciousness, including already-published as well as new material. I have endeavored to glorify Kṛṣṇa and His devotees for my own purification, to water my own *bhakti-latā-bīja*. At the same time, if some spray or droplets of water touch the devotional creepers in your hearts—the hearts of the readers—I will consider my effort to be supremely successful.

Hare Kṛṣṇa.

Giriraj Swami

Acknowledgements

I would like to thank the following persons who contributed to the publication of this book:

Śacīnandana Swami for suggesting this revised and enlarged edition;

Bhakta Carl Herzig for editing and standardizing the text and for encouraging and advising me at every stage of production;

Viśākhā Priyā for editing, proofreading, and standardizing the text;

Vārṣabhānavī for transcribing recordings, formatting, and numerous other production contributions;

Acyuta, Bhakti Bṛhat Bhāgavata Swami, Dāmodara, Gaurī, Karuṇāmayī, Kṛśāṅgī, Kuntīdevī, Mira, Nāma Cintāmaṇi, Nikuñja Vilāsinī, Rādhā-pada-dhūli, Śikhi Māhiti, Svarūpa Dāmodara, Ṭhākura Haridāsa, and others too numerous to mention by name who have helped directly or indirectly.

I pray that Śrīla Prabhupāda will continue to inspire them in their service to *guru* and Gaurāṅga.

May God bless them.

Hare Kṛṣṇa.

Prologue

Finding a Perfect Master

During my college years I had the idea to attain perfection. I began reading spiritual books and learned I needed a *guru*, someone who could bring me to an enlightened state of consciousness. So whenever I heard about a *guru* anywhere—even a thousand miles away—I would go to meet him. One teacher I met was a Zen master, supposedly enlightened and certified by another enlightened master in Japan. I had read a book he had written, *The Three Pillars of Zen*, and he was holding a three-day retreat at his ashram in Rochester, New York, so I went. Upon my arrival there I found that his students were not very happy. But I thought, "Anyway, they're just students. Let me meet the master."

During the retreat he held meditation sessions in which everyone had to sit up very straight and look at the wall, concentrating on some object he would give us. The master walked around with a stick, and if he thought any of us was falling asleep or that his or her mind was wandering, he would hit us. After one such session, some of his students asked him about his recently having become angry. "Yes, it's true," he said. "I lost my temper; I shouldn't have." I started to doubt whether he was my *guru*. But because I had read that a Zen master might appear ordinary and that one might not recognize him, I thought, "Maybe this is part of it." But my doubt remained. Later he came to Boston, near Brandeis University, where I was in my last year as a psychology major. After his talk and demonstration, someone in the audience asked about *Vedānta*. "I have enough trouble keeping up with Zen," he answered. "How do you expect me to know about *Vedānta*?" My previous doubt was confirmed; I realized, "He is not my perfect master."

Then a *haṭha-yogī* came to Brandeis to give a lecture. He had long hair and a beard and flowing robes. He said that by yoga you could attain complete mastery over your bodily functions, including the movements of the bowels. You could actually command your intestines: "Ascending colon, advance! Transverse colon, advance! Descending colon, advance!" and finally, "Rectum, pass!" I was really looking for a *guru*, so I thought, "Anyway, maybe."

After the lecture, I tried to meet the swami, but he was leaving for the airport. I wanted to ride with him in his car, but there was no room. Instead, I rode in a car with some of his students. On the way, they discussed the various foods they missed since they had joined the ashram. So I started to have some doubts. But then I thought, "Anyway, they are just the students; the master may be on a much higher level." Then, when we arrived at the airport, I beheld the swami. There he was—long flowing hair, beard, draping orange robes, a flower in his hair, a twinkle in his eyes—the very picture of Indian spirituality. But then I saw him tightly embracing his women disciples. And I knew: "He is not my perfect master. I have to keep looking."

Next I heard of an "enlightened" psychology professor who was teaching at Antioch College, in Ohio, which was known as a progressive university. I wanted to meet him immediately. Ready to do anything to find my *guru*, I got in my car and drove the seven hundred miles. When I arrived, with great anticipation and eagerness I searched out the professor's office and inquired about him from his secretary. "He's playing golf," she informed me. "Playing golf?" I asked incredulously. "I thought he was supposed to be enlightened." "That is his Zen," she replied. "Oh, no!" I thought. "Playing golf? He is not my perfect master."

Although I was disappointed about the professor, the Antioch campus was full of people interested in spiritual life, and while I was there I spoke with some of them. Some students in the Student Union told me about a swami who had recently visited the campus. "The *guru* is in the heart," he had said, "where he sits on a lotus flower. You can actually see him and speak with him." "Wow," I thought; *that* sounded attractive. That night I tried to really focus on my heart. And indeed, I got a very strong impression that there *was* a divine personality there, with whom I could have a sublime, personal relationship. And He seemed just about to speak. I was very excited, and I became eager to meet Him.

Back at Brandeis, my psychology professor invited J. Krishnamurti to speak. I attended his lecture, and during a break I told my professor I wanted to meet him. "Why?" my professor asked. "I may want him as my *guru*," I replied. "Oh, he doesn't accept disciples," my professor said. "He doesn't even touch money." My professor was impressed. But I wasn't. I thought, "If he is actually able to help people, why should he refuse? Just to be renounced? He is not my perfect master."

Still, I kept searching. I had gotten the idea from reading books that you don't have to find your *guru* or choose him; he is already there. All I had to do was recognize him. I even had a mental picture of what my *guru* looked like—and he didn't have hair. All the swamis and yogis I had encountered had long hair and beards, so I was starting to despair: "How am I ever going to meet my *guru*?"

Then one day I saw a poster on campus: Lecture—Bhagavad-gita As It Is—Swami Bhaktivedanta. Although my friends and I were supposed to go to the movies that night, I wanted to attend the lecture instead. When I suggested that, however, one friend in particular got really upset. "Why can't you be normal like other people?" she complained. "All you want to do is see swamis and yogis." And the argument became so intense that I decided not to go. I didn't want to disappoint my friends, so I tried to go along with their idea. But there was something inside me that kept impelling me to go to the lecture. Finally I said, "Okay, let's go to a later show. First I have to go to the lecture by the swami. I promise, he will be the last one I ever go to."

My friends reluctantly came along, but because we'd been arguing, we arrived at the auditorium late and missed the lecture.

Entering the auditorium, I beheld an elderly Indian gentleman sitting on a cushion on stage—Swami Bhaktivedanta. As soon as I saw him, two things struck me: he was so effulgent I could hardly focus on his form, and he had no hair; he was clean-shaven. To the side a young devotee, Satsvarūpa dāsa, sang into a microphone, and other devotees were dancing in a circle around the *guru*. Satsvarūpa was singing right into the microphone, and the sound was reverberating off the bare brick walls. One by one students from the audience jumped onto the stage and joined in, and I also felt like going up, but I knew my friends wouldn't approve; that would have been too much. More students were jumping up, climbing on the stage, and joining the circle, dancing. I kept trying to focus my eyes on the *guru*, but I couldn't; his effulgence was too great.

When the *kīrtana* ended, Satsvarūpa announced from the stage that if anyone was driving to Boston or Harvard Square, the devotees needed a lift. As my friends and I were still going to the movie and it was at Harvard Square, I invited the devotees to ride with us, and everyone piled into my red Rambler station wagon. I was the driver, and also in front were two ladies. In the back seat were three or four devotees and in the rear compartment I don't even know how many—I don't think we could have fit anyone else.

Satsvarūpa was squeezed in the rear with my best friend, Gary. Because of our impersonal readings, my friend was saying that ultimately everything is void. And Satsvarūpa was saying, "There is no void in the creation of God." But my friend kept insisting: "Everything is ultimately void." I was overhearing them from the front, and puffed up as I was, I thought, "Oh, how silly that they are arguing over this." I thought I had it all figured out. So I turned to the back and announced something

I had read in some Zen book: "It is not void, and it is not not-void, but to give it a name, we call it the void." I thought I had resolved the whole controversy. But still, they kept arguing; my pronouncement didn't stop them.

One of the ladies in the front seat was named Jāhnavā. I had been trying to understand all the different paths and philosophies, so I asked her about Zen. She told me, "This world seems real, but it is illusory, like images on a movie screen. Now, if you withdraw your consciousness from the screen, you will find there is a beam of light." And I thought, "This is the best explanation I've ever heard, even better than the Zen books." "And if you keep following that beam of light back," she continued, "you come to a point." I thought, "Wow, this is getting to the void." But then she said, "But behind that point there is a projector, and behind the projector there is a person." Then I thought, "This philosophy encompasses everything that Zen does, and more."

Then I asked her about Yogananda. She dismissed him out of hand: "Oh, he is just a shopkeeper. Whatever you want, he keeps in stock. You want yoga, he will give you that. Whatever you ask for, he pulls off the shelf." Then she said, "At his ashram in California he has a Gandhi peace memorial. But Gandhi wasn't a worker for world peace. He was a politician who wanted to drive the British out of India." She just dismissed Yogananda: "He doesn't even know who Gandhi is."

I thought, "She is speaking with authority." But I sensed it couldn't all be coming from her. How was it possible for such a young girl of twenty or so years to have so much knowledge and speak with such authority? But she did have authority. And I knew it wasn't coming from her. Then I thought, "This must be coming from her teacher. I want to meet him."

When we got to Harvard Square, I let the devotees out. But as I was driving away, I realized I didn't know how to get in touch with them. How would I meet the *guru*? I immediately stopped the car at the center of Harvard Square, jumped out, and ran after them. I caught up to one, Patita-pāvana. When he stopped, he turned his head and pointed to the crowd around us. "You see these people?" he said. "They're all sleepwalkers. They don't know what they're doing, or why. They're just conforming." His words were so intriguing and deep; I wanted to hear more. Suddenly I became aware of the honking of horns all around us. I'd left my car in the middle of the roundabout, and the traffic at Harvard Square was backed up. The honking kept getting louder. "I want to meet the *guru*," I said quickly. "Quick, give me the address." "Come at seven," he said, "tomorrow night." I could hardly wait.

The next evening when I arrived, the small storefront temple was packed with young people. At the far end, Śrīla Prabhupāda sat on a cushion. The walls were decorated with exotic paintings, and the aroma of incense filled the air. When he began speaking, I had difficulty understanding what he was saying. He had a thick Bengali accent, and the philosophy was new to me. But I did hear him say that out of many thousands of men, one will seek perfection. "That's me!" I thought. "He's talking about me!"

After the lecture, Śrīla Prabhupāda called for questions. Someone asked, "Since everything comes from God, or Kṛṣṇa, does *māyā* also come from Kṛṣṇa?" Śrīla Prabhupāda replied that everything comes from Kṛṣṇa, just like everything comes from the sun. The cloud also comes from the sun, although it covers our vision of the sun. But the sun is never covered by the cloud; only our vision is covered.

Burning to ask my question, I raised my hand. "There are so many swamis and yogis," I began, "and each recommends a different process of self-realization, and each says that his is the best. So how do I know which is actually best?"

Prabhupāda responded, "What is your goal? Do you want to serve God, or do you want to become God? If you want to become God, that means you are not God now. And how can not-God become God? God is God. He is always God. He doesn't have to become God by meditation. Kṛṣṇa is always God. He is God when He is playing on the lap of Mother Yaśodā; He is God when He is fighting at Kurukṣetra; He's God when He's speaking the *Bhagavad-gītā* to Arjuna. That is God. So, if you want to serve God and you sow the seed of devotional service and water it by chanting, God will provide the sunlight and all other favorable conditions to make it grow. But if you want to become God, then why should God help the competition?" Then he said, "God is in your heart. He is ready to help you. You can become godly—but you cannot become God. If you want to become God, you are only cheating yourself."

As Śrīla Prabhupāda spoke, I got the clear impression that he knew everything about me, that he was seeing right into me, into Waltham, into my apartment, into my bathroom, right to the wall on which I had pasted a sign I had inscribed in beautiful ornate lettering: You Are God.

"So what do you think?" Śrīla Prabhupāda asked gravely. "Do you want to serve God, or do you want to become God?" I felt so ashamed. My abominable desire to become God had been exposed. Still, I didn't want to admit it. "I want to serve God," I said. But I knew that I couldn't fool Śrīla Prabhupāda. He knew everything. How could I cheat him? Within a second I admitted, "I want to serve God, but I can see that I was trying to become God." And Śrīla Prabhupāda affirmed emphatically, "Yes!"

My search was over. I offered my obeisances. I had found my spiritual master.

The devotees put their heads on the floor and offered obeisances. I also kept my head on the floor in surrender, for a long time. I felt so glad. I had finally found my perfect master and wanted to surrender fully. At the same time I also felt ashamed and humiliated—everyone there knew I had wanted to become God. After some time I heard sounds that indicated that devotees were distributing food, *prasāda*, to the guests and other devotees. Something inside prompted me to look up. I expected everyone would be glaring at me, but no. People were blissfully taking *prasāda*, and when they saw me get up they simply smiled. The *prasāda* looked like everything else in the temple—colorful, attractive, and variegated. Because of macrobiotics and other speculations, I had not expected a feast. But where to begin? I picked up what must have been a cauliflower *pakorā*, put it in my mouth, bit into it . . . and felt an explosion of taste. One by one I sampled the preparations: *vaḍa*, sweet rice—every taste new, incomparable. I thought everything was perfect: the *guru*, the *prasāda*, the chanting.

I loved the chanting. The devotees had a sign with the Hare Kṛṣṇa *mantra* written in Indian style lettering. During the *kīrtana*, as I was looking at the letters on the sign, they started to move, dissolve, form, and unform themselves. These were the things I was looking for, and everything indicated that this was it.

From the time Śrīla Prabhupāda answered my question and I bowed my head, I surrendered. From that first meeting, my whole life's purpose became to bring people to meet Śrīla Prabhupāda. And I was able to do that for many years. But when he passed away, I wondered, *What will be my service now?* My whole service had been to bring people to Śrīla Prabhupāda.

Now I understand that Śrīla Prabhupāda is always present, and that by speaking of him, hearing about him, remembering him, and, most significantly, by studying his books and following his instructions, we can experience his presence. So I can continue doing what I was doing when he was personally present—introducing souls to Śrīla Prabhupāda—and that is what I feel most natural doing. Because I know that somehow or other, if someone comes in touch with Śrīla Prabhupāda, his life will be successful.

Śrīla Prabhupāda in the Boston temple, 1969

"You can become godly, but you cannot become God."

Devotees chanting the holy names in Boston

"If you chant Hare Kṛṣṇa, all your problems will be solved—materially and spiritually."

Śrīla Prabhupāda chanting at the first Bombay paṇḍāl

"The process of cleansing in this age is the *saṅkīrtan yajña*. It is authorized by the *śāstra*. And because it is being properly performed, it is taking effect all over the world."

Śrīla Prabhupāda reading Śrīmad-Bhāgavatam at Juhu

"By reading the book *Bhāgavata* or by serving the person *bhāgavata*, one gets the same result."

Śrīla Prabhupāda at Cheviot Hills Park, Los Angeles

A disciple said to Śrīla Prabhupāda, "Everyone likes you so much," and Prabhupada replied, "Yes, because I like everyone."

Śrīla Prabhupāda with Dr. Patel and friends on Juhu Beach

"Our duty is to engage everyone."

Śrīla Prabhupāda praying before Śrī Śrī Rādha-Rāsabihārī

"We are successful because we try to please Kṛṣṇa."

Śrīla Prabhupāda accepting guru-pūjā in Juhu

"He who has opened our eyes with transcendental knowledge is our lord, birth after birth."

Śrīla Prabhupāda walking on Juhu Beach
"Whatever I may be, I am an eternal servant of Kṛṣṇa."

Śrīla Prabhupāda with disciples on Juhu Beach

"When we have our perfect master to serve we become peaceful, *praśānta*, and jubilant."

Śrīla Prabhupāda in his new quarters in Juhu, 1977

"He lives forever by his divine instructions, and the follower lives with him."

1

Anecdotes

Service to Man and Service to God

Before I met Śrīla Prabhupāda, I had the desire to serve humanity. Then from Śrīla Prabhupāda I heard about the importance of service to Lord Kṛṣṇa. Still the question remained—How does God's service relate to man's?

In May of 1969, after one week of hearing from Śrīla Prabhupāda, I got the chance to ask.

Śrīla Prabhupāda had just concluded his lecture:

sa vai puṁsāṁ paro dharmo
yato bhaktir adhokṣaje
ahaituky apratihatā
yayātmā suprasīdati

"Without spiritual realization, you cannot have peace of mind. If you want to have peace of mind, peace in the world, peace in your society, peace in your family, simply by amassing money, by material advancement, it will never be possible. But if you improve a little in spiritual life, you will immediately become happy. . . .

"So now, if you have any questions, you can ask."

"You talk about service to Lord Kṛṣṇa," I began. "How does service to our fellow man come in?"

"Why are you and others coming here?" Śrīla Prabhupāda replied. "Are we not rendering service? To deliver one from the illusory material existence and bring him to Kṛṣṇa consciousness is the best service.

"What is the meaning of service? To give relief from suffering. And Kṛṣṇa consciousness gives the best relief, as confirmed in the *Bhāgavatam* [1.2.6]: 'The best service, the best religion, the best philosophy is that which teaches one how to serve God.' And as soon as one comes to serve God without any motive, immediately he becomes satisfied (*yayātmā suprasīdati*).

"As a five-year-old boy, Dhruva Mahārāja was insulted by his stepmother. Still he wanted his father's kingdom. So his mother advised him, 'Only God can help you.' Immediately Dhruva went to the forest to find God. But when actually he saw God he said, 'My Lord, I do not want anything. I am fully satisfied. I came looking for some pieces of broken glass, but now I have found the most valuable jewel.' When one discovers his eternal relationship with God, he feels, 'I have nothing more to ask.' And to bring a man to feel 'I have no more demands, I am fully satisfied' is the best service.

"What is this so-called material service? Suppose I am hungry and you give me some food; will I not be hungry again? Of course, the Kṛṣṇa conscious movement also gives food. But we are giving food that will make one satisfied forever. No more hunger, no more demands. 'I am fully satisfied' (*svāmin kṛtārtho 'smi*). 'I have no more demands' (*varaṁ na yāce*). To think you can satisfy your hunger materially is simply illusion. America is materially advanced. But are you satisfied? So many frustrated young people, hippies, are there. Still, the rascals think, 'If we become rich like America, we shall become happy.' One will never be satisfied by material adjustment.

"Actual happiness comes when you learn to love God, and that can be achieved without any material advancement. Anywhere you are, in any condition of life, you can simply chant Hare Kṛṣṇa and develop such love. Then you will say, 'Now I am fully satisfied. I do not want anything else. No more stealing, no more pick-pocketing, no more cheating. Because I have no want, why shall I cheat?'"

Śrīla Prabhupāda's words entered deep in my heart. Although I prided myself on my honesty, I had one weakness: I had been turned on to shoplifting, pocketing little things here and there. But Śrīla Prabhupāda's statement "no more pick-pocketing" made me realize how fallen I actually was—and how I could be saved by Kṛṣṇa consciousness.

Śrīla Prabhupāda continued, "Perhaps you know the story. A saintly person was sitting in a solitary place, almost naked.

Alexander the Great asked him, 'Can I do something for you?' He replied, 'Please stand aside. You are making a shadow. That's all.' Because he was fully satisfied, what could Alexander the Great do for him?

yaṁ labdhvā cāparaṁ lābhaṁ
manyate nādhikaṁ tataḥ
yasmin sthito na duḥkhena
guruṇāpi vicālyate

You will find in *Bhagavad-gītā* [6.22] that if you are situated in the transcendental position, you have no more demands and are not disturbed even in the greatest difficulty. This is life—to be satisfied in any condition. And this peace can be achieved only by Kṛṣṇa consciousness."

I was satisfied. There was no need to look any further. Śrīla Prabhupāda could answer every question.

The only way to be peaceful and happy in life was to follow Śrīla Prabhupāda and become Kṛṣṇa conscious. And the best way to serve others was to give them Kṛṣṇa consciousness.

Śrīla Prabhupāda had shown the way perfectly. Now I simply had to follow.

If I Tell You I Am God, Will You Believe Me?

Every Sunday in Boston we used to go to Cambridge Commons to do *kīrtana*. Different rock bands used to come and perform, and thousands of young people used to come and hear, dance, picnic, wander around and mingle, or just sit. So on Sundays Satsvarūpa would lead the devotees to an area in the commons where they would chant and dance in a circle, joined by other young people. And some devotees used to wander around the crowd to distribute books and get donations.

At that time, 1969–1970, there was a lot of interest in spiritual life, and one boy I approached was especially friendly. He said he was interested and had an Indian *guru* who was God. I said, "How do you know he is God?"

"He says he's God."

"Just because he says he's God you believe him?"

"Yes."

"So if I tell you I am the president of the United States you will also believe me? Being president is not as great as being God."

"Yes, I will believe you."

"Very good. So if I am the president you have to do what I say."

"Yes."

So I said, "Take all your money from your pocket."

He took out all his money. There was a lot! In those days young people didn't have much money, but he pulled out ninety-seven dollars.

"You accept that I am the president?"

"Yes." He was stubborn; he didn't want to admit his philosophy was wrong. He persisted just to maintain his false prestige.

So I said, "Okay, give me all your money." He gave me his money, and in return I gave him a book, invited him to the temple, and disappeared in the crowd.

About two hours later the boy found me, still distributing. "You know, I just gave you my whole pay, and tomorrow I have to pay the rent. Could you give me twenty dollars?"

Śrīla Prabhupāda heard about the incident and was pleased. He even mentioned it in one conversation in Los Angeles: "Our Giriraj took some money. Yes. Somebody said, 'Everyone is God.' So Giriraj said, 'I am God?' 'Yes, you are God.' 'Then I can take your money?' 'Yes.' And he gave him some money, all the money. Out of sentiment, whatever money he had in his pocket, he gave him." When one devotee commented that the boy had been caught in his own philosophy Śrīla Prabhupāda agreed, "Yes."

Śrīla Prabhupāda preached vehemently against the impersonal philosophy, following his own spiritual master, Śrīla Bhaktisiddhānta Sarasvatī Ṭhākura, for whom, in appreciation, he wrote:

> Absolute is sentient, thou hast proved,
> Impersonal calamity, thou hast moved.

Śrīla Bhaktisiddhānta Sarasvatī Ṭhākura in turn appreciated how Śrīla Prabhupāda had understood his mission. We can similarly be recognized by our spiritual master, Śrīla Prabhupāda, if we understand his mission and execute it to the best of our ability.

So this is our line, *paramparā*, and this is our mission: to demolish the *māyāvāda* philosophy and establish the *bhakti-siddhānta*—the conclusion of pure devotion—through Śrīla Prabhupāda's books.

Śrīla Prabhupāda's Equal Vision

One of the most wonderful experiences in my life came when I accompanied Śrīla Prabhupāda on his tour of India from October 1970 to February 1972. While every experience with Śrīla Prabhupāda was wonderful, traveling with him as he spread Kṛṣṇa consciousness was especially so. We visited Bombay, Amritsar, Indore, Surat, Allahabad, Gorakhpur, Calcutta, Delhi, Madras, and Māyāpur.

In December 1970, on the invitation of the Gita Bhavan, Śrīla Prabhupāda and a party of disciples traveled to Indore to participate in the week-long celebration of Gītā Jayantī. Unfortunately, most of the speakers were Māyāvādī impersonalists, who did not preach the *Bhagavad-gītā* as it is or present Kṛṣṇa as He is.

In Indore, many gentlemen would come to meet Śrīla Prabhupāda in his room—usually with their own ideas of spiritual life. In fact, Śrīla Prabhupāda had even complained, "They come to the *guru* with their own opinions to see if the *guru* will agree. If the *guru* agrees, he is very good. But if the *guru* disagrees, they think, 'He is not good.'"

One argument between Śrīla Prabhupāda and some guests was especially instructive. On the previous night, Śrīla Prabhupāda had delivered a lecture at the Gita Samiti Hall, where Śrīla Prabhupāda was appalled to find there was no picture of Kṛṣṇa. The next day Śrīla Prabhupāda raised the issue with his guests to point out that persons are not properly understanding and presenting the *Bhagavad-gītā* and its speaker, Lord Kṛṣṇa. Śrīla Prabhupāda explained that his mission was to present the *Bhagavad-gītā* properly, as it is—and to expose those who did not.

PRABHUPĀDA: Bona fide spiritual master means one who carries out the order of higher authorities. We are carrying out the order of Caitanya Mahāprabhu, or Kṛṣṇa. Kṛṣṇa taught the *Bhagavad-gītā*, and He stated, "Anyone who preaches the confidential message of the *Bhagavad-gītā* is very dear to Me."

GUEST: We believe in an incorporeal God, *nirākāra*.

PRABHUPĀDA: Who says, "incorporeal?" Who says?

GUEST: You find it all over India, that incorporeal form—*jyotir-liṅga*.

PRABHUPĀDA: That's all right. You are bringing something besides the *Bhagavad-gītā*. Just try to understand. In this International Society for Krishna Consciousness we are preaching the *Bhagavad-gītā*. *Jyotir-liṅga*—these theories may be in other literatures. But we are particularly interested in preaching the *Bhagavad-gītā*. And because the *Bhagavad-gītā* is being preached wrongly all over the world, with nonsense commentation, we want to rectify it. Therefore our society is especially named "Kṛṣṇa conscious."

GUEST: What is wrongly preached about *Gītā*?

PRABHUPĀDA: Just like yesterday, I went to that Gita Samiti. There is a lamp. Why a lamp instead of Kṛṣṇa? Kṛṣṇa is a lamp? Therefore I say it is being wrongly preached. Why there is a lamp? Does Kṛṣṇa say?

GUEST: Lamp has been with us for more than . . .

PRABHUPĀDA: That's all right. Kṛṣṇa has also been there.

GUEST: They must evolve . . .

PRABHUPĀDA: No, no. The first thing is that the *Bhagavad-gītā* is spoken by Kṛṣṇa. So why there is no picture of Kṛṣṇa? That means you have not understood Kṛṣṇa. Therefore your so-called Gita Society is not bona fide. Even in ordinary affairs, if there is some political meeting, you keep Gandhi's photo, Nehru's photo, because they are the political leaders. Gita Samiti is preaching the *Bhagavad-gītā*, and there is not a single picture of Kṛṣṇa. This is misguided.

Now Gita Bhavan, they have invited me because we are teaching the *Bhagavad-gītā*, and that was the *Gītā's jayantī*—and the speaker of the *Gītā* is not present? Therefore I say that there are so many places, even here, that are wrongly representing the *Bhagavad-gītā*. So our position is to rectify that wrong propaganda.

GUEST (2): What is that wrong propaganda?

PRABHUPĀDA: That is one instance. There are many. Just like in the ninth chapter, there is *man-manā bhava mad-bhakto mad-yājī māṁ namaskuru*. Lord Kṛṣṇa says, "Engage your mind always in thinking of Me, become My devotee, offer obeisances to Me, and worship Me." But Dr. Radhakrishnan says, "It is not to the person Kṛṣṇa." Where does he get this nonsense idea?

GUEST (1): No, Vivekananda has also said that.

PRABHUPĀDA: Therefore I say they are all nonsense. They are all nonsense who deviate from the original text of the *Bhagavad-gītā*.

The guests challenged Śrīla Prabhupāda's statement that his presentation of the *Bhagavad-gītā* was correct whereas others' presentations were not. They said he should see and treat others with "equal vision."

GUEST (5): If each and every person has an individual identity of soul above the body, unless you treat him as equal . . .

PRABHUPĀDA: There are three *guṇas*, and *Bhagavad-gītā* analyzes, "These persons are in *sattva-guṇa*, these persons are in *rajo-guṇa*, these persons are in *tamo-guṇa*."

GUEST (5): That is not the personality of the *ātmā*. The *ātmā* is everybody's soul. If you have the potency to rise and go higher and higher . . .

PRABHUPĀDA: You are not in the *ātmā* stage; I am not in the *ātmā* stage. You are in the bodily stage.

GUEST (5): Both—body and soul together.

Śrīla Prabhupāda in turn challenged the guests—if they saw everyone equally, why did they find fault with him? "If you are in the *ātmā* stage," he asserted, "you have no argument with me. *Paṇḍitāḥ sama-darśinaḥ*. This is stated in the *Bhagavad-gītā* (5.18):

vidyā-vinaya-sampanne
brāhmaṇe gavi hastini
śuni caiva śva-pāke ca
paṇḍitāḥ sama-darśinaḥ

'The humble sage, by virtue of true knowledge, sees with equal vision a learned and gentle *brāhmaṇa*, a cow, an elephant, a dog, and a dog-eater.'"

Another GUEST (3) agreed, "That is the correct position."

PRABHUPĀDA: That is correct position. But if you find that "Swamiji is not on the standard," that means you are not in the position, *sama-darśinaḥ*.

GUEST (3): But that means that if a person commits a murder, a sinner . . .

PRABHUPĀDA: Yes, that is very high stage, *sama-darśinaḥ*. *Sama-darśinaḥ* means there is no distinction between what is sin and what is virtue. As soon as you see "This is virtue and this is sin," it is not *sama-darśinaḥ*. Here it is said clearly, *vidyā-vinaya-sampanne brāhmaṇe*. A *brāhmaṇa* is learned and *vinaya*, "very humble"—these are signs of goodness. *Vidyā-vinaya-*

sampanne brāhmaṇe gavi hastini śuni. Śuni means "dog." He sees a dog and a learned *brāhmaṇa* the same. Now, the dog is supposed to be sinful, and this learned *brāhmaṇa* is supposed to be virtuous. Therefore in his vision, the virtuous and the sinful are the same. That is *sama-darśī.*

GUEST (1): I think they have made many mistakes in writing the *ślokas.*

PRABHUPĀDA: That's all right. Now you are finding faults in Vyāsa, so who can talk with you? Please excuse me. Please go out. You are finding faults with Vyāsa.

GUEST (4): We only want you to be understood here.

PRABHUPĀDA shouted: I am not *sama-darśī.* I don't say I am *sama-darśī.* You say *sama-darśī.*

GUEST (2): You should be *sama-darśī.*

PRABHUPĀDA: But I'm not in that stage. I say because you don't surrender to Kṛṣṇa, you are sinful. That is my *darśaṇa.*

GUEST (5): You should also be seeing as *sama-darśinaḥ.*

PRABHUPĀDA: No, why shall I? I am not in that position. I am simply repeating the words of Kṛṣṇa. That is my point. I may be *sama-darśī*; I may not be *sama-darśī.* My position is simply to repeat. That's all.

In his books Śrīla Prabhupāda had explained that one on the highest platform does not make distinctions. He sees everyone engaged in the service of the Lord. But when one takes the position of *ācārya,* or preacher, he must make distinctions for the sake of instructing others and delivering them. Even the highest devotee acts on the intermediate platform when he preaches.

I remembered Śrīla Prabhupāda's strong criticism of persons who are still in the bodily concept of life but who try to imitate the highest devotee. "The *uttama-adhikārī* [highest devotee] knows that there is no difference between a vastly learned *brāhmaṇa* and a dog in the street, because both of them are of the Lord, although they are embodied differently according to the qualities of material nature. . . . Such a learned devotee is not misled by material bodies but is attracted by the spiritual within the respective entities.

"Those who imitate an *uttama-adhikārī* by flaunting a sense of oneness or fellowship but who behave on the bodily platform are actually false philanthropists. . . . The *uttama-adhikārī* sees the living entity's soul and serves him as spirit. Thus the material aspect is automatically served." (*Īśopaniṣad* 6 purport)

Finally, a sixth guest raised one last question.

> GUEST (6): But every successive teacher has added some interpretations of the knowledge, no?
>
> GUEST (4): You are the successor of somebody.
>
> PRABHUPĀDA: Yes. Yes.
>
> GUEST (5): Then what is your contribution? That is what we are asking. What is *sama-darśī*? Have you become *sama-darśī*?
>
> GUEST (6): You are teaching others to be *sama-darśī*.
>
> PRABHUPĀDA: My *sama-darśī* is that why should only Hindus know Kṛṣṇa. The whole world should know Kṛṣṇa. But if you, the Hindus, refuse to know, what can I do?

Here Śrīla Prabhupāda answered their challenge. By his practical work he had made Kṛṣṇa consciousness available to all persons all over the world. That was his equal vision, and that was his contribution—to his predecessors, and to us. Śrīla Prabhupāda had presented Kṛṣṇa as the Supreme Personality of Godhead and the *Bhagavad-gītā* as it is, and people all over the world were accepting and becoming Kṛṣṇa's devotees. The guests were impressed. And if they wanted, they could also follow and benefit.

Special Prerogative

Generally, on his tour Śrīla Prabhupāda would address large public gatherings in the evening and meet individuals or small groups during the day. While speaking about Kṛṣṇa consciousness to Indians, Śrīla Prabhupāda touched one young American who was touring India. The young man began to travel with us, and sometimes he would sit next to me when we took our meals of *kṛṣṇa-prasāda*. "Kṛṣṇa is definitely God!" he would exclaim. "Otherwise, how could I—such a lowly creature—get such nice *prasāda* every day? Kṛṣṇa is truly merciful."

After associating with us for some days, the young man had learned enough of the philosophy to ask Śrīla Prabhupāda a question: "If all service is absolute, why do we have to chant sixteen rounds?" Śrīla Prabhupāda answered, but somehow the young man was not satisfied and repeatedly pressed his point.

Finally, Śrīla Prabhupāda sat erect, and in a grave voice said, "Why chant sixteen rounds? Because the Supreme Personality of Godhead wants you to!" Even then the young man persisted.

> YOUNG MAN: Why is any one activity of Kṛṣṇa consciousness better than another? Take, for example, chanting sixteen rounds. Suppose you've served Kṛṣṇa twenty-three hours, and in the last hour you can either finish your rounds or enroll someone as a life member of ISKCON. Instead of chanting your sixteen rounds . . .
>
> ŚRĪLA PRABHUPĀDA: You cannot concoct. You have to abide by the orders of Kṛṣṇa.
>
> YOUNG MAN: Then why . . .
>
> ŚRĪLA PRABHUPĀDA: There is no question of "why." It is the order of Kṛṣṇa's representative. You have to abide by that. You cannot say, "Why?" As soon as you say, "Why?" then you are not fully surrendered. Surrender

means there is no "Why?" It is ordered; it has to be done. That's all.

Young Man: Suppose, for example, last night I was chanting. Then I thought, "Oh, I'm not concentrating on the chanting anymore. Now I should go to sleep."

Śrīla Prabhupāda: Therefore we have prescribed rules for chanting. You must finish sixteen rounds. Then go to sleep. You finish sixteen rounds and sleep the whole day. I have no objection. [laughter]

Young Man: But then . . .

Śrīla Prabhupāda: There is no "then." If you are so addicted to sleeping, you simply chant sixteen rounds and sleep the whole day. But then, also, don't take food. [laughter] Don't get up for taking *prasāda*: "Now I have to honor *prasāda*. Let me eat sumptuously and then again sleep." Still, if you cannot do anything else, simply chant sixteen rounds, take *prasāda*, and sleep. It is a special prerogative for you.

Śrīla Prabhupāda's words were always full of truth, and sometimes full of humor. Subsequently, while studying *Śrī Caitanya-caritāmṛta* (*Madhya* 22.113), I found a philosophical truth underlying Śrīla Prabhupāda's humorous reply. The basic principle of regulative devotional service is to always remember Kṛṣṇa and never forget Him:

smartavyaḥ satataṁ viṣṇur
vismartavyo na jātucit
sarve vidhi-niṣedhāḥ syur
etayor eva kiṅkarāḥ

Commenting on this verse from the *Padma Purāṇa*, Śrīla Prabhupāda writes: "There are many regulative principles in the *śāstras* and directions given by the spiritual master. These regulative principles should act as servants of the basic principle—that is, one should always remember Kṛṣṇa and never forget Him. This is possible when one chants the Hare Kṛṣṇa *mantra*. Therefore one must strictly chant the Hare Kṛṣṇa *mahā-mantra* twenty-four hours daily. One may have other duties to perform under the direction of the spiritual master, but he must first abide by the spiritual master's order to chant a certain number of rounds. In our Kṛṣṇa consciousness movement, we have recommended that the neophyte chant at least sixteen rounds. This chanting of sixteen rounds is absolutely necessary if one wants to remember Kṛṣṇa and not forget Him. Of all the regulative principles, the spiritual master's order to chant at least sixteen rounds is most essential."

Although Śrīla Prabhupāda had instructed the young man not to ask why, here Śrīla Prabhupāda gives the answer. Though we may have other important duties, the basic principle is to always remember Kṛṣṇa. And to always remember Kṛṣṇa, we must regularly chant sixteen rounds.

As Kṛṣṇa's empowered representative, Śrīla Prabhupāda understood the necessity for us to chant sixteen rounds. But is it true, as Śrīla Prabhupāda said, that he would have no objection if the young man did nothing more than chant sixteen rounds, eat, and sleep?

Let us consider the meaning of the *mahā-mantra*. When we chant we are addressing Kṛṣṇa and His energy. If Kṛṣṇa were to respond and ask, "Yes? You called? What do you want?" what would we reply? "A VCR"? "A new house"? "An imported car"? "A beautiful wife"? "A better job"? "A husband for my daughter"? No. A pure devotee will not ask for anything material. He will ask only for service to Kṛṣṇa and Kṛṣṇa's devotees: "O Lord Kṛṣṇa! O Śrīmatī Rādhārāṇī! Please engage me in Your devotional service."

Śrīla Prabhupāda knew that if the young man chanted sixteen rounds every day, Kṛṣṇa would hear his prayer and fulfill his desire. Kṛṣṇa would give him more and more service at the lotus feet of His dear representative, Śrīla Prabhupāda.

Why Do You Sleep?

In Gorakhpur, in 1971, Śrīla Prabhupāda was speaking from the *Bhāgavatam* on the history of Ajāmila and the significance of the holy name, reading from the original Sanskrit commentary of Śrīpāda Śrīdhara Svāmī. After one class, Haṁsadūta said to Śrīla Prabhupāda, "That was a wonderful lecture." Śrīla Prabhupāda remarked, "Do you think so? What do the other devotees think?" Haṁsadūta replied, "Well, frankly speaking, Śrīla Prabhupāda, most of the devotees were asleep in the class." "Yes, I know," said Śrīla Prabhupāda. "Practically, I am speaking to only a few sincere disciples."

Day after day, the problem persisted: So many devotees—including me—were falling asleep during class.

During one morning class, when Śrīla Prabhupāda noticed a devotee dozing, he stopped speaking from the *Bhāgavatam* and told him, "You can go and lie down. Why you are sitting and sleeping? This is not good. Sleeping from ten to four is not sufficient? Why do you do like this—whole day and night, whenever you sit down? What is this? Every one of you more or less. What is the reason?"

Yamunā-devī ventured, "Inattentive." But Śrīla Prabhupāda responded, "Inattentive means like this? No. Unless one is tired or has had no sufficient sleep, one will not do like that. It is not inattentiveness."

Then Guru dāsa suggested, "Not enough sleep." But Śrīla Prabhupāda retorted, "Enough sleep. You require twenty-four hours sleep? If you sleep for ten hours, that is not sufficient? Your business is to sleep only. So ten hours' or eight hours' sleep is not sufficient. Kumbhakarṇa. Just like Kumbhakarṇa. He was sleeping six months."

Tamal Krishna interjected, "Hibernation."

Śrīla Prabhupāda chuckled and continued, "We are also sleeping six months in a year, because we generally sleep ten to twelve hours. So if you sleep half day, that means half year. We are all Kumbhakarṇas. Anyone who sleeps more than six or seven hours is a Kumbhakarṇa. Kumbhakarṇa was the brother of Rāvaṇa. He was sleeping six months, and six months he was awake. That means that anyone who sleeps half the time, twelve hours out of twenty-four, he's a Kumbhakarṇa.

"One should not sleep more than seven hours utmost. That is sufficient. You can sleep six hours at night and one hour to rest in the daytime. That is sufficient. And if you sleep more, you are Kumbhakarṇa.

"So you should adjust things. *Nidrāhāra-vihārakādi-vijitau.* That's the Gosvāmīs.

saṅkhyā-pūrvaka-nāma-gāna-natibhiḥ kālāvasānī-kṛtau
nidrāhāra-vihārakādi-vijitau cātyanta-dīnau ca yau
rādhā-kṛṣṇa-guṇa-smṛter madhurimānandena sammohitau
vande rūpa-sanātanau raghu-yugau śrī-jīva-gopālakau

['I offer my respectful obeisances unto the Six Gosvāmīs, namely Śrī Rūpa Gosvāmī, Śrī Sanātana Gosvāmī, Śrī Raghunātha Bhaṭṭa Gosvāmī, Śrī Raghunātha dāsa Gosvāmī, Śrī Jīva Gosvāmī, and Śrī Gopāla Bhaṭṭa Gosvāmī, who were engaged in chanting the holy names of the Lord and bowing down in a scheduled measurement. In this way they utilized their valuable lives, and in executing these devotional activities they conquered over eating and sleeping and were always meek and humble, enchanted by remembering the transcendental qualities of the Lord.' (*Ṣaḍ-gosvāmy-aṣṭaka* 6)]

"We are followers of the Gosvāmīs. Their whole time, twenty-four hours, was used in Kṛṣṇa consciousness by chanting Hare Kṛṣṇa *mantra* regularly, fixed up, on big beads. So, we have reduced that to sixteen. Haridāsa Ṭhākura was chanting three times sixty-four, or one hundred and ninety-two, rounds.

And we are giving you only sixteen. We don't ask you to imitate Haridāsa Ṭhākura. But he would not sleep or eat unless he had finished his 192 rounds. And Raghunātha dāsa Gosvāmī was offering obeisances around the whole Rādhā-kuṇḍa: 'So many times I shall fall down.' He was falling down, *daṇḍavat*. From the point where your head is touching, you have a line, stand there, and again fall down. Again stand, and again fall down. Just see how much good exercise it is.

"This is called *tapasya*, austerity. We should not take it very easily that we are going back to Godhead. Of course, there are so many concessions. . . . But at the same time, we should be very much aware of the responsibility, that we have decided to go back to Godhead after leaving this body, so we have to perform some austerities. The austerity in our Gauḍīya-sampradāya is very simple: following the four principles, restrictions, avoiding the offenses, and chanting regularly on beads. And hearing. Chanting and hearing, both. Not only chanting; we have to hear *Śrīmad-Bhāgavatam*. In this way we should engage twenty-four hours. Hear and chant. When you speak, when you go to lecture for preaching, that is also chanting. And automatically there is hearing. If you chant, there is hearing also. *Śravaṇaṁ kīrtanaṁ viṣṇoḥ smaraṇaṁ*. (*SB* 7.5.23) And there is memorizing also. Unless you memorize all the conclusions of *Śrīmad-Bhāgavatam*, *Bhagavad-gītā*, you cannot speak. *Śravaṇaṁ kīrtanaṁ viṣṇoḥ smaraṇaṁ pāda-sevanam arcanaṁ*. *Arcanaṁ*, this is *arcanaṁ*." Śrīla Prabhupāda indicated the Deities of Rādhā-Kṛṣṇa that were traveling with him and then continued: "*Vandanaṁ*, offering prayers. Hare Kṛṣṇa is also prayer. Hare Kṛṣṇa, Hare Kṛṣṇa: 'O Kṛṣṇa, O energy of Kṛṣṇa, please engage me in Your service.' This Hare Kṛṣṇa is simply prayer. So, *śravaṇaṁ kīrtanaṁ viṣṇoḥ smaraṇaṁ pāda-sevanam arcanaṁ vandanaṁ dāsyaṁ*. Always remain engaged as a servant, *dāsyaṁ*. *Sakhyam*—always think that Kṛṣṇa is your best friend. And *ātma-nivedanam*—dedicate everything to Kṛṣṇa. This is our process. And we have to be engaged in these processes twenty-four hours.

"Because we have got this body, it requires eating, sleeping, mating. So the arrangement is there: eating is there; sleeping is there; mating is there; defending is there—but not excessively. *Nidrāhāra-vihārakādi-vijitau.* The very word is used, *vijita.* You should not be conquered by them. Eating, sleeping, mating, and defending are required, but you should not be conquered by them. You should conquer them.

"So we should be always conscious of our responsibility. That will help us. We must stay awake. *Uttiṣṭhata.* Always remain awakened."

Śrīla Prabhupāda was referring to a Vedic injunction:

> *uttiṣṭhata jāgrata*
> *prāpya varān nibodhata*
> *kṣurasya dhārā niśitā duratyayā*
> *durgaṁ pathas tat kavayo vadanti*

"Please wake up and try to understand the boon that you now have in this human form of life. The path of spiritual realization is very difficult; it is sharp like a razor's edge. That is the opinion of learned transcendental scholars." (*Kaṭha Upaniṣad* 1.3.14)

He continued, "So, regularly, seven hours sleep is sufficient. Why more? What is the cause? One cause may be that if we eat more, then we sleep more. So to reduce the sleeping process, the eating process should be reduced. If you fast for one day, don't take anything, you will see that there will be less sleep. Is it not? Yes. So six hours, from ten to four, is complete, and one hour during daytime. Then no more sleeping unless you are sick. But why you young boys and girls should fall sick? There is no question of falling sick.

"When one is engaged in some serious business, he sleeps less. So one should be engaged in serious business; then sleeping will be less. If we become lazy, if we have no sufficient engagement, then sleeping will come.

"We have to adjust things personally, not by dictation or by rules and regulations. Personal affairs cannot be adjusted by rules and regulation. They can be adjusted by oneself. And then everything will be all right.

saṅkhyā-pūrvaka-nāma-gāna-natibhiḥ kālāvasānī-kṛtau
nidrāhāra-vihārakādi-vijitau cātyanta-dīnau ca yau
rādhā-kṛṣṇa-guṇa-smṛter madhurimānandena sammohitau
vande rūpa-sanātanau raghu-yugau śrī-jīva-gopālakau

The Six Gosvāmīs used their time in this way. And *rādhā-kṛṣṇa-padāravinda-bhajanānandena mattālikau.* They were jolly in the service of Rādhā-Kṛṣṇa, *bhajanānanda.* That should be the basis of jolliness. Our real pleasure should be in *rādhā-kṛṣṇa-padāravinda-bhajana.*

"We have taken a very serious job. In this life we want to finish this material existence for good. If you take responsibility in this way, everything will be adjusted. My *guru mahārāja* used to say, 'Finish this business in this life. Don't delay for the next life.' He also said, 'Don't give me trouble to again come here to deliver you.' Serious. We have taken a very, very responsible task, to finish this so-called lording over this material nature. Our business is not to lord it over but to serve Kṛṣṇa.

"We have to become Viṣṇudūtas. Our preachers are Viṣṇudūtas, just to give protection to any person who is slightly inclined to worship the Supreme Personality of Godhead. We shall give all help, all assistance, to such persons. That is our business—not sleeping business, not lazying business. We should be always active. We shall always make plans, think how to protect people from this miserable condition of material existence. They cannot understand. They are fools. They are rascals. So you have to give them knowledge. You have to give them help. That is missionary activity. Missionary activity is not laziness or sleeping. My *guru mahārāja* used to say, *prāṇa āche yāra sei hetu pracāra*: one who has life will preach. 'I have got some disciples, I have got a temple, and people are contributing. Now I have got good arrangement for eating and sleeping. Now I am perfect. Because I am getting some food without any work, and honor, I am perfect'—this is not the mentality. *Prāṇa āche yāra.* You must be engaged continually for these missionary activities. The Gauḍīya Mission failed in preaching work because they adopted this principle—as soon as they got a little shelter under the name of Maṭha, or temple, and a few dozen—not a few dozen, one dozen—disciples, then he is settled. And he is doing *bhajana*, 'Hare Kṛṣṇa, Hare Kṛṣṇa, Hare Kṛṣṇa, Hare Kṛṣṇa, Hare Kṛṣṇa,' showing that he is very great chanter. And what is your preaching? Lord Caitanya ordered, *pṛthivīte āche yata nagarādi-grāma sarvatra pracāra haibe mora nāma*: 'In as many towns and villages as there are on the surface of the earth, My holy name will be preached.' Why don't you go?

"Therefore my *guru mahārāja* condemned this policy. *Mana, tumi kisera vaiṣṇava*: 'What kind of Vaiṣṇava you are?' *Pratiṣṭhāra tare, nirjanera ghare*: 'Simply for cheap popularity—'Oh, he is a Vaiṣṇava. He is chanting. All right.' No botheration. If there is no preaching, there is no botheration. You can sit down and show people, 'I have now become a very liberated soul' and chant and meditate. That means sleeping. This sort of business is condemned by my *guru mahārāja*. This is simply cheating.

duṣṭa mana! tumi kisera vaiṣṇava?
pratiṣṭhāra tare, nirjanera ghare,
tava hari-nāma kevala kaitava

'My dear sinful mind, what kind of devotee are you? Simply for cheap adoration you sit in a solitary place and pretend to chant the Hare Kṛṣṇa *mahā-mantra*, but this is all cheating.'

"He did not approve of this kind of business. He wanted to see everyone engaged in preaching work, some sort of preaching work, either indoor or outdoor. Indoor you have to be busy writing articles and proofreading and so many things. And outdoor you have to go door to door, make people members, interest them in this movement, collect money for expenses.

"Preaching means you have to meet opposing elements. So many will criticize; so many will attack. Nityānanda Prabhu was hurt personally, but still, outdoor. This is missionary work, not 'Whenever I find some opportunity, go to some solitary place and sleep.' This is not missionary life.

"So we should adjust things. You have got very responsible business, this Kṛṣṇa consciousness. It is genuine, it is authorized, and Lord Caitanya wants us to do it all over the world. Things should be adjusted to keep us always alive to our responsibility. That is missionary life."

While Śrīla Prabhupāda was speaking, I was struggling to stay awake. But he spoke so strongly, so ferociously—like a lion, like Nṛsiṁhadeva—that we were practically forced to stay awake and be attentive to his words.

After the talk I commented to Tamal Krishna that Śrīla Prabhupāda had spoken so forcefully that we were almost forced to stay alert and pay attention, and Tamal Krishna replied, "Yes, by our own power we cannot even stay awake. It is only by Śrīla Prabhupāda's potency and mercy that we are able to stay awake."

Where Is Kṛṣṇa?

In December of 1971 I arranged a speaking program for Śrīla Prabhupāda in Madras. For five nights, thousands of people came to hear him, and the leading newspaper carried a summary of his lecture every day. Then the chief justice of Madras invited him to speak before a large gathering of high court judges, advocates, and other leading citizens. Śrīla Prabhupāda appealed to the audience to follow the examples of Śrī Sanātana Gosvāmī and Rūpa Gosvāmī, who in the sixteenth century had given up their exalted posts as prime minister and finance minister in the Bengal government to help Śrī Caitanya Mahāprabhu spread the Kṛṣṇa consciousness movement.

"I offer my respectful obeisances unto the Six Gosvāmīs, namely Śrī Rūpa Gosvāmī, Śrī Sanātana Gosvāmī, Śrī Raghunātha Bhaṭṭa Gosvāmī, Śrī Raghunātha dāsa Gosvāmī, Śrī Jīva Gosvāmī, and Śrī Gopāla Bhaṭṭa Gosvāmī, who kicked off all association with aristocracy as insignificant. In order to deliver the poor conditioned souls, they accepted the garments of mendicants, but they were always merged in the ecstatic ocean of the *gopīs'* love for Kṛṣṇa, and they bathed always and repeatedly in the waves of that ocean." (*Ṣaḍ-gosvāmy-aṣṭaka* 4)

After the program, the chief justice invited Śrīla Prabhupāda and his disciples to dinner at his home, and he disclosed that he wanted to join Śrīla Prabhupāda's movement as soon as possible. Śrīla Prabhupāda again began to glorify the Six Gosvāmīs, but this time in a different way. He explained how after going to Vṛndāvana, the Gosvāmīs were always longing for Lord Kṛṣṇa and His eternal consort Śrīmatī Rādhārāṇī. "They never said, 'Now I have seen God! Now I'm satisfied!' No! Rather, they were saying, 'Where is Rādhā? Where is Kṛṣṇa?'"

"I offer my respectful obeisances unto the Six Gosvāmīs,

who chanted very loudly everywhere in Vṛndāvana, shouting, 'O Queen of Vṛndāvana, Rādhārāṇī! O Lalitā! O Kṛṣṇa, son of Nanda Mahārāja! Where are you all now? Are you just on the hill of Govardhana, or are you under the trees on the bank of the Yamunā? Where are you?' These were their moods in executing Kṛṣṇa consciousness." (*Ṣaḍ-gosvāmy-aṣṭaka* 8)

The chief justice respectfully presented Śrīla Prabhupāda a sandalwood garland and a small statue of Kṛṣṇa. Then, to demonstrate the ecstasy the Gosvāmīs felt in separation from Kṛṣṇa, Śrīla Prabhupāda did something wonderful. He held the statue of Kṛṣṇa in front of Sarasvatī, his secretary's three-year-old daughter, and said, "Who is this, Sarasvatī?"

"Kṛṣṇa!" Sarasvatī exclaimed.

He held the statue in front of Sarasvatī's eyes and then slowly moved it around to the side, until he had hidden it behind his back. Then Śrīla Prabhupāda said, "Sarasvatī, where is Kṛṣṇa?"

When Sarasvatī realized that Kṛṣṇa was gone, a startled look of anxiety crossed her face. Her eyes darted in all directions—"Where is Kṛṣṇa?"

But Kṛṣṇa was nowhere to be found. She appealed to the faces of the devotees, glanced at their hands, and looked around behind their backs, searching everywhere. Unable to find Kṛṣṇa, she became stunned.

Śrīla Prabhupāda's grave voice broke the silence. "Sarasvatī, where is Kṛṣṇa?"

Sarasvatī began again to look anxiously all over the room, but still she could not find Him.

Then a devotee said, "Sarasvatī, where is Kṛṣṇa? *Who* has Kṛṣṇa?"

Sarasvatī's mind awakened with a realization. She opened her eyes wide, eyebrows raised, and exclaimed, "Prabhupāda has Kṛṣṇa!" She immediately turned to Śrīla Prabhupāda and rushed to his lotus feet. "Prabhupāda has Kṛṣṇa!"

Śrīla Prabhupāda carefully brought the statue of Kṛṣṇa from behind his back and gradually moved it before the expectant eyes of Sarasvatī.

"Prabhupāda has Kṛṣṇa!"

As we observed this touching exchange, we all gained the clear realization that Śrīla Prabhupāda held Kṛṣṇa in his hand and that he could deliver Kṛṣṇa to us when he felt our desire for Kṛṣṇa was sufficiently intense. We also understood that Śrīla Prabhupāda knew our inner feelings. He knew the heart of everyone perfectly. Although Sarasvatī was only three years old, Śrīla Prabhupāda could understand her heart. He knew just how to engage her in Kṛṣṇa consciousness.

And finally, we could witness Śrīla Prabhupāda as the supreme preacher, engaging everything and everybody in spreading Kṛṣṇa consciousness. Śrīla Prabhupāda had wanted to demonstrate transcendental anxiety in separation from Kṛṣṇa and thus created a situation wherein a three-year-old girl could instruct a chief justice. As a result of Śrīla Prabhupāda's grace, everyone—from little Sarasvatī to the chief justice of Madras—became fully absorbed in Kṛṣṇa consciousness and completely attached to the lotus feet of Kṛṣṇa's dearmost servant, His Divine Grace Śrīla Prabhupāda.

The incident brought to mind Śrīla Bhaktivinoda Ṭhākura's devotional song about the glories of the Kṛṣṇa conscious spiritual master.

kṛṣṇa se tomāra, kṛṣṇa dite pāro
tomāra śakati āche

"Kṛṣṇa is yours, and you have the power to give Him to me."

āmi to' kāṅgala, 'kṛṣṇa 'kṛṣṇa' boli',
dhāi tava pāche pāche

"I am simply running behind you, shouting, 'Kṛṣṇa! Kṛṣṇa!'"

Intelligent

In October of 1971 my parents came to see me in Calcutta. While Śrīla Prabhupāda was talking with some of his disciples in his quarters, my parents entered. Śrīla Prabhupāda received them warmly. After hearing him speak for some time, they finally came to the point: they wanted me back.

Śrīla Prabhupāda said: "I have no objection; ask your son."

I said, "I want to stay with Śrīla Prabhupāda."

"We want to set up a big trust for Giriraj," my father said. "And we want him to come home to sign the papers."

"Yes, you can send the papers," Śrīla Prabhupāda replied. "He can sign."

My parents said that they had no objection to my remaining in the movement but that they did not want my health to deteriorate. So they wanted me to be stationed near home.

Śrīla Prabhupāda said, "Do not worry; I will take personal care of him."

My parents were still apprehensive, so Śrīla Prabhupāda said, "Let him stay with me in India for some months more, and I will take personal care of him. Then, when I return to America in April, he can come with me."

With my parents somewhat relieved, I said, "Just see how intelligent Śrīla Prabhupāda is. In the winter, when the Western countries are cold and dark, Śrīla Prabhupāda stays in India. And in the summer, when the West is warm and sunny, Śrīla Prabhupāda goes there."

My father was becoming enlivened by Śrīla Prabhupāda, and he affirmed, "Yes, he is very intelligent."

Śrīla Prabhupāda said, "No, your son is—he has understood my strategy."

My father said, "No—you are intelligent, actually."

Śrīla Prabhupāda replied, "Yes, I must be intelligent; otherwise how could I attract so many intelligent young men like your son?"

My mother was still thinking of my poor health and long absence from home, and she began to cry.

To cheer her, Śrīla Prabhupāda gave her a *sandeśa* (milk sweet). At first my mother wouldn't accept, but Śrīla Prabhupāda's kind and gentle persistence prevailed. Then he told her, "These sweets—*sandeśa* and *rasagullā*—are made of cheese and are very high in protein." Then he said, "Giriraj, you must take at least two dozen *sandeśa* and *rasagullā* every day. Then you will become strong and healthy."

Śrīla Prabhupāda assured my parents, "I will personally see that he is supplied with sufficient *sandeśa*. Do not worry."

Everyone was thoroughly pleased and satisfied by Śrīla Prabhupāda's loving dealings. As my father was leaving the room, he remarked, "Well, I can say two things about your Prabhupāda. He is a brilliant organizer, and he really knows how to deal with people." And in my father's system of values, those were the highest compliments.

Remember Prabhupāda's Instructions and Distribute

The Birla family had traditionally been the richest in India. Śrīla Prabhupāda called them "the best organized family in the world" and said, "Nobody can measure their wealth."

In 1971 one of the devotees in Calcutta made an appointment for Śrīla Prabhupāda to meet Mr. L. N. Birla, the first son of the senior Birla, G. D. When the devotees informed Śrīla Prabhupāda about the appointment, he called me to his room. "They have made the appointment, but I want you to go." I inquired why. "In Bombay recently I asked some big men for help, but they refused. If he refuses also, it won't be good for him and it won't be good for me." I replied, "But what if he refuses me?" "Oh, you are just a young boy! That doesn't matter."

Mr. Birla received us cordially. We showed him Śrīla Prabhupāda's books. Immediately he asked, "How much do I pay for these books?" I thought, "He can't just buy the books. He has to do more." So I replied, "We don't actually sell the books. We only give them to life members." "What do I have to do to become a life member?" I explained and gave him the form. He called his secretary, issued the check, and enrolled as a life member. Then I came to the real point—Māyāpur. But he replied, "Presently we are building hospitals." And that was the end of the meeting.

Back at the temple Śrīla Prabhupāda asked for the report. I thought I had been clever enough not to allow Mr. Birla to just buy the books, but when Śrīla Prabhupāda heard the story he said, "You did wrong. When he asked how much the books cost, you should have replied, 'These are our presentation to you. Now we are building one temple in Māyāpur. Kindly help us.'"

Years later in Bombay I got an appointment with Mr. G. D.

Birla, L. N. Birla's father. My assistant, Purīdāsa, and I took the special lift to the top floor of the Birla office building. The floor was laid with spectacular swirling green marble, and the walls were lined with mirrors so everything looked like marble. One could not distinguish between marble and glass, horizontal and vertical. It was bewildering.

Mr. Birla's secretaries were expecting us. A few minutes later Mr. Birla came in.

He began by admitting that for many years he had held some prejudice against us. "I don't know why. I just had some prejudice. But now it is gone." Suddenly an important overseas call came, and Mr. Birla left the room.

I started to think, "What to do now? What to do?" Then I remembered I had some sets of *Śrīmad-Bhāgavatam* and *Śrī Caitanya-caritāmṛta* in the back of the car.

It was the third day of December, and we had just begun our annual book distribution marathon. For two days I had gone out on the street to distribute books and was relishing the nectar of *saṅkīrtana*. But I also began to consider that with so much effort I had distributed one or two hundred small books but that with much less effort I could meet a big man and with his donation distribute so many more books. Finally I concluded, "Anyway, it's the marathon, so let me meet some big men with sets." Thus the trunk of the car was filled with sets of Prabhupāda's books.

"Purīdāsa! Quick! Run and bring the sets of books. Don't worry how many boxes there are. The Birla people will help you." (In those days the *Bhāgavatam* was thirty volumes and the *Caitanya-caritāmṛta* seventeen.) I was anxiously waiting for Purīdāsa, fearing that Mr. Birla might return first. Finally Purīdāsa came rushing in with five large cartons of books—just moments before Mr. Birla.

As soon as Mr. Birla took his place I started showing him the books. And he was perusing them and appreciating. After some time he said, "How much do I owe you for these books?" His words suddenly called to mind my previous meeting with the other Birla—and Śrīla Prabhupāda's instructions. "Oh, no! These books are our presentation to you. We can't take anything for them." Mr. Birla countered, "These are such beautiful books. I can't take them for free. I must pay you." "Oh, no! These are our presentation to you. We can't take money for them." He was insisting. And me, I was still relatively young and inexperienced. How could I argue with Mr. Birla? But still I stuck to my point. "No. In our mind we have already given these books to you as our gift. We cannot take payment for them under any circumstance." He relented, but still he was not satisfied. So I added, "But we are building a *gurukula* school in Juhu. If you like, you may help us." I explained the project and showed him the plans and budget. He said, "All right, you leave these with me and we'll see what we can do."

Two days later Mr. Birla's secretary phoned, "Mr. Birla would like to meet you. He has something for you." We were pleased to return to his office to accept his kind and generous donation.

We can thus see how perfect and potent Śrīla Prabhupāda's instructions are. Ten years after the original incident, the same instruction worked wonderfully. And we can see also how just by distributing Śrīla Prabhupāda's books, everything else follows, including *lakṣmī*. Thus we should faithfully remember Śrīla Prabhupāda's instructions and distribute his books as he desired.

Simple

In late 1971 a prominent businessman, Mr. A. B. Nair, offered Śrīla Prabhupāda some land in Juhu, on the outskirts of Bombay. Later we discovered that Mr. Nair was very tricky and cunning. Before taking money for the land from Śrīla Prabhupāda, he had already taken—and kept—money from two other parties.

After Śrīla Prabhupāda signed the purchase agreement and left Bombay, Yadubara dāsa and I had to deal with Mr. Nair. We would meet him at his home in Juhu and talk with him, but we couldn't understand: was he our friend or our enemy?

Ultimately, from thousands of miles away in Los Angeles, Śrīla Prabhupāda concluded that Mr. Nair was trying to cheat us.

Eventually, Prabhupāda came to Bombay to deal with the matter. Tamal Krishna Goswami told him how Mr. Nair had bluffed me. Perhaps he expected Śrīla Prabhupāda to reproach me. But Śrīla Prabhupāda replied, "Giriraj is simple. What can be done?"

Śrīla Prabhupāda's words stayed in my mind: "Giriraj is simple." I considered my simplicity a fault, a disqualification.

Some months later, while reading the *Kṛṣṇa* book to Śrīla Prabhupāda during his daily morning walk on Juhu Beach, I came to the chapter "The Salvation of Tṛṇāvarta," in which Lord Kṛṣṇa defeats a demon who had assumed the form of a whirlwind. There I read, "After observing such wonderful happenings, Nanda Mahārāja began to think of the words of Vasudeva again and again."

Previously we had read how Nanda Mahārāja considered Vasudeva a great sage and mystic *yogī* because Vasudeva had foretold an incident that happened in Vṛndāvana, where Kṛṣṇa was living. Śrīla Prabhupāda had remarked, "Vasudeva is a *kṣatriya*, a ruler. With political eyesight, Vasudeva predicted, 'This may happen,' but Nanda Mahārāja, as a *vaiśya*, a simple agriculturalist, thought, 'Oh, Vasudeva is a foreseer.'"

I noticed that Śrīla Prabhupāda was applying the word "simple" to a pure devotee—Nanda Mahārāja—and I was surprised. I wondered how a pure devotee like Nanda Mahārāja could have a disqualification such as being simple. So I asked Śrīla Prabhupāda, "Simplicity is not considered a bad quality?"

Śrīla Prabhupāda replied, "No. For him it is all right. He is a *vaiśya*, so he should believe like that. And a politician should act like Vasudeva. One should not imitate. For example, a physician does operations, but I should not imitate and take the knife and operate. That is not my business." Then Śrīla Prabhupāda explained, "But Vasudeva was thinking of Kṛṣṇa, and Nanda Mahārāja was also thinking of Kṛṣṇa. As a simple agriculturalist, Nanda Mahārāja was thinking of Kṛṣṇa. And Vasudeva, when he was asking Nanda Mahārāja, 'Go and take care of your children there,' he was also thinking of Kṛṣṇa. If thinking of Kṛṣṇa is there, then whether *kṣatriya* or *vaiśya* or *brāhmaṇa*, it doesn't matter. Everyone gets the same benefit.

"Everyone should understand, 'Whatever I may be, I am an eternal servant of Kṛṣṇa.' If this consciousness is maintained and everyone is engaged in the service of Kṛṣṇa by his work and by his occupational duty, then he is perfect."

Śrīla Prabhupāda's answer was deep. He said that for a person in a certain position simplicity may be a good qualification, and for another it may not. For a *vaiśya* or a *brāhmaṇa* to be simple may be good, but not for a *kṣatriya*, who has to deal with politics and diplomacy. Yet ultimately it doesn't matter whether one is a *brāhmaṇa*, a *kṣatriya*, a *vaiśya*, or whatever. What matters is that one works in Kṛṣṇa's service and thinks of Kṛṣṇa in love—Kṛṣṇa consciousness.

Always Remain Śrīla Prabhupāda's Dog

Almost every morning in Bombay Śrīla Prabhupāda used to walk on Juhu Beach. One morning I was feeling especially wretched and miserable. Although so many other devotees were present, Śrīla Prabhupāda began to speak as if he were addressing me personally.

He quoted a Sanskrit verse and said there are two words—*a-nātha* and *sa-nātha*. *Nātha* means "master," so *a-nātha* means "without master" and *sa-nātha* means "with master." The whole goal of life is to become *sa-nātha*, "with master."

In the morning on Juhu Beach many gentlemen used to walk their dogs. Śrīla Prabhupāda pointed to a fat and fit gentleman walking with an equally fat and fit dog. The man was walking briskly and confidently with his dog on his leash, and the dog was walking equally briskly and confidently with his master by his side. Śrīla Prabhupāda commented that every dog wants a good master. If the dog has a good master he is happy. He holds his head high; he wags his tail. He knows that his master will maintain and protect him, so he has no anxiety.

But the street dog—"The poor fellow has no master. Therefore he is always suffering." Śrīla Prabhupāda then pointed to some stray dogs. "They have no master. They do not know where they will sleep, how they will get food. Other dogs bark at them; children throw stones at them. They are always in anxiety."

Śrīla Prabhupāda stopped walking. He planted his cane firmly in the sand of Juhu Beach. Although I stood behind many of the devotees who moved close around him, with his eyes laden with love and compassion he looked in my eyes. "So we should be *sanātha*, protected, not *anātha*—orphan. We should have our master and be exclusively devoted to him. Then we will feel confident in his protection and always be happy."

Quoting the verse again, Śrīla Prabhupāda explained each Sanskrit word. *Mano-ratha*: the chariot of the mind. Mental concoction is driving us here, there, here, there. We have no peace. But when we have our perfect master to serve, we become peaceful, *praśānta*, and jubilant: "I have got my master. I have no cares and anxiety." This is the ideal of life, to become *sanātha-jīvitam*, living with hope that "I have got my master who will give me protection."

I knew that Śrīla Prabhupāda was speaking directly to me, addressing my present need in Kṛṣṇa consciousness. Without my even asking or saying anything, he knew my heart and gave the perfect solution through his instructions. Thus he exemplified the verse from *Śrīmad-Bhāgavatam* (3.7.36):

anuvratānāṁ śiṣyāṇāṁ
putrāṇāṁ ca dvijottama
anāpṛṣṭam api brūyur
guravo dīna-vatsalāḥ

"Those who are spiritual masters are very kind to the needy. They are always kind to their followers, disciples, and sons, and without being asked by them, the spiritual master describes all that is knowledge."

Thereafter, I always tried to remember and follow the instructions Śrīla Prabhupāda gave me on Juhu Beach.

Although I had caught some of the words from the verse and Śrīla Prabhupāda's explanation, I very much wanted to find the verse—but could not. Then several years later I came across the same verse quoted in *Śrī Caitanya-caritāmṛta*:

bhavantam evānucaran nirantaraḥ
praśānta-niḥśeṣa-manorathāntaraḥ
kadāham aikāntika-nitya-kiṅkaraḥ
praharṣayiṣyāmi sanātha-jīvitam

"By serving You constantly, one is freed from all material desires and is completely pacified. When shall I engage as Your permanent eternal servant and always feel joyful to have such a fitting master?" (Cc *Madhya* 1.206)

Reading the purport, I found the same instructions Śrīla Prabhupāda had given on Juhu Beach: "Just as a dog or servant is very satisfied to get a competent, perfect master, or as a child is completely satisfied to possess a competent father, so the living entity is satisfied by completely engaging in the service of the Supreme Lord. He thereby knows that he has a competent master to save him from all kinds of danger."

I realized that Śrīla Prabhupāda is so perfect that he always spoke on the basis of scripture. At the same time, because of his tremendous compassion and humanity, he could say just the right thing in the right way to deeply touch the heart of the listener.

Now whenever I walk on Juhu Beach and see the different types of dogs—those with masters and those without—I remember Śrīla Prabhupāda's instructions and pray that I will always remain Śrīla Prabhupāda's dog.

A Prayer

Early in 1977 Śrīla Prabhupāda became seriously ill. Although he had come to Juhu in September to see the completion of the temple construction and to organize and bless the grand opening of the complex, he apprehended his imminent death and consulted the devotees about what to do. Finally everyone agreed: Śrīla Prabhupāda should travel to Vṛndāvana to "wait for Kṛṣṇa's decision."

In Vṛndāvana, we wanted to pray to Kṛṣṇa to allow Śrīla Prabhupāda to remain with us, but at the same time, as surrendered servants, we did not want to place demands or impose upon Kṛṣṇa. Always dependent on Śrīla Prabhupāda for guidance, we asked him if and how we could pray. In response, he suggested the prayer, "My dear Lord Kṛṣṇa, if You so desire, please cure Śrīla Prabhupāda."

Day and night we prayed, sometimes with Śrīla Prabhupāda's words and sometimes with our own. Finally I wrote a prayer, which I wanted to read to Śrīla Prabhupāda.

On November 3, I entered Śrīla Prabhupāda's room, where he lay on his bed as usual, and approached his secretary, Tamal Krishna Goswami. Śrīla Prabhupāda heard me whisper and inquired, "Hmm?"

I replied, "Śrīla Prabhupāda, I wrote a prayer to Lord Kṛṣṇa for your health. It's in the next room. I was thinking of bringing it to read to you."

"Oh, yes."

When I returned, Tamal Krishna Goswami asked Śrīla Prabhupāda if he would like to hear my prayer, and Prabhupāda replied, "Yes."

I began: "My dear Lord Kṛṣṇa, You are known as Yogeśvara, the master of all mystic powers. So it is very easy for You to perform the impossible, as You have done many times in the past. By Your merciful glance You restored life to the boys and cows who died by drinking the water of the Yamunā River, which was poisoned by Kāliya. You swallowed a devastating forest fire to protect the inhabitants of Vṛndāvana. In the *rāsa* dance, You expanded Yourself to be simultaneously present by the side of each *gopī*. And as *guru-dakṣiṇā,* You recovered the dead son of Your teacher. When the hunchback maidservant of Kaṁsa smeared You with sandalwood pulp, You made her straight and beautiful. And as a householder in Dvārakā, You expanded Yourself into sixteen thousand Kṛṣṇas and simultaneously satisfied each of Your sixteen thousand wives. When Sudāmā Brāhmaṇa offered You chipped rice, You transformed his poor cottage into a beautiful palace suitable for the king of heaven. To satisfy Mother Devakī, You returned her six dead sons from the kingdom of Bali. And to appease the Dvārakā *brāhmaṇa,* You also reclaimed his dead sons from Mahā-viṣṇu.

"When Śrīla Prabhupāda sat with seven dollars under a tree in Tompkins Square Park, You transformed that tree into so many regal palaces, and You expanded that seven dollars into millions. When Śrīla Prabhupāda spoke Your message, You turned the *mlecchas* and *caṇḍālas* who heard him into Your devotees. And when Śrīla Prabhupāda went all by himself to sell his *Śrīmad-Bhāgavatam* sets, You expanded him into ten thousand loving salesmen who worked day and night without asking any salary, and You expanded his suitcase of books into fifty-five million pieces of literature in twenty-three different languages. And then, when Hare Krishna Land was lost to the demons, You returned it to His Divine Grace.

"From these examples we can understand that for You, the impossible is not difficult. Rather, You have performed so many impossible feats for Your devotees. Therefore, if You desire, please give Śrīla Prabhupāda a new body."

Śrīla Prabhupāda was pleased to encourage me: "Excellent. Print in *Back to Godhead.* I am getting a little glimpse—He may agree to your prayer. Yes."

2

Spiritual Solutions to Material Problems

Kṛṣṇa and Humanity

In December of 1971, Giriraj Swami gave the following speech at the Rotary Club of Madras, India.

Our love is expanding like concentric rings around a pebble dropped in a pond. If you offer a baby some food, he will immediately pop it into his mouth, but if you offer the food to a child a few years older, he will think of sharing it with his parents, and then later with his brothers and sisters. In this way our radius of interest is expanding to include our friends, our community, our nation, and eventually, finally, all of humanity.

But what about the cows? We are thinking about the welfare of our fellow countrymen, who have taken birth in India, but the cows are also born in India, and they perform valuable service. So why do we allow the cow to be mercilessly slaughtered? Our love is not perfect, and every day we are killing millions of cows and plants and animals without a thought, inflicting untold misery upon their societies, and then when so many "innocent" members of our society are caused to suffer, we act surprised.

We are suffering because we do not know where to place our love, our service, so everybody can be happy. Our radius of interest is doubtlessly expanding, but because we have missed the center, there is conflict. Your communalism conflicts with my communalism, my nationalism conflicts with your nationalism, your humanitarianism conflicts with my humanitarianism. Because we do not know the center, there is conflict, just as when we drop pebbles in different points in a pond the waves and ripples overlap and conflict.

The International Society for Krishna Consciousness is teaching the science of how to serve and love everybody by the easy method of loving Kṛṣṇa, God. If we love God, then automatically our love and service are distributed to all the living entities, just as when we water the root of a tree, the part and parcel leaves and branches automatically receive the nourishment. If we neglect the root and simply try to water some particular leaves and twigs, the whole tree will die. This science of how to love all living beings by the process of loving God has been taught in India for thousands of years, and until the present age of Kali, when Indians (and people all over the world) have chosen to neglect their God consciousness, there was perfect peace and prosperity in the world, and India was venerated as the greatest civilization.

Now, unfortunately, India has neglected her duty of spreading *bhāgavata-dharma*, and she and the whole world are suffering because of it. In my travels I have found that India is regarded as a beggars' country; your ministers go simply to beg—give me food, give me money, give me armament, give me this, give me that. But if India simply distributes this most priceless treasure of Kṛṣṇa consciousness, for which the rest of the world is hankering, then India will be glorified all over the world, and all of you—your families, your communities, your states, your nation, humanity—everybody will be blessed with happiness and plenty.

One Indian, His Divine Grace A. C. Bhaktivedanta Swami Prabhupāda, has taken up this work of spreading Kṛṣṇa consciousness throughout the world, and since he founded the International Society for Krishna Consciousness in New York in 1966, he has revolutionized the lives of millions of persons around the world. ISKCON now has centers in over seventy cities, and all of its students strictly refrain from eating meat, fish, and eggs; from illicit sex; from all intoxicants, including coffee, tea, and cigarettes; and from gambling. This positive alternative for our confused youth is being appreciated in all quarters, and if one man alone, at the age of seventy, could do so much service for the world, just imagine what the country of India could do if she were united under the banner of Kṛṣṇa consciousness.

So our proposal is that there is no scarcity in the world—the only scarcity is of Kṛṣṇa consciousness. If we really want brotherhood (and a solution to all our problems), then we must accept a common father, and that father is God Himself. If we love God and serve Him according to His instructions in the *Bhagavad-gītā*, He will be satisfied, and automatically all of His children (us) will enjoy lives in harmony, filled with abundance.

South Africa: What's the Problem?

In the early 1980s, when South Africa's policy of apartheid, separate development, led the world to impose economic sanctions, Giriraj Swami gave the following response to a reporter's question about the Hare Kṛṣṇa movement's viewpoint.

All problems are caused by ignorance of spiritual knowledge and by a deficiency of love of God. Our movement is meant to enlighten the world with spiritual understanding and give people a practical method for developing transcendental love for God. We have already written a letter to the state president, giving him our idea of how the problem can be solved. We are awaiting his answer.

The letter to the state president:

His Honor, the State President, Mr. P. W. Botha,

Please accept my greetings and the blessings of God Almighty.

I am a disciple of His Divine Grace A. C. Bhaktivedanta Swami Prabhupāda, the late founder and spiritual master of the International Society for Krishna Consciousness and author of numerous authoritative translations of important writings from India's Vedic literatures.

The problems in South Africa are many and complex. As national secretary for our Society in South Africa, I would like to offer some observations.

Since each individual has his own intellectual and physical capacity, the strong must protect the weak. If instead of protecting the weak the strong exploit them, there will be trouble. Before God we are all weak. Therefore, for the solution to our problems we must take shelter of Him.

In the *Bhagavad-gītā*, a Vedic scripture recorded five thousand years ago, the Lord states that He is the father of every living entity. As the supreme father, He wishes well for all His children. By nature's arrangement some are stronger (or more intelligent) and others weaker. The stronger brothers must protect the weaker ones on behalf of the supreme father.

Of course, by our own ability, we cannot protect anyone; only God can protect. We must help people take shelter of God. In this age the best way to attain the Lord's shelter is to chant His holy name. One can chant any name of God found in any bona fide scripture. We chant Hare Kṛṣṇa, Hare Kṛṣṇa, Kṛṣṇa Kṛṣṇa, Hare Hare/ Hare Rāma, Hare Rāma, Rāma Rāma, Hare Hare.

When people chant the holy name of the Lord, they come into contact with the Lord, and because the Lord is all-blissful, the chanters also become happy and satisfied. On the other hand, no amount of political, social, or economic adjustment can make people happy.

It is your duty—as the leader of the twenty-five million people of South Africa—to give them the Lord's association. Then they will be peaceful and happy. Otherwise their frustrations and anxieties will only increase.

For the well-being of all concerned, we recommend a vigorous program of engaging the entire population in chanting the Lord's holy names. All facilities are at your command, and if you use them in the service of God for the benefit of all, you will be blessed and the entire population will become successful.

If you are doubtful about the effectiveness of chanting God's names, why don't you try it? You have nothing to lose. And the gain is very great: you will get peace in God.

If you would like to know more about how to apply this process on a large scale, or on a personal level, we are at your service. We would also like to invite you to visit the magnificent Temple of Understanding we recently opened in Durban. In the meantime we enclose a book by our spiritual master that may help you in dealing with the difficult problems you face.

Thank you for your consideration.

Hare Krishna!

Yours in the service of the Lord,
Giriraj Swami

Often, people come to us and ask, What is your solution to the drug problem? What is your solution for crime? What is your solution to the hunger problem? But we offer the same solution for every problem, because we see every problem as a variation of one problem, *yayā sammohito jīva*: The living entities are bewildered by the illusory energy of the Lord (*māyā*), and thus they suffer so many problems. Although the living entities are transcendental to material nature, they falsely identify with the material body and think, "I am white" or "I am black," and "I am dependent on so many material things."

In the *Bhagavad-gītā*, Lord Śrī Kṛṣṇa states that this illusory energy, consisting of the three modes of material nature (goodness, passion, and ignorance), is very difficult to overcome but that one who surrenders unto Him can easily surpass it. Similarly, in *Śrīmad-Bhāgavatam* Śrīla Vyāsadeva declares, *anarthopaśamaṁ sākṣād bhakti-yogam adhokṣaje*: The material miseries of the living entity, which are superfluous to him, can be directly mitigated by linking with God through the process of devotional service. Therefore Śrīla Vyāsadeva compiled the Vedic literatures to explain the science of rendering devotional service to Kṛṣṇa.

When we learn how to serve Kṛṣṇa, all our problems disappear. For example, take the economic problem. Where is the problem? Anywhere in the world you can cultivate the land and keep some cows. The cows give milk and fertilizer, and the bulls pull the plows and do other work. There is no problem. Kṛṣṇa gives this formula in the *Bhagavad-gītā*: cows and land.

If someone asks us for the solution to the crime problem, we will give the same solution: follow *bhakti-yoga* and chant Hare Kṛṣṇa—and people's hearts will be cleansed. And by following *bhakti-yoga*, we also address the health problem, because the life of the *yogī* is very regulated and clean, so he is naturally healthy and happy. All problems are solved in Kṛṣṇa consciousness—health problems, social problems, economic problems, political problems—all problems.

So there is no problem. The only problem is that we have forgotten our eternal relationship with God, Kṛṣṇa. The *Īśopaniṣad* states, *oṁ pūrṇam adaḥ pūrṇam idaṁ pūrṇāt pūrṇam udacyate*: "The Personality of Godhead is perfect and complete, and because He is completely perfect, all emanations from Him, such as this phenomenal world, are perfectly equipped as perfect wholes." We want to be happy, but we are incomplete. Kṛṣṇa is *pūrṇam*, complete. If we link with Kṛṣṇa through *bhakti-yoga*, we become complete.

We cannot fulfill our desires through *māyā*, material adjustment. This material world is like a great desert, and we are thirsting for happiness. If someone says, "I shall supply water—one drop," what is that drop? How can it satisfy us? That one drop is the sense gratification offered by *māyā* in return for our illusory pursuit of material advancement of life. Due to *māyā* we imagine we need so many material things, and when we do not have them we think we have so many problems. But that thinking is simply *māyā*, illusion. External arrangements can never fulfill our inner desires.

Because the general populace is bewildered by *māyā*, they think that this material world is everything, and thus they have created so many problems. But for persons practicing *bhakti-yoga* there is no problem. For example, in our International Society for Krishna Consciousness we have hundreds of branches, but we have no problem—because Kṛṣṇa is there. We are spending millions of dollars. From where is the money coming? Kṛṣṇa is sending. We are not working in factories. We are living together—blacks, whites, Indians, Africans, Christians, and Muslims—but we have no problems. In South Africa we have a beautiful plot of land in a wonderful location, and we recently constructed a magnificent temple for the spiritual upliftment of all. The land was given to us for the equivalent of one dollar, and the center was built at a cost of one million dollars. We can see practically that when we come to Kṛṣṇa consciousness, there is no problem. All problems are solved: Kṛṣṇa is there.

"But," one may ask, "if all problems are solved just by surrendering to Kṛṣṇa, by *bhakti-yoga*, why don't more people do it? There are many famous and intelligent persons; why don't they surrender to Kṛṣṇa?" The answer is given in *Śrīmad-Bhāgavatam*. People cannot take to Kṛṣṇa consciousness unless they bow down to the dust of the lotus feet of the exalted devotees of Kṛṣṇa, who have nothing to do with this material world. *Niṣkiñcanānāṁ na vṛṇīta yāvat*: Unless human society accepts the dust of the lotus feet of Kṛṣṇa's devotees (in other words, unless they learn the science of serving Kṛṣṇa from Kṛṣṇa's devotees), they cannot turn their attention to the lotus feet of wonderful Kṛṣṇa.

Therefore the devotees of the Kṛṣṇa consciousness movement go from door to door and country to country just to give people the chance to take to Kṛṣṇa consciousness. And if they take, all their problems will be solved.

Titanic Disasters

As I wait at the dentist's office, my eyes fall on the cover of an issue of *Life* magazine. A huge ship, half submerged, heads down into a vast, dark ocean. People gather frantically around the railings of her upward-poised stern. In the foreground, other people sit stunned in a lifeboat, watching. Lights from the ship reflect dimly on the water and the small lifeboat as its passengers row away from the destiny awaiting those left on board. Superimposed on the night sky, an eye stares, captivated by the ghastly spectacle.

A haunting picture with a title to match: "Titanic Fever—Why we can't look away from disasters."

The article describes various disasters in history: the eruption of Mount Vesuvius in 79 CE, which buried Pompeii and its 20,000 citizens under twenty feet of volcanic ash; the Great Chicago Fire of 1871, which ravaged 2,000 acres of the city and killed 250 people; the Lisbon earthquake of 1755, in which 60,000 died; the great Boston Molasses Flood, in which a fountain of molasses burst out of a distillery's cast-iron tank and oozed through the streets, suffocating 21 people; the 1986 explosion of the space shuttle Challenger, telecast live before millions; and almost fifty years before that, the crash of the zeppelin Hinderberg, broadcast live over the radio to millions of listeners. There is no dearth of disaster in world history.

The article focuses on people's fascination with the Titanic. "Titanimania" has given rise to dozens of books, a CD-ROM, a television movie, a Broadway musical, a blockbuster Hollywood film, a multimillion-dollar exhibition of Titanic artifacts, and even a cookbook: *Last Dinner on the Titanic.*

Although advertised as a ship that could never sink, the Titanic sank on her maiden voyage after just four days at sea.

Built as the largest, most luxurious ocean liner of that time, her construction cost $7.5 million and engaged thousands of workers. She boasted a crew of 892—two for every three passengers—and, remarkable for 1912, amenities such as a gymnasium, a swimming pool, and Turkish baths. The passengers would have everything they could need or want, and dine on delicacies.

Everything seemed set for a comfortable and pleasurable voyage. Among the elite on board were millionaire realtor John Jacob Aster, entrepreneur Isidor Straus, industrialist George Widener, and English artist Francis Millet. Passengers' spirits were high as the Titanic left the Southampton port. One thing was sure in their minds: the journey would be safe.

After two days at sea, the captain began to receive warnings of ice and bad weather ahead. Two days later, on Sunday, April 14, 1912, there was not much sign of weather change, so the captain retired early, leaving the ship in the hands of other crewmembers. He told them to rouse him if the situation became "at all doubtful."

Crewmen posted in the crow's nest had no binoculars, and the ship's wireless operator, overburdened by demands from passengers, failed to respond to repeated bad-weather warnings. While life on the great luxury liner carried on with abandon, she was moving into treacherous waters. The crew of the 46,329 tons of Titanic, plowing through the Atlantic waves at twenty-one knots, spotted the iceberg too late to divert the ship from inevitable disaster.

At first, none of the passengers took the collision seriously. But as water gushed into five of her front compartments and her nose started to dip, reality took hold: the Titanic was sinking.

More than 1,500 people would go down with the Titanic that night. Those who got away in life boats lived to tell the tale. The rest held on till the last minute, before plunging into the icy North Atlantic waters as the ocean swallowed the great ship.

Reading the article, I recalled Prahlāda Mahārāja's prayer to Nṛsiṁhadeva (Lord Kṛṣṇa's half-man, half-lion incarnation) in *Śrīmad-Bhāgavatam* (7.9.19):

bālasya neha śaraṇaṁ pitarau nṛsiṁha
nārtasya cāgadam udanvati majjato nauḥ
taptasya tat-pratividhir ya ihāñjaseṣṭas
tāvad vibho tanu-bhṛtāṁ tvad-upekṣitānām

"My Lord Nṛsiṁhadeva, O Supreme, because of a bodily conception of life, embodied souls neglected and not cared for by You cannot do anything for their betterment. Whatever remedies they accept, although perhaps temporarily beneficial, are certainly impermanent. For example, a father and mother cannot protect their child, a physician and medicine cannot relieve a suffering patient, and a boat on the ocean cannot protect a drowning man."

In the purport Śrīla Prabhupāda writes, "Through parental care, through remedies for different kinds of disease, and through means of protection on the water, in the air, and on land, there is always an endeavor for relief from various kinds of suffering in the material world, but none of them are guaranteed measures for protection. . . . Ultimately the shelter is the Lord, and one who takes shelter of the Lord is protected. This is guaranteed. . . .

"In the history of the world, no one has been successful in conquering the miseries imposed by material nature. . . . Our humble attempt to propagate the Kṛṣṇa consciousness movement all over the world is the only remedy that can bring about a peaceful and happy way of life."

Although everyone in the material world is trying to deflect the attacks of material nature, the efforts have never succeeded. In the *Bhagavad-gītā* the creator Himself certifies the material world as a place of misery (*duḥkhālayam aśāśvatam*). Only surrender to the Lord can save us.

Śrīla Prabhupāda says, "The material world is full of dangers *(padaṁ padaṁ yad vipadām)*. For example, if one is on the ocean, one may have a very strong ship, but that ship can never be safe; because one is at sea, there may be dangers at any time. The Titanic was safe, but on its first voyage it sank, and many important men lost their lives. So danger must be there, because we are in a dangerous position. The material world itself is dangerous. Therefore our business now should be to cross over this sea of danger as soon as possible." (*Teachings of Queen Kuntī*)

Instead of being disturbed by the waves in the material ocean, which perpetually come and go, we should tolerate the waves and try to cross the ocean to safety, to the shore of the spiritual world. How? By the boat of Lord Kṛṣṇa's lotus feet:

samāśritā ye pada-pallava-plavaṁ
mahat-padaṁ puṇya-yaśo murāreḥ
bhavāmbudhir vatsa-padaṁ paraṁ padaṁ
padaṁ padaṁ yad vipadāṁ na teṣāṁ

"For those who have accepted the boat of the lotus feet of the Lord, who is the shelter of the cosmic manifestation and is famous as Murāri, the enemy of the Mura demon, the ocean of the material world is like the water contained in a calf's hoofprint. Their goal is *paraṁ padam*, Vaikuṇṭha, the place where there are no material miseries, not the place where there is danger at every step." (*SB* 10.14.58)

Shall we make no practical effort to protect ourselves? We should take normal precautions. Yet, as Śrīla Prabhupāda writes, "Although as a matter of routine duty one must of course accept other remedial measures, no one can protect one who is neglected by the Supreme Personality of Godhead."

If Kṛṣṇa wants to save someone, no one can kill him, and if Kṛṣṇa wants to kill someone, no one can save him (*rākhe kṛṣṇa māre ke māre kṛṣṇa rākhe ke*). "Unless one is protected by the mercy of the Lord," Śrīla Prabhupāda writes, "no remedial measure can act effectively. One should consequently depend fully on the causeless mercy of the Lord."

A person completely surrendered to Lord Kṛṣṇa is confident of Kṛṣṇa's protection in all circumstances. Knowing that Kṛṣṇa is ultimately the well-wishing protector of His devoted servant, the devotee accepts any situation as the Lord's mercy. Śrīla Prabhupāda explains that we should not think, "Because I have become a devotee there will be no danger or suffering." Devotees like Prahlāda Mahārāja, the Pāṇḍavas, Vasudeva and Devakī, and Haridāsa Ṭhākura apparently suffered greatly. But they never gave up faith in Kṛṣṇa. Rather, when a devotee faces difficulty, he humbly thinks he deserves worse but Kṛṣṇa is just giving him a token reaction so he can learn from his past mistakes and come closer to Kṛṣṇa:

tat te 'nukampāṁ su-samīkṣamāṇo
bhuñjāna evātma-kṛtaṁ vipākam
hṛd-vāg-vapurbhir vidadhan namas te
jīveta yo mukti-pade sa dāya bhāk

"My dear Lord, any person who is constantly awaiting Your causeless mercy to be bestowed upon him, and who goes on suffering the resultant actions of his past misdeeds, offering You respectful obeisances from the core of his heart, is surely eligible to become liberated, for it has become his rightful claim." (*SB* 10.14.8)

The Lord explains in the *Bhāgavatam* (10.88.8) that sometimes to show special mercy to His devotee He takes away material things to which the devotee is attached. Kṛṣṇa thereby induces the devotee to take full shelter of Him and thus achieve the highest happiness and perfection.

The material world is fraught with danger; the only shelter is Kṛṣṇa and Kṛṣṇa consciousness.

The *Life* article points out that man has always been fascinated by disasters. Why? I'd say it's because we know that a disaster may strike any of us at any moment. Although in recent years a whole field of risk management has developed to counteract risks and dangers, still the only shelter is the Lord's lotus feet. And to take shelter of the lotus feet of Kṛṣṇa in the present age, one need only chant His holy names—Hare Kṛṣṇa, Hare Kṛṣṇa, Kṛṣṇa Kṛṣṇa, Hare Hare/ Hare Rāma, Hare Rāma, Rāma Rāma, Hare Hare—and follow His instructions in the *Bhagavad-gītā* and *Śrīmad-Bhāgavatam*.

The alternative is disaster—titanic disaster.

Harmony in the Holy Names

The park resounded. The musicians were very careful in listening to the mantra *. . . The Swami sang Hare Kṛṣṇa, Hare Kṛṣṇa, Kṛṣṇa Kṛṣṇa, Hare Hare/ Hare Rāma, Hare Rāma, Rāma Rāma, Hare Hare . . . "Hey," they would say, "listen to this holy monk."*

—Śrīla Prabhupāda-līlāmṛta

The practice of chanting God's names in public was begun by Lord Caitanya—who is God Himself—five hundred years ago in Bengal, India. And the Lord predicted that in every town and village of the world God's names would be sung. But how His prediction would be fulfilled nobody knew. Then in 1965 His Divine Grace A.C. Bhaktivedanta Swami Prabhupāda, at the age of seventy, set sail from India to America to bring the Hare Kṛṣṇa movement to the West.

Because people in this age have no time (or no interest) to go to church or temple, God comes to them in the form of His holy name. Therefore, when in New York City one of Śrīla Prabhupāda's first followers suggested they take the chanting out of the temple and into the park, Śrīla Prabhupāda readily agreed.

It was a strange sight for New Yorkers. Śrīla Prabhupāda sat under a tree and began singing. Strollers and musicians joined him. He entered their world with the holy names, and he entered their hearts. A headline in *The New York Times* declared, SWAMI'S FLOCK CHANTS IN PARK TO FIND ECSTASY.

Every day, devotees go into streets and parks throughout the world and chant Hare Kṛṣṇa. Once, when we went to chant in downtown Johannesburg, we came across several musical groups playing in the promenade outside the Market Theatre. We joined in with some of them, and some of them joined in with us. When we joined some Zulus in tribal dress, they danced around their drums and chanted Kṛṣṇa's names. Looking into the crowd that had gathered, I perceived a deep sense of appreciation. Here were blacks, whites, coloreds, and Indians, all united in God's names. And this coming together of peoples is exactly what everyone is hankering to see.

After we had chanted with some Rastafarians, one of them exclaimed, "We really liked playing with you. People are surprised: 'How is it that the Hare Kṛṣṇas and the Rastafarians are getting together, singing and dancing?' They couldn't believe it. So I told them, 'God speaks in different languages, but He's the same God. We chant in our language, and they chant in theirs, but it all goes to the same place. So what's the difficulty getting together and singing God's names?'" Another musician suggested we hold big festivals together, with chanting and dancing, speaking about God, and lots of food.

Perhaps nobody really understood what happened that afternoon, why everyone felt so pleased, but it was the presence of Lord Kṛṣṇa that brought everyone together in such a nice way. Śrīla Prabhupāda explains: "As living spiritual souls, we are all originally Kṛṣṇa conscious entities, but due to our association with matter from time immemorial, our consciousness is now polluted. The transcendental vibration established by chanting Hare Kṛṣṇa, Hare Kṛṣṇa, Kṛṣṇa Kṛṣṇa, Hare Hare/ Hare Rāma, Hare Rāma, Rāma Rāma, Hare Hare is the sublime method for reviving our transcendental consciousness. The chanting is a spiritual call for the Lord and His energy to give protection to the conditioned soul, and the Lord reveals Himself to the devotee who chants this *mantra* sincerely.

"No other means of spiritual realization is as effective in this age of quarrel and hypocrisy as the chanting of the *mahā-mantra*: Hare Kṛṣṇa, Hare Kṛṣṇa, Kṛṣṇa Kṛṣṇa, Hare Hare/ Hare Rāma, Hare Rāma, Rāma Rāma, Hare Hare."

3

Appeals and Messages

Not to Beg, But to Give

An address given at the Fourth World Conference of The Friends of India Society International in Bombay.

sā devakī sarva-jagan-nivāsa-
nivāsa-bhūtā nitarāṁ na reje
bhojendra-gehe 'gni-śikheva ruddhā
sarasvatī jñāna-khale yathā satī

"Devakī then kept within herself the Supreme Personality of Godhead, the cause of all causes, the foundation of the entire cosmos, but because she was under arrest in the house of Kaṁsa, she was like the flames of a fire covered by the walls of a pot, or like a person who has knowledge but cannot distribute it to the world for the benefit of human society." (*SB* 10.2.19)

Until recently, the knowledge of devotional service to Lord Kṛṣṇa contained in the *Bhagavad-gītā* was more or less imprisoned in India. That knowledge had not been distributed to the world. But *sarasvatī jñāna-khale*—one who has knowledge but does not distribute it cannot be appreciated. Therefore it is our duty to take the knowledge of the *Bhagavad-gītā* and distribute it for the benefit of the world. I think that this will be the greatest service we can do for humanity in general.

The *Caitanya-caritāmṛta* (*Ādi* 9.41) states,

bhārata-bhūmite haila manuṣya janma yāra
janma sārthaka kari' kara para-upakāra

Anyone who has taken his birth in Bhārata-varṣa, or India, should make his life successful according to the standard of the *Bhagavad-gītā* and perform the greatest welfare activity by spreading the knowledge of the *Bhagavad-gītā* for the benefit of the entire human society.

This is India's mission—*para-upakāra*, performing welfare activities. So many Indians want to find a place where they can make money, get some big position, and enjoy. But this is not their real duty. Their real duty is to go and preach Kṛṣṇa consciousness for the benefit of others.

Generally speaking, people all over the world have the idea that India is a backward, poverty-stricken country of beggars. Foreigners come to India and see so many beggars in the street, so many people lying on the footpath. And Indians who go abroad are also like beggars if they simply want to get something material for themselves and don't teach the spiritual knowledge of the *Bhagavad-gītā*. Even India's ambassadors tend to neglect the treasure of India's knowledge and try to benefit their country materially.

But our spiritual master, His Divine Grace A.C. Bhaktivedanta Swami Prabhupāda, went to the Western world all alone at the age of sixty-nine, not to beg, but to give. He sat down under a tree in Tompkins Square Park, in New York City, and began chanting Hare Kṛṣṇa and preaching the *Bhagavad-gītā*. And from that humble beginning he established more than one hundred centers all over the world, published and distributed millions of books, and made millions of people Kṛṣṇa conscious.

And Śrīla Prabhupāda was loved and respected wherever he went. Why? Because he didn't go to the West to beg something or to take something but to give something sublime: the knowledge of the *Bhagavad-gītā*.

So, on behalf of Śrī Caitanya Mahāprabhu and Śrīla Prabhupāda, my request to all of you is that you make your lives perfect according to the standard of the *Bhagavad-gītā*. And what is that standard of perfection?

janma karma ca me divyam
evaṁ yo vetti tattvataḥ
tyaktvā dehaṁ punar janma
naiti mām eti so 'rjuna

From the *Bhagavad-gītā* you must understand the transcendental nature of Kṛṣṇa's appearance and activities in this world.

Then, at the end of this lifetime you will not be forced to take birth again in this miserable world; you will go back home, back to Godhead. So make your life successful according to this standard and then benefit others by giving them the same knowledge.

Every nation should contribute something to the world. Despite the technology that India has developed in recent years, I don't think people are really interested in coming to India to learn how to manufacture airplanes or motorcycles or transistor radios. But people from all over the world *are* interested in coming to India to understand spiritual life, to understand the *Bhagavad-gītā*.

It is common sense that a businessman will export his best product. And the best product India has is the spiritual knowledge contained in the *Bhagavad-gītā*. So we should promote that product. Many times Śrīla Prabhupāda requested India's leaders to create a Department of the *Bhagavad-gītā* that would train men in Kṛṣṇa consciousness and then send them throughout the world to teach this knowledge. But unfortunately India's leaders have not taken up this work.

Now the responsibility has come to all of you gathered here. You are the leaders among the Indians dispersed throughout the world. So please take up this mission of spreading Kṛṣṇa consciousness. You will do the greatest benefit for yourselves, for your families, for your community, for the entire world. You will increase the glory of India throughout the world, and in the end Lord Kṛṣṇa will be pleased with you and you will go back home, back to Godhead.

Hare Kṛṣṇa.

Reverence for All Life

Late in 1997 I received a phone call from Sri Bhari B. R. Malhotra, a prominent industrialist based in Pune, India, inviting me to speak at a conference on "Reverence for All Life." Considering the Malhotras' relationship with Śrīla Prabhupāda—he had called them "our good friends"—and wanting to present the message of Kṛṣṇa, I accepted.

The list of the conference organizers was impressive. Prominent representatives from various fields and cultures had joined together to promote vegetarianism. The conference was held on the grounds of the most prestigious hotel in Pune. Gathered on stage were distinguished leaders from the fields of religion, politics, science, business, social work, and even the military. Thousands of delegates from around the world sat in the audience.

The program began with a representative from each religion reciting a short prayer of invocation. Then all the participants on stage joined to light a sacred lamp. One after another, the distinguished speakers appealed for compassion, nonviolence, and reverence for all life. Finally my turn came to speak:

"I am very pleased to be with you today and wish to express my gratitude to the organizers, especially my dear friend Sri Bhari Malhotra; his older brother, Sri S. P. Malhotra; and all the other great souls who have helped organize and make this function so successful.

"We are here to appreciate and develop reverence for all life. The *Bhagavad-gītā,* which is a scientific explanation of the Supreme Soul and His relationship with the individual soul, explains that all life emanates from the supreme life, or God, known in Sanskrit as Kṛṣṇa. When we have reverence for God, naturally we have reverence for all life. If we love God, naturally we will love all living entities, who come from Him. Lord Kṛṣṇa states in the *Bhagavad-gītā, mamaivāṁśo jīva-loke jīva-bhūtaḥ sanātanaḥ*: 'All living entities are My fragmental parts and parcels, and they are eternal.'

"The *Bhagavad-gītā* also explains that a learned person sees all living entities equally—*paṇḍitāḥ sama-darśinaḥ*—because he sees the same soul within the different varieties of bodies. My spiritual master, His Divine Grace A.C. Bhaktivedanta Swami Prabhupāda, used to say, 'We want brotherhood, but what does it mean to be brothers? It means we have the same father.' Only when we recognize God as the supreme father can we have real brotherhood. Knowing God to be the supreme father, we can understand that if we deal with God's other children nicely, God will be pleased. But if we try to exploit and commit violence upon one another, how will the supreme father be pleased? And if God is not pleased, how can we expect peace and prosperity in the world?

"Animals are also children of God, although they have less developed intelligence. They resemble human children, who also do not have developed intelligence, or developed speech. Nor can they defend themselves. But in a family the strong are meant to protect the weak. For a stronger, older brother to torture or massacre a baby is a terrible crime. How upset and angry the father would be! Animals should be treated like our younger brothers or sisters, to be protected, not exploited or slaughtered so we can eat their flesh.

"By Kṛṣṇa consciousness, by realizing that God is the supreme father of all living entities, we can actually achieve brotherhood and unity among all living beings.

"Now, we have heard many wonderful talks today. I felt enlightened by hearing the noble thoughts expressed by the esteemed participants. We have heard about the need for love, for compassion, for reverence for all life. We have heard of the horrors of cruelty and violence inflicted on less fortunate living beings. But we are faced with the practical fact that so many human beings do not love as much as they should. Nor do they have as much compassion or reverence as they should. So how to create the love and other finer sentiments we value? There must be some process.

"The *Gītā* and other scriptures of the world advise us that to develop love for God, which naturally includes love for all living entities, we must adopt a spiritual process. And the best process recommended for the present age is the chanting of the holy names of God. The Vedic scriptures advise:

harer nāma harer nāma
harer nāmaiva kevalam
kalau nāsty eva nāsty eva
nāsty eva gatir anyathā

'One should chant the holy names, chant the holy names, chant the holy names. There is no other means of success in the age of Kali [the present age].' (*Bṛhan-nāradīya Purāṇa* 38.126)

"The Koran too advises that one should chant the names of God. For many years I had the opportunity to go to Pakistan and teach Kṛṣṇa consciousness. I was pleased to meet some very learned Muslim friends of ours. Just as the Hindus have *Viṣṇu-sahasra-nāma*, 'The Thousand Names of Viṣṇu,' the Muslims have 'Ninety-Nine Names of God.' The Koran (7.180) states, 'The most beautiful names belong to God, so call on Him by them.' And learned Muslims understand that they can achieve the perfection of life by chanting the holy name of God at death. I even learned from my Muslim friends how vegetarianism is part of the teachings of the Koran, and I saw a book by a Muslim physician entitled *Vegetarianism and the Koran*.

"Similarly, the Bible enjoins that one should praise the name of the Lord with cymbals and drums. And in the teachings of Buddha, one is advised to chant the holy names of God:

'All who sincerely call upon My name will come to Me after death, and I will take them to paradise.' (*Buddhist Sūtras*, Vow of Amida Buddha, 18)

"So the chanting of the holy names of the Lord is a universal process recommended in all scriptures for the current age, and unless we adopt a practical means for purifying the heart of hatred and anger and violence, our pontification and platitudes will not really bring the desired results. So I appeal to you all. Many of you are important leaders in society. Even if you are not very big leaders, you are leaders in your society, in your community, in your family. Please consider the need to chant the holy names of God to purify the heart of the sinful desire to commit violence on other living entities.

"All over the world we have practical experience of the effects of chanting the names of God. The Vedic literature explains that in this age, the Age of Kali, the Lord Himself, Śrī Kṛṣṇa, appears as Śrī Kṛṣṇa Caitanya. Five hundred years ago Caitanya Mahāprabhu predicted:

pṛthivīte āche yata nagarādi grāma
sarvatra pracāra haibe mora nāma

'In every town and village of the world, My name will be sung.' (*Cb* 3.4.126)

"ISKCON's founder and spiritual master, His Divine Grace A.C. Bhaktivedanta Swami Prabhupāda, was instrumental in fulfilling the desire and prediction of Lord Caitanya. And what has been the consequence of chanting throughout the world? People addicted to all sorts of bad habits have given up their vicious activities and are following regulative principles: no meat, fish, or eggs; no intoxication; no gambling; and no illicit sex. Those who from babyhood were fed meat, without any consideration that meat-eating is wrong, have become vegetarians, or 'Kṛṣṇatarians,' who eat only sanctified food offered to the

Lord. The potency of chanting the names of God is so great. And I believe that our aspirations for reverence for all life, for an end to unnecessary violence, can be successful only if people are engaged on a large scale in chanting the holy names of God.

"Thank you very much. Hare Kṛṣṇa."

Sri Bhari Malhotra interjected, "Why don't we all chant!"

I continued: "Actually, these names of God are not sectarian. There is no question of a Hindu God or a Muslim God or a Christian God. There is only one God, who is the supreme father of all of us. And He is not Hindu, Christian, or Muslim, but He is the supreme spirit soul.

"So now we'll chant Hare Kṛṣṇa, and later, if any of you want to lead the chanting of any other name of God, we will also be happy to join in."

I led the audience in chanting the Hare Kṛṣṇa *mantra* responsively, first two words at a time, then four, then eight, and finally all sixteen words. Eventually almost everyone in the audience—respectable ladies and gentlemen of various faiths—were standing and clapping and singing: Hare Kṛṣṇa, Hare Kṛṣṇa, Kṛṣṇa Kṛṣṇa, Hare Hare/ Hare Rāma, Hare Rāma, Rāma Rāma, Hare Hare.

I thought, "Now the conference is successful. The participants have chanted the holy names of Kṛṣṇa, the origin of all life."

The Lord's Special Mercy

anugrahāya bhaktānāṁ
mānuṣaṁ deham āsthitaḥ
bhajate tādṛśīḥ krīḍa
yāḥ śrutvā tat-paro bhavet

"The Supreme Lord Kṛṣṇa manifests His humanlike form to show mercy to His devotees, and He performs such wonderful pastimes that anyone who hears them will become exclusively devoted to Him."

—*Śrīmad-Bhāgavatam* 10.33.36

Some persons believe that the Lord is ultimately impersonal and that the impersonal "One" assumes various temporary forms. But Vedic scripture, the *Bhagavad-gītā*, describes such persons as follows:

avyaktaṁ vyaktim āpannaṁ
manyante mām abuddhayaḥ
paraṁ bhāvam ajānanto
mamāvyayam anuttamam

"Unintelligent men, who do not know Me perfectly, think that I, the Supreme Personality of Godhead, Kṛṣṇa, was impersonal before and have now assumed this personality. Due to their small knowledge, they do not know My higher nature, which is imperishable and supreme." (*Bg* 7.24)

Yāmunācārya, a great devotee in the disciplic succession of Rāmānujācārya, has written:

tvāṁ śīla-rūpa-caritaiḥ parama-prakṛṣṭaiḥ
sattvena sāttvikatayā prabalaiś ca śāstraiḥ
prakhyāta-daiva-paramārtha-vidāṁ mataiś ca
naivāsura-prakṛtayaḥ prabhavanti boddhum

"My dear Lord, devotees like Vyāsadeva and Nārada know You to be the Personality of Godhead. By understanding different Vedic literatures, one can come to know Your characteristics, Your form, and Your activities, and one can thus understand that You are the Supreme Personality of Godhead. But those who are in the modes of passion and ignorance—the demons, the nondevotees—cannot understand You. However expert such nondevotees may be in discussing *Vedānta* and the *Upaniṣads* and other Vedic literatures, it is not possible for them to understand the Personality of Godhead." (*Stotra-ratna* 12)

Persons who believe that the Absolute Truth is impersonal are described as *abuddhayaḥ*, less-intelligent persons who do not know the ultimate feature of the Absolute Truth. *Śrīmad-Bhāgavatam* states that supreme realization begins from impersonal Brahman and then rises to localized Paramātmā—but the last word in the Absolute Truth is the Supreme Personality of Godhead. Modern impersonalists are even less intelligent, for they do not even follow their great predecessor Śaṅkarācārya, who stated specifically that Kṛṣṇa is the Supreme Personality of Godhead. Impersonalists, therefore, not knowing the Supreme Truth, think Kṛṣṇa to be only the son of Devakī and Vasudeva, or a prince, or a powerful living entity. This is further condemned by Lord Kṛṣṇa in the *Bhagavad-gītā* (9.11): *Avajānanti māṁ mūḍhā mānuṣīṁ tanum āśritam*—"Only fools regard Me as an ordinary person."

The fact is that no one can understand Kṛṣṇa without engaging in devotional service and developing Kṛṣṇa consciousness. The *Bhāgavatam* (10.14.29) confirms this:

athāpi te deva padāmbuja-dvaya-
prasāda-leśānugṛhīta eva hi
jānāti tattvaṁ bhagavan-mahimno
na cānya eko 'pi ciraṁ vicinvan

"My Lord, if one is favored by even a slight trace of the mercy of Your lotus feet, he can understand the greatness of Your personality. But those who speculate to understand the Supreme Personality of Godhead are unable to know You, even though they continue to study the *Vedas* for many years." One cannot understand the Supreme Personality of Godhead, Kṛṣṇa, or His form, quality, or name simply by mental speculation or by discussion of Vedic literature. One can understand Him only by devotional service.

Therefore the Lord descends to attract the fallen conditioned souls to His transcendental loving service, so they can understand the Supreme Lord in truth and experience supreme bliss in relation to Him.

The Lord appears in different incarnations—as a fish, tortoise, and boar, as Paraśurāma, Lord Rāma, Buddha, and so on—to reciprocate the different appreciations of living entities in different stages of evolution. Although inconceivable to the human brain, incarnations of the Personality of Godhead appear in all species of life. But the Supreme Lord bestows His most merciful benediction to human society when He appears in His human form, thus giving human beings the opportunity to engage in different varieties of eternal service to Him.

That the humanlike form of Kṛṣṇa is the original form of Godhead is confirmed in *Śrīmad-Bhāgavatam* (1.3.28): *ete cāṁśa-kalāḥ puṁsaḥ kṛṣṇas tu bhagavān svayam*—"All of the above-mentioned incarnations are either plenary portions or portions of the plenary portions of the Lord, but Lord Śrī Kṛṣṇa is the original Personality of Godhead."

Even the Bible states, "Man is created in the image of God." Although in one sense all species are created in the image of God, the human species, the highest, is created specifically in the image of Kṛṣṇa, the original Supreme Personality of Godhead.

The human form of life has special significance because only in the human form can the living entity revive his eternal relationship with the Supreme Personality of Godhead. The human form is the best position for devotional service. If one takes advantage of the more highly developed consciousness in human life, one can regain his position of devotional service to Kṛṣṇa.

Adoration, servitorship, friendship, parental affection, and conjugal love are the five primary relationships with Kṛṣṇa. The highest perfectional stage of conjugal love, called *parakīya-rasa*, is the highest loving relationship exhibited between Lord Kṛṣṇa and His devotees.

The Lord is by nature eternal, full of knowledge, and full of bliss, and when we revive our eternal relationship with Him, we regain our original position of eternity, knowledge, and bliss. When we hear of the pastimes of the Lord, our inherent natural propensity to serve the Lord becomes awakened. "Special natural appreciation of the description of a particular pastime of Godhead indicates the constitutional position of a living entity." (Cc *Ādi* 4.34 purport) Therefore, we *must* hear about the pastimes of the Lord, so that our eternal loving service mood can be revived.

Śrī Caitanya-caritāmṛta (*Ādi* 4.35) states that the use of the verb *bhavet*, which is in the imperative mood, indicates that one must certainly hear about the pastimes of Kṛṣṇa and develop one's inclination to serve Him. If one does not do so, he disobeys the injunction of the scripture.

The original commentator on *Śrīmad-Bhāgavatam*, Śrīla Śrīdhara Svāmī, comments that in order to attract the minds of persons attached to the taste of sense gratification, Śrī Kṛṣṇa displays His eternal pastimes. The absolute world is transcendental. There are no activities of material sense gratification in the spiritual world. The transactions between lover and beloved in the spiritual world are pure transcendental love and bliss, far different from the perverted reflection in the material world.

Therefore Śrīla Prabhupāda concludes: "One who has not

been attracted by the transcendental beauty of *rasa* will certainly be dragged down into material attraction, thus to act in material contamination and progress to the darkest region of hellish life. But by understanding the conjugal love of Rādhā and Kṛṣṇa, one is freed from the grip of attraction to material so-called love between man and woman. Similarly, if one understands the pure parental love of Nanda and Yaśodā for Kṛṣṇa, he will be saved from being dragged into material parental affection. If one accepts Kṛṣṇa as the supreme friend, the attraction of material friendship will be finished for him, and he will not be dismayed by so-called friendship with mundane wranglers. If he is attracted by servitorship to Kṛṣṇa, he will no longer have to serve the material body in the degraded status of material existence with the false hope of becoming master in the future. Similarly, one who sees the greatness of Kṛṣṇa in neutrality will certainly never again seek the so-called relief of impersonalist or voidist philosophy. If one is not attracted by the transcendental nature of Kṛṣṇa, one is sure to be attracted to material enjoyment, thus to become implicated in the clinging network of virtuous and sinful activities and continue material existence by transmigrating from one material body to another. Only in Kṛṣṇa consciousness can one achieve the highest perfection of life." (*Cc Ādi* 4.35 purport)

Out of His mercy, Kṛṣṇa has descended to display His eternal pastimes, just to attract us to His service. So we should make the Lord's mission successful: we should hear His pastimes and engage in His transcendental loving service.

Ratha-yātrā Message

Although Giriraj Swami was expected to be guest of honor at Ratha-yātrā in Durban, South Africa, circumstances obliged him to remain in Bombay and thus miss the festival. He sent the following message to be read at the celebrations:

My dear devotees and friends,

The Ratha-yātrā festival is an ancient celebration dating back many thousands of years. The deities of Jagannātha, Baladeva, and Subhadrā represent the Supreme Personality of Godhead, His first expansion, and His internal potency. Kṛṣṇa is the Absolute Truth, the Supreme Personality of Godhead, and He expands Himself into various incarnations and energies, all of whom work according to His will. He is the possessor of all energies, and these energies are also persons who wish only to serve the will of Kṛṣṇa and give pleasure to the Lord.

Five thousand years ago Lord Kṛṣṇa descended on earth with His various expansions and energies. Lord Baladeva appeared as Kṛṣṇa's older brother and Subhadrā-devī appeared as His sister. Just after appearing in this world, Kṛṣṇa was transferred to a small cowherd village named Vṛndāvana. Although Kṛṣṇa is the Supreme Personality of Godhead, He acted as ordinary children do: growing and playing just like them. All of the residents of Vṛndāvana were devotees of Kṛṣṇa, and they loved Him more than anything—even more than their own life's breath. They were prepared to do anything for Kṛṣṇa's pleasure.

Of all the devotees of Kṛṣṇa, God, the best are the *gopīs* of Vṛndāvana. They had no thought other than the happiness of Kṛṣṇa. When Kṛṣṇa would go to herd the cows in the pastures during the day, the *gopīs* would stay at home and cry. Why were they crying? They were thinking of the soft soles of Kṛṣṇa's lotus feet—that they may be pricked by pebbles or thorns on the way—and feeling pained, they would cry.

Of course, Kṛṣṇa is the Supreme Personality of Godhead. He has an eternal, blissful spiritual body. He cannot experience any pain as we do. But because He was playing like an ordinary human being to reciprocate in love with His devotees, they, in extreme love, thought that Kṛṣṇa might feel pain, Kṛṣṇa might feel fatigue, Kṛṣṇa might feel hunger. And so the devotees would try to relieve His hunger and fatigue. Sometimes they would massage His lotus feet; sometimes they would fan Him; sometimes they would cook delicious foodstuffs to satisfy His hunger. Because Kṛṣṇa is the Supreme Personality of Godhead, the Absolute Truth, He is perfect and complete. He does not want or lack anything. The only thing He wants or desires is our love, pure love, *prema*. Kṛṣṇa is not hungry for anything except our love, and when the devotee prepares some offering for Him, Kṛṣṇa does not actually accept the material ingredients. What He accepts is the pure love of the devotee.

Because the residents of Vṛndāvana served Kṛṣṇa with pure love, Kṛṣṇa was completely satisfied with their service. However, as fate sometimes ordains, Kṛṣṇa's devotees were separated from Him. Kṛṣṇa left Vṛndāvana for other places.

Then, many years later, there was a solar eclipse, and persons from throughout India went to the holy place known as Kurukṣetra to observe it with various ritualistic ceremonies. When the residents of Vṛndāvana heard that Kṛṣṇa was going to Kurukṣetra, they also wanted to go, not because they were interested in any Vedic rituals but because they wanted to meet Kṛṣṇa. Not only the residents of Vṛndāvana, but all sorts of sages, saintly persons, kings, and others traveled to Kurukṣetra to see the Supreme Personality of Godhead.

We can just imagine the ecstatic exchange between Kṛṣṇa and the residents of Vṛndāvana when they met after so many years of separation. After meeting His other friends and relatives,

Lord Kṛṣṇa then met the *gopīs*. The *gopīs* had been almost dead in separation from Kṛṣṇa, but seeing Him again they felt that their lives had returned to their bodies. But they were not content to see Kṛṣṇa for just a few moments at Kurukṣetra. In fact, they were not at all happy to see Kṛṣṇa dressed as a royal prince with horses and elephants and chariots and soldiers and servants. They preferred to see Kṛṣṇa dressed as a cowherd boy in the rural atmosphere of the Vṛndāvana forest, beautiful with blossoming flowers, chirping birds, humming bees, the Yamunā River, and Govardhana Hill. They wanted to bring Kṛṣṇa back to Vṛndāvana, even as He was mounted on His royal chariot with Baladeva and Subhadrā. So, the Ratha-yātrā we are celebrating today commemorates the meeting of Kṛṣṇa and His devotees at Kurukṣetra.

Śrī Caitanya Mahāprabhu celebrated the Ratha-yātrā at Jagannātha Purī five hundred years ago in the same mood. When Lord Caitanya was pulling the chariot of Jagannātha, He was experiencing the same ecstasy as Śrīmatī Rādhārāṇī, who wanted to take Kṛṣṇa back to Vṛndāvana. So Gauḍīya Vaiṣṇavas appreciate the inner feelings of Lord Caitanya at the Ratha-yātrā, and people in general can also appreciate the beauty and mercy of the Lord—how He comes out of the temple, lotus face smiling, lotus eyes glancing, giving benediction to all. So on this occasion we are sure that Lord Jagannātha will bestow His most gracious blessings upon all of you who are so fortunate to be present for the Lord's Chariot Festival.

Unfortunately, I am not one of those souls fortunate enough to be present at the festival this year, so on this occasion you should also pray for me, that I will be able to attend next year.

Thank you very much.

Hare Kṛṣṇa, Hare Kṛṣṇa, Kṛṣṇa Kṛṣṇa, Hare Hare/ Hare Rāma, Hare Rāma, Rāma Rāma, Hare Hare.

Yours in the service of the Lord,
Giriraj Swami

The Real Cure

My dear devotees, guests, and friends,

Please accept my best wishes on the occasion of the opening of the Bhaktivedanta Hospital. All glories to His Divine Grace, A. C. Bhaktivedanta Swami Prabhupāda.

Many months ago I committed myself to be in South Africa on this date; thus I am unable to be with you now. But although I cannot be with you in person, I am with you in spirit.

We are grateful to His Grace Kṛṣṇacandra Prabhu and the other organizers of the Bhaktivedanta Hospital for their great contribution to the spiritual and material well-being of both the general populace and the devotees, under the spiritual guidance of His Holiness Radhanath Swami Mahārāja.

In the *Bhāgavatam* Śrī Prahlāda Mahārāja prays to the Supreme Personality of Godhead Kṛṣṇa in the form of Lord Nṛsiṁhadeva, *bālasya neha śaraṇaṁ pitarau nṛsiṁha nārtasya cāgadam udanvati majjato nauḥ*: "My Lord Nṛsiṁhadeva, O Supreme, because of a bodily conception of life, embodied souls neglected and not cared for by You cannot do anything for their betterment. Whatever remedies they accept, although perhaps temporarily beneficial, are certainly impermanent. For example, a father and mother cannot protect their child, a physician and medicine cannot relieve a suffering patient, and a boat on the ocean cannot protect a drowning man." (*SB* 7.9.19)

Commenting on the above verse, Śrīla Prabhupāda remarks, "We are opening hospitals with beds. We may do that, but at the same time the patients must be Kṛṣṇa conscious. We have practical examples. Some of our devotees go to the hospitals, and the patients purchase our books and become devotees. Even in the hospital beds they're reading *Śrīmad-Bhāgavatam* and *Bhagavad-gītā* and benefiting. That is the real remedy, so after being cured they'll become devotees. This literature is the cure. . . . Kṛṣṇa consciousness is the real cure. Without Kṛṣṇa's protection, all other measures are useless. Therefore we have to teach people how to take shelter of Kṛṣṇa." (SP lecture on *SB* 7.9.19)

We are pleased that the Bhaktivedanta Hospital will give patients the real cure—Kṛṣṇa consciousness—along with the ordinary medicine. Here patients will be blessed with the association of the Lord's devotees. Although material life entails suffering, the association of Lord Kṛṣṇa's devotees and the shelter of Lord Kṛṣṇa's lotus feet can save us. As confirmed by Prahlāda Mahārāja, *mahīyasāṁ pāda-rajo-'bhiṣekaṁ niṣkiñcanānāṁ na vṛṇīta yāvat*: "Unless human society accepts the dust of the lotus feet of great devotees who have nothing to do with material possessions, mankind cannot turn its attention to the lotus feet of Kṛṣṇa. Those lotus feet vanquish all the unwanted miserable conditions of material life." (*SB* 7.5.32)

We also feel indebted to the devotees of the hospital for the great service they will render to other devotees. Although devotees do not identify with the body, they engage the body in the Lord's service. So for the sake of Kṛṣṇa's service they take care of the body. Thus the hospital will serve the devotees and ultimately the Lord by affording devotees complete medical care in a spiritual atmosphere. Devotees from throughout the world may come and avail themselves of the facilities.

We wish the Bhaktivedanta Hospital and all associated with it all success. May Śrīla Prabhupāda, Śrī Caitanya Mahāprabhu, and Śrī Śrī Rādhā and Kṛṣṇa bless this great effort.

Hare Kṛṣṇa!

Your servant,
Giriraj Swami

Prabhupāda's Gifts

On December 23, 1995, over 30, 000 people attended the inauguration of Śrīla Prabhupāda's Centennial in the NSCI Stadium in central Bombay—the largest gathering for a single function in the history of ISKCON in India. The glittering event drew leading industrialists, celebrities, and VIPs to honor Śrīla Prabhupāda's contributions to India and the world. The chief minister of Maharashtra and its minister of Cultural Affairs expressed their appreciation of Śrīla Prabhupāda and his movement, and the chief minister ended his talk by loudly proclaiming three times, "Śrīla Prabhupāda ki jaya!" *("All glories to Śrīla Prabhupāda"). All four GBCs for Bombay—His Holiness Giriraj Swami, His Holiness Gopal Krishna Goswami, His Holiness Radhanath Swami, and His Holiness Sridhar Swami—were personally present. Giriraj Swami was asked to give blessings.*

I do not know what blessings I can give personally, but I can tell you about Śrīla Prabhupāda's blessings and hope you will take advantage of them.

According to Vedic literature, five processes of devotional service are most potent. By even a slight contact with any one of them, one can awaken dormant love for Kṛṣṇa and attain the supreme goal of life. Through ISKCON Śrīla Prabhupāda has given us the best facility to engage in those activities. First is *sādhu-saṅga*, the association of devotees. Śrīla Prabhupāda said he created the International Society for Krishna Consciousness to give people the opportunity to associate with devotees. So please take advantage of this blessing of Śrīla Prabhupāda and associate with pure devotees of Śrī Kṛṣṇa.

Then, *nāma-kīrtana*, the chanting of the holy names of the Lord. Especially in Kali-yuga,

harer nāma harer nāma
harer nāmaiva kevalam
kalau nāsty eva nāsty eva
nāsty eva gatir anyathā

"One should chant the holy names, chant the holy names, chant the holy names. There is no other way, no other way, no other way for success in the present age." (*Bṛhan-nāradīya Purāṇa* 38.126)

The Lord Himself, Śrī Kṛṣṇa Himself, has incarnated in the Age of Kali as Śrī Kṛṣṇa Caitanya Mahāprabhu, as confirmed in *Śrīmad-Bhāgavatam* and other Vedic *śāstras*. And He predicted and desired,

pṛthivīte āche yata nagarādi grāma
sarvatra pracāra haibe mora nāma

"In every town and village of every country in the world, the name of Kṛṣṇa will be sung and preached." (*Cb* 3.4.126) So we may say with confidence that Śrīla Prabhupāda is the person who appeared on earth to fulfill the desire and prediction of the Supreme Personality of Godhead, Śrī Kṛṣṇa Caitanya. So we should all take advantage of this blessing of Śrīla Prabhupāda and chant Hare Kṛṣṇa.

Then *bhāgavata-śravaṇa*, hearing *Śrīmad-Bhāgavatam*. As Sri Shrichand Hindujaji mentioned, Śrīla Prabhupāda went to the United States practically without any possessions. He had just forty rupees, about seven dollars then, or as Śrīla Prabhupāda said, "just one day's spending in New York." Now it's not even one minute's spending! But he also brought with him the most valuable treasure of *Śrīmad-Bhāgavatam*. In addition to translating *Śrīmad-Bhāgavatam*, Śrīla Prabhupāda translated *Bhagavad-gītā As It Is*, *Śrī Īśopaniṣad*, *Śrī Caitanya-caritāmṛta*, and summary studies of many other Vedic scriptures, which all present the same conclusions as *Śrīmad-Bhāgavatam*. So we request you, please take advantage of this blessing of Śrīla Prabhupāda and read his translations of *bhāgavata* philosophy.

Then *mathurā-vāsa*, living in holy places. Śrīla Prabhupāda established the most wonderful temples, guesthouses, and *gurukulas* in Vṛndāvana and Māyāpur. So we request all of you—everyone likes to travel and see places—take the opportunity and visit these holy places, the holiest places in Kṛṣṇa consciousness, Śrī Vṛndāvana-dhāma and Śrī Māyāpur-dhāma; stay at our ISKCON centers; and enhance your Kṛṣṇa consciousness.

And finally, *śrī-mūrtira śraddhāya sevana*, worshiping the Deity with faith and veneration. Śrīla Prabhupāda established Deities of Rādhā and Kṛṣṇa all over the world, so you may visit any ISKCON temple in practically any city of the world and participate in the worship of Śrī Śrī Rādhā and Kṛṣṇa. Here in Bombay alone we have three temples: At Juhu, Śrī Śrī Rādhā-Rāsabihārījī Mandir; at Chowpatti, Śrī Śrī Rādhā-Gopīnātha; and at Bhayandar, Śrī Śrī Rādhā-Giridhārī. So please take advantage of this blessing of Śrīla Prabhupāda and worship Rādhā and Kṛṣṇa as They are being worshiped according to authorized scriptures in all ISKCON centers.

Śrīla Prabhupāda is so munificent. Just as Lord Caitanya is described as the most munificent incarnation of Godhead, even more merciful than Kṛṣṇa Himself, because He came to give freely what no other incarnation ever gave before, pure love of Kṛṣṇa, similarly Śrīla Prabhupāda, as the perfect representative of Śrī Caitanya Mahāprabhu, is most mercifully giving the greatest benediction of all, pure love of Godhead, *kṛṣṇa-prema*, through the process of chanting the holy names and pure devotional service—specifically through the medium of ISKCON.

So we thank you all for coming here tonight to glorify Śrīla Prabhupāda and take his blessings. In conclusion, I request you to please repeat after me: Hare Kṛṣṇa, Hare Kṛṣṇa, Kṛṣṇa Kṛṣṇa, Hare Hare/ Hare Rāma, Hare Rāma, Rāma Rāma, Hare Hare.

Śrīla Prabhupāda's Incessant Mercy

A lecture given at the Prabhupāda Festival in Los Angeles, May 25, 1998.

svayaṁ samuttīrya sudustaraṁ dyuman
bhavārṇavaṁ bhīmam adabhra-sauhṛdāḥ
bhavat-padāmbhoruha-nāvam atra te
nidhāya yātāḥ sad-anugraho bhavān

"O Lord, who resemble the shining sun, You are always ready to fulfill the desire of Your devotee, and therefore You are known as a desire tree [*vāñchā-kalpataru*]. When *ācāryas* completely take shelter under Your lotus feet in order to cross the fierce ocean of nescience, they leave behind on earth the method by which they cross, and because You are very merciful to Your other devotees, You accept this method to help them."(*SB* 10.2.31)

PURPORT by Śrīla Prabhupāda

This statement reveals how the merciful *ācāryas* and the merciful Supreme Personality of Godhead together help the serious devotee who wants to return home, back to Godhead. Śrī Caitanya Mahāprabhu, in His teachings to Rūpa Gosvāmī, said:

brahmāṇḍa bhramite kona bhāgyavān jīva
guru-kṛṣṇa-prasāde pāya bhakti-latā-bīja
(*Cc Madhya* 19.151)

One can achieve the seed of *bhakti-latā*, devotional service, by the mercy of *guru* and Kṛṣṇa. The duty of the *guru* is to find the means, according to the time, the circumstances, and the candidate, by which one can be induced to render devotional service, which Kṛṣṇa accepts from a candidate who wants to be successful in going back home, back to Godhead. After wandering throughout the universe, a fortunate person within this material world seeks shelter of such a *guru*, or *ācārya*, who trains the devotee in the suitable ways to render service according to the circumstances so that the Supreme Personality of Godhead will accept the service. This makes it easier for the candidate to reach the ultimate destination. The *ācārya's* duty, therefore, is to find the means by which devotees may render service according to references from *śāstra*. Rūpa Gosvāmī, for example, in order to help subsequent devotees, published such devotional books as *Bhakti-rasāmṛta-sindhu*. Thus it is the duty of the *ācārya* to publish books that will help future candidates take up the method of service and become eligible to return home, back to Godhead, by the mercy of the Lord. In our Kṛṣṇa consciousness movement, this same path is being prescribed and followed. Thus the devotees have been advised to refrain from four sinful activities—illicit sex, intoxication, meat-eating, and gambling—and to chant sixteen rounds a day. These are bona fide instructions. Because in the Western countries constant chanting is not possible, one should not artificially imitate Haridāsa Ṭhākura but should follow this method. Kṛṣṇa will accept a devotee who strictly follows the regulative principles and the method prescribed in the various books and literatures published by the authorities. The *ācārya* gives the suitable method for crossing the ocean of nescience by accepting the boat of the Lord's lotus feet, and if this method is strictly followed, the followers will ultimately reach the destination, by the grace of the Lord. This method is called *ācārya-sampradāya*. It is therefore said, *sampradāya-vihīnā ye mantrās te niṣphalā matāḥ (Padma Purāṇa)*. The *ācārya-sampradāya* is strictly bona fide. Therefore one must accept the *ācārya-sampradāya*; otherwise one's endeavor will be futile. Śrīla Narottama dāsa Ṭhākura therefore sings:

tāṅdera caraṇa sevi bhakta-sane vāsa
janame janame haya, ei abhilāṣa

One must worship the lotus feet of the *ācārya* and live within the society of devotees. Then one's endeavor to cross over nescience will surely be successful.

LECTURE

We are gathered today at the lotus feet of the *ācārya*, whose mercy and mission are described here. Śrī Caitanya Mahāprabhu advised that one should make one's life successful by becoming Kṛṣṇa conscious and do good for others by helping them to become Kṛṣṇa conscious. Śrīla Prabhupāda, as the *ācārya*, has shown the example: he followed a system of devotional service and successfully crossed the ocean of nescience, and in crossing he left behind the same method for us to utilize to cross and meet him on the other side.

In the purport, Śrīla Prabhupāda gives the essence of the method he left behind: chanting sixteen rounds of the Hare Kṛṣṇa *mahā-mantra* daily and following the regulative principles, especially no illicit sex, no intoxication, no meat-eating, and no gambling. The process Prabhupāda left is so simple that some people doubt whether that method is sufficient to cross the ocean of nescience and go back to Godhead. Some say that Śrīla Prabhupāda did not give us everything we need for going to Kṛṣṇa, that we must add something from somewhere else. But here Śrīla Prabhupāda affirms that the method he has left for us is bona fide and sufficient to carry us across the ocean of birth and death back to Godhead. (Of course, Śrīla Prabhupāda does not say "he," but we know he is the *ācārya* who did it for us.)

Śrīla Prabhupāda also explains why: Lord Kṛṣṇa is very favorable to His devotees. We cannot even imagine how favorably disposed Kṛṣṇa is to a devotee like Śrīla Prabhupāda, who risked everything and gave his life to preach Kṛṣṇa consciousness, following the order of superior authorities, the order of his spiritual master and Śrī Caitanya Mahāprabhu. There is nothing, I believe, that Kṛṣṇa would not do for Śrīla Prabhupāda. And Śrīla Prabhupāda desired that every living entity go back home, back to Godhead—what to speak of the disciples who surrendered unto him or unto the devotees who even now are surrendering unto his lotus feet by following his instructions and serving his mission.

Because Kṛṣṇa has so much love for Śrīla Prabhupāda, He will do anything for him. He will fulfill Śrīla Prabhupāda's desire that all who take shelter of his lotus feet and follow his instructions will go back home, back to Godhead.

Some years ago I wondered, "Is Śrīla Prabhupāda's promise true, that just by chanting sixteen rounds, following the regulative principles, and doing our best to spread Kṛṣṇa consciousness we can go back to Godhead?"

Then I thought of Śrīla Prabhupāda's purport to the verse *kaunteya pratijānīhi na me bhaktaḥ praṇaśyati.* Prabhupāda raises the question, "Why did Kṛṣṇa tell Arjuna to make the declaration? Why did He not make it Himself?" Śrīla Prabhupāda explains that of all of Kṛṣṇa's qualities, His quality of being favorable to His devotees is considered best. For the sake of protecting His devotee, Kṛṣṇa is ready to sacrifice a lesser principle, even the principle of truthfulness. So although Kṛṣṇa is most truthful, for the sake of His devotee He may even break His own promise.

We have one such instance when, during the Battle of Kurukṣetra, Duryodhana criticized Bhīṣmadeva that because of his affection for the Pāṇḍavas he was not doing his best in the battle. This was a great insult to Grandfather Bhīṣma. So Bhīṣma took a vow that he would either kill Kṛṣṇa's friend Arjuna or force Kṛṣṇa to break His vow of not taking part in the fighting—in order to save Arjuna. During the next day's fighting, Bhīṣma fought so heroically that Arjuna was actually in trouble;

he was on the verge of being killed by Bhīṣmadeva. So Lord Kṛṣṇa, in order to protect the life of Arjuna, as well as the vow of Bhīṣma, took up a broken chariot wheel as a weapon and rushed toward Bhīṣma as if to kill him. Lord Kṛṣṇa, for the sake of His devotees, for Arjuna and Bhīṣma, broke His own promise. Kṛṣṇa will never allow the word of His devotee to be broken, and so, breaking His own promise not to fight, the Lord upheld the word of Bhīṣma and thus fulfilled His promise to always protect His devotee.

Coming back to Śrīla Prabhupāda's promise to us that if we chant sixteen rounds, follow the regulative principles, and do our best to spread Kṛṣṇa consciousness, we will go back home, back to Godhead, I considered, "Yes, Śrīla Prabhupāda has given this promise, and Lord Kṛṣṇa, whether personally He would want to or not, is obliged by His own nature to fulfill Śrīla Prabhupāda's promise to us."

Thus, although the method is easy, by the mercy of Śrīla Prabhupāda, it is also effective, by the mercy of Kṛṣṇa, who wants to fulfill Śrīla Prabhupāda's desires and the desires of Śrīla Prabhupāda's followers who are serious about going back to Godhead.

Śrīla Prabhupāda, the *ācārya*, is described in the verse as *adabhra-sauhṛdāḥ*, "incessantly friendly to the fallen souls." We probably all have some experience of Śrīla Prabhupāda's mercy. We experience Śrīla Prabhupāda's mercy when we follow the process strictly. But Śrīla Prabhupāda is so merciful that we can also experience his mercy even when we do not follow so strictly: He always keeps track of us, always looks for the opportunity to help us and bring us back to the boat of devotional service, the boat of the Lord's lotus feet. Somehow or other, through his books, through his followers, or from within the heart, he will bring us back to the boat of Lord Kṛṣṇa's lotus feet, which for us means Śrīla Prabhupāda's lotus feet. Thus he is incessantly merciful; he never gives up on anyone.

When we were with Śrīla Prabhupāda at Kartikeya Mahadevia's house in Bombay, Śrīla Prabhupāda received a phone call from the temple president in Calcutta, who informed Śrīla Prabhupāda that one of Prabhupāda's oldest disciples had fallen into difficulty in India and was smoking ganja. Śrīla Prabhupāda told the authority to tell him that if he didn't stop smoking ganja, Prabhupāda would reject him. When Śrīla Prabhupāda got off the phone, Tamal Krishna Goswami asked, "Śrīla Prabhupāda, is it true that you will reject him if he doesn't stop smoking ganja?" Śrīla Prabhupāda replied, "No. I cannot reject anyone." Then Tamal Krishna Goswami questioned, "But Śrīla Prabhupāda, don't you have to draw the line somewhere? Is there not some limit?" And Śrīla Prabhupāda said, "No. The mercy of Lord Nityānanda is unlimited."

In big or small ways we may all cross the line of what we should and should not do. Still, Śrīla Prabhupāda extends his mercy to us and somehow or other makes us think of him, even when we feel helpless and incapable, under the circumstances, to remember and follow him. But somehow, if we keep the desire somewhere in our hearts to one day again follow, even if we feel too weak to follow now, Śrīla Prabhupāda will understand our heart's desire, excuse us, and look for the opportunity to bring us back to his instructions.

In one sense, Śrīla Prabhupāda's simple instructions are easy to follow. Anyone, even a child, can chant Hare Kṛṣṇa, Hare Kṛṣṇa, Kṛṣṇa Kṛṣṇa, Hare Hare/ Hare Rāma, Hare Rāma, Rāma Rāma, Hare Hare. Our process is not difficult like Vedic sacrifices or the mental and physical gymnastics of the *jñānīs* and *yogīs*. Chanting is simple, as is following the regulative principles. But to have the determination to follow and chant is not so easy. Therefore we need the association of devotees.

Association has such a strong influence. As Śrīla Prabhupāda said, "Man is a social animal. He cannot live without company." And if we associate with nondevotees, we will naturally become inclined to engage in the same activities as they. But if we associate with devotees who follow Śrīla Prabhupāda's instructions, such association will inspire us also to follow. So following the regulative principles also means taking *kṛṣṇa-prasāda* and associating with devotees who are also following.

Although the verse and purport speak primarily about the *ācārya*, at the end of the purport Śrīla Prabhupāda quotes Śrīla Narottama dāsa Ṭhākura:

tāṅdera caraṇa sevi bhakta-sane vāsa
janame janame haya, ei abhilāṣa

"Birth after birth I desire to serve the lotus feet of the *ācāryas* and live in a society of devotees." And in conclusion, Śrīla Prabhupāda comments, "One must worship the lotus feet of the *ācārya* and live within the society of devotees. Then one's endeavor to cross over nescience will surely be successful."

In the early days of ISKCON, living in the association of devotees meant living in the temple. Almost all the devotees who joined then were young and lived like *brahmacārīs*—even the married ones. But as devotees have matured in age and in their understanding of *varṇāśrama-dharma*, and as more older persons have come to Kṛṣṇa consciousness, living in the association of devotees now does not necessarily mean living in the temple. Still, we must live in association with devotees wherever we may be.

In Nārada's instructions on *varṇāśrama-dharma* in the Seventh Canto, he mentions that the householders must again and again hear from saintly persons about the pastimes of the Lord. Śrīla Prabhupāda comments that householders should simplify their lives to spare at least three hours every day to hear and chant about the glories of the Lord, especially in the association of devotees. Once, Śrīla Prabhupāda told me, "We do not expect everyone to live in the temple; very few will live in the temple. Then why have a temple? Just to show the example how they can worship at home." Prabhupāda's method is so simple and sublime that practically we can do at home everything the devotees do in the temple. It is not very difficult. Only we have to have the determination to do it, and that determination develops through association, through the association of Śrīla Prabhupāda's books and the association of Śrīla Prabhupāda's followers. Such association will give us the inspiration to follow strictly.

Events like the Prabhupāda Festival are wonderful occasions for us to come together and see Śrīla Prabhupāda as the center of our lives—as everything for us—and to think very deeply about him, how he was incessantly friendly to the fallen souls, how he sacrificed everything for the mission of Kṛṣṇa consciousness, how he came to America from Vṛndāvana at the age of seventy to save us. And I feel fortunate that I could come here and remember Śrīla Prabhupāda in the association of those who love him.

Hare Kṛṣṇa.

Śrīla Prabhupāda *ki jaya!*

Juhu Silver Jubilee Message

My dear friends and devotees, godsisters and godbrothers,

When Śrīla Prabhupāda held the first meeting for life members in Bombay, in the Akash Ganga building on Warden Road in 1971, he quoted a verse from the *Upadeśāmṛta*:

dadāti pratigṛhṇāti
guhyam ākhyāti pṛcchati
bhuṅkte bhojayate caiva
ṣaḍ-vidhaṁ prīti-lakṣaṇam

"Offering gifts in charity, accepting charitable gifts, revealing one's mind in confidence, inquiring confidentially, accepting *prasāda*, and offering *prasāda* are the six symptoms of love shared by one devotee and another." (*NOI* 4)

Śrīla Prabhupāda went on to explain how we engage in the six reciprocations of love with our life members: We invite them to our temples and serve them *prasāda*, and they invite us to their homes and offer us *prasāda*. They give us charity in the form of donations, and we give them the gift of the holy name. They disclose their minds to us and inquire about devotional service, and we try our best to explain the science and engage them in service.

Then Śrīla Prabhupāda quoted a verse from *Śrīmad-Bhāgavatam* (10.22.35):

etāvaj janma-sāphalyaṁ
dehinām iha dehiṣu
prāṇair arthair dhiyā vācā
śreya-ācaraṇaṁ sadā

"It is the duty of every living being to perform welfare activities for the benefit of others with his life, wealth, intelligence, and words." He explained that if one is able, he should give his whole life. But if he thinks, "How can I give my life? I have my family, my responsibilities," then he can give his wealth. And if one thinks, "I have no money; how can I give?" then he can offer his intelligence: he can suggest, "Oh, you can approach that person. He will help you." And if one thinks, "I have no intelligence; what can I do?" then he can offer his words: he can tell his friends and colleagues, "Oh, these Hare Kṛṣṇa people are very nice. You should go to their temple." Thus Śrīla Prabhupāda explained how we apply these verses in practical activities.

Over the years, Śrīla Prabhupāda engaged in these six reciprocations of love with you—as did we—and thus our relationships developed. And over the years you rendered service to the great cause of Kṛṣṇa consciousness in the various ways cited above, and we became even closer.

I always wanted, on behalf of Śrīla Prabhupāda, to thank you, and to express our appreciation for your service, especially in the early days when Śrīla Prabhupāda was beginning the preaching in Bombay and developing the Juhu project. And I thought the best way to glorify Śrīla Prabhupāda and your service to him would be through writing one or more books about his struggles to get the Juhu land and build the Juhu project. In fact, on the night Śrīla Prabhupāda finally succeeded in getting the land, after the signing of the documents and the sharing of *prasāda*, he reclined back on the bolsters of his *āsana* and remarked, "It was a good fight!" And then he added, "Someone should write a book about it." So I always had it in my mind to write such a book, and by the grace of Śrīla Prabhupāda I may do so.

But now I feel gladdened by the opportunity to glorify all of you and your service to Śrīla Prabhupāda and his mission—and at the same time glorify Śrīla Prabhupāda—through the Silver Jubilee Celebrations. And from the recollections and discussions at the celebrations I hope to get more information and more inspiration to glorify you all in the book or books to come.

When the Juhu temple opened in 1978, *Newsweek* magazine ran a full-page color story about it. The article included a picture of Śrīla Prabhupāda with the caption, "From rags to riches." The story of the Juhu temple really is a story of coming from rags to riches, as everyone can see—and not just for Śrīla Prabhupāda but, in a way, for all of us, even Śrī Śrī Rādhā-Rāsabihārījī. And we gained not only externally but also internally, the greatest treasure, in the reciprocation of service and love.

Śrī Śrī Rādhā-Rāsabihārī began Their stay at Juhu in a *paṇḍāl*. Then, after the *paṇḍāl*, They were moved to a makeshift arrangement of bamboo and cloth. Then They were moved to a semi-permanent structure of bricks and steel tubes covered by asbestos sheets. And finally, on January 14, 1978, They were installed in Their beautiful new marble temple.

When Śrīla Prabhupāda entered the agreement to purchase the land from Mr. Nair, he was concerned about the future of the transaction, and he wanted to secure our possession of the land. So practically as soon as he got possession of the land, Śrīla Prabhupāda brought the Deities. (Later, His Holiness Tamal Krishna Goswami would comment, "We often hear of devotees performing austerities for the sake of the Lord, but in Juhu the Lord performed austerities for the sake of His devotee.") The reciprocation between the devotee and the Lord, and in particular between Śrīla Prabhupāda and Śrī Śrī Rādhā-Rāsabihārī, was gradually, and fully, manifest in Śrīla Prabhupāda's struggle to serve Them in Juhu, with the assistance of his devotees and friends.

Śrīla Prabhupāda had invited the Deities to come to Juhu and told Them, "Please come and sit down here, and I will build a temple for You." Later, when so many difficulties arose with the landlord and the Municipal Corporation, even our best friends and life members suggested that we give up the Juhu land, Hare

Krishna Land, and look for some other place. Eventually Śrīla Prabhupāda explained why he had been so insistent to keep the land. He said, "Actually, I was not so interested in this land. But because Kṛṣṇa came to stay here, it would have been a great insult to drive Him away." Śrīla Prabhupāda could not bear the thought of such an insult to his Lord, and so he struggled to the end to get the land—and in the end he got it.

Śrīla Prabhupāda was the ideal teacher (*ācārya*), and he showed by his own example how to fight for Kṛṣṇa. He was willing to take any pain, go to any extent, take any risk, and perform any austerity for the sake of the Lord. And by his example and his words he inspired us to do as he did.

Once, Śrīla Prabhupāda spoke on a verse from *Śrīmad-Bhāgavatam* about the qualities and behavior of a saintly devotee (*sādhu*):

titikṣavaḥ kāruṇikāḥ
suhṛdaḥ sarva-dehinām
ajāta-śatravaḥ śāntāḥ
sādhavaḥ sādhu-bhūṣaṇāḥ

"The symptoms of a *sādhu* are that he is tolerant, merciful, and friendly to all living entities. He has no enemies, he is peaceful, he abides by the scriptures, and all his characteristics are sublime." (*SB* 3.25.21)

Although Śrīla Prabhupāda himself perfectly exemplified the verse, he related the verse to the devotees in Juhu:

"Here all the boys and girls, the devotees, they are concerned with Rādhā-Kṛṣṇa. That's all. Their whole business, day and night, is Rādhā-Kṛṣṇa. From early morning, three o'clock, to night, ten o'clock, their only business is Rādhā-Kṛṣṇa. That's all. Therefore they are *sādhu*.

"And so many people are criticizing. We are not getting the sanction to build, because we have so many enemies. They say we are creating a 'nuisance.' We are chanting the Hare Kṛṣṇa *mantra*, and that is a 'nuisance.' This complaint is going to the police. So that is very difficult."

Then Śrīla Prabhupāda became emotional and exclaimed: "Therefore a *sādhu* is advised, *titikṣavaḥ*, tolerate! Tolerate all this nonsense! What can be done? We have no other alternative but to tolerate. Nobody's coming to help us. Our business is so thankless. Because we are trying to create one temple, so many enemies are giving hindrance: 'You cannot do it.' Therefore *titikṣavaḥ*. You have to remain *sādhu*. You cannot become *asādhu*. You have to tolerate. What can be done?

"At the same time, you have to become merciful. You know what has happened in this place, Hare Krishna Land? So much attack by the police, by the municipality: 'Break this temple.' We could have gone, concluding, 'What is the use of taking so much botheration? We have hundreds of temples outside India. If people here are not liking, let us go away.' No. *Kāruṇikāḥ*. We have come to distribute Kṛṣṇa consciousness. We must tolerate and give this message to the people. *Kāruṇikāḥ*: very merciful, in spite of all trouble.

"These American boys and girls have come to help me—not that they have come because they are hungry. No. My mission is, 'You Americans, you chant Hare Kṛṣṇa so the people of India will see, "Oh, Americans are also chanting. Why not we?"' But unfortunately—such dull brains—that thought is not coming. But still, we have to do it. We have to tolerate, and we have to become *kāruṇikāḥ*, merciful.

"Why should you want to be merciful? *Para-duḥkha-duḥkhī. Kṛpāmbudhir yas tam ahaṁ prapadye*. A Vaiṣṇava understands, 'These people are engaged like cats and dogs in sense gratification. They are misguided, and in the next life they'll be punished. Let us do something for them.' This is *kāruṇikāḥ*: out of mercy. There is no question of getting something, money. No. We have got sufficient money. But just to become merciful upon these fallen, conditioned souls, who are suffering on account of becoming animalistic, without Kṛṣṇa consciousness, the preacher, the *sādhus* . . . These are *sādhus—titikṣavaḥ*, tolerant: 'Never mind. Whatever hindrances and tribulations they are offering to us, never mind. Tolerate.'

"And *suhṛdaḥ*. *Suhṛdaḥ* means the heart is so nice. . . . The Vaiṣṇava is always thinking how a man can be saved from the clutches of *māyā*. He has no other desire. The Vaiṣṇava is so kind that *suhṛdaḥ sarva-dehinām*: he is kind not only to the human beings but to all embodied souls—cats, dogs, trees, plants, insects. A Vaiṣṇava will hesitate to kill even a mosquito. *Sarva-dehinām*. Not that 'I shall take care of my brother only. I am good, and my brother is good.' No. *Suhṛdaḥ sarva-dehinām*.

"And *ajāta-śatravaḥ*. When one is living in that way, as a *sādhu*, why will others become enemy? The *sādhu* does not create enemies, but people become enemies out of their own character. How can a *sādhu* create enemies? Kṛṣṇa says, *sarva-dharmān parityajya mām ekaṁ śaraṇaṁ vraja* [Bg 18.66], and we are simply teaching, 'My dear human being, my dear friend, you become a surrendered soul to Kṛṣṇa.' So what is our fault? So we don't create any enemy, but they become enemy. Why shall I create enemy? *Suhṛdaḥ sarva-dehinām*. But they become, out of their own nature. . . .

"So we are in this society, human society, and because we are spreading Kṛṣṇa consciousness, the envious, who are more dangerous than snakes, are putting so many impediments. But we have to tolerate. We have no other alternative. You see? *Ajāta-śatravaḥ śāntāḥ*. Be peaceful. What can be done? Depend on Kṛṣṇa.

"These are the ornaments of a *sādhu*: *titikṣavaḥ kāruṇikāḥ suhṛdaḥ sarva-dehinām*. You must know what is a *sādhu*. First, a *sādhu* is a devotee. And if he is a devotee, then all the symptoms are there. Now, you find a *sādhu* and associate with him. Then your path of liberation will be open." (Lecture given at Hare Krishna Land, Juhu, on November 23, 1974)

Of course, Śrīla Prabhupāda was that *sādhu*. And by his words and his example, he encouraged us to try to become *sādhus*. And by the service of such a *sādhu*, one actually develops the qualities of the *sādhu*.

Thus, just as Śrīla Prabhupāda performed great austerities, many devotees in the early stage of the project performed great austerities for the sake of Śrīla Prabhupāda, and for the sake of the Deities. I would not even attempt to mention all your names here. You know who you are, and, more important, Śrīla Prabhupāda and Śrī Śrī Rādhā-Rāsabihārī know who you are. For you, the gates to liberation are open.

Here I think of Lord Kṛṣṇa's words to the *gopīs*, recorded in *Śrīmad-Bhāgavatam* (10.32.21–22): *evaṁ mad-arthojjhita-loka-veda svānām hi vo*: "Simply for My sake you rejected the authority of worldly opinion, of the *Vedas*, and of your relatives."

na pāraye 'haṁ niravadya-saṁyujāṁ
sva-sādhu-kṛtyaṁ vibudhāyuṣāpi vaḥ
yā mābhajan durjara-geha-śṛṅkhalāḥ
saṁvṛścya tad vaḥ pratiyātu sādhunā

"I am not able to repay My debt for your spotless service, even within a lifetime of Brahmā. Your connection with Me is beyond reproach. You have worshiped Me, cutting off all domestic ties, which are difficult to break. Therefore please let your own glorious deeds be your compensation."

I cannot say exactly how Śrīla Prabhupāda and Śrī Śrī Rādhā-Rāsabihārī feel about you, although I know they love you and will shower their sublime mercy upon you. But I do know how I feel. And I pray to remain eternally engaged in the service of Śrīla Prabhupāda and Śrī Śrī Rādhā-Rāsabihārī—and eternally in the service of all of you, their beloved servants.

Thank you. Hare Kṛṣṇa.

Your eternal servant,
Giriraj Swami

4

Lectures

Kṛṣṇa's Gifts

According to *śāstra*, there are two Kṛṣṇas. One is Kṛṣṇa, and the other is the name Kṛṣṇa, and both are Kṛṣṇa equally. We may distinguish between the two because of imperfect or incomplete realization, but when we actually realize the holy name of Kṛṣṇa, we will know that it is Kṛṣṇa and everything associated with Him. *Hare* indicates Śrīmatī Rādhārāṇī, the energy of Kṛṣṇa. When we chant the holy name of Kṛṣṇa, Kṛṣṇa is actually present, and as we progress in chanting we will realize more and more that there is no difference between Kṛṣṇa and Kṛṣṇa's name. And Kṛṣṇa is always accompanied by His entourage in His *dhāma*. So everything—the whole spiritual world, including Kṛṣṇa and His associates as they enjoy pastimes in Kṛṣṇa's abode—is there in the holy name.

All of Kṛṣṇa's qualities are also there in the holy name because the holy name of Kṛṣṇa and Kṛṣṇa Himself are the same in every respect. Whatever attributes we can ascribe to Kṛṣṇa can also be ascribed to His holy name:

nāma cintāmaṇiḥ kṛṣṇaś
caitanya-rasa-vigrahaḥ
pūrnaḥ śuddho nitya-mukto
'bhinnatvān nāma-nāminoḥ

"The holy name of Kṛṣṇa is transcendentally blissful. It bestows all spiritual benedictions, for it is Kṛṣṇa Himself, the reservoir of all pleasure. Kṛṣṇa's name is complete, and it is the form of all transcendental mellows. It is not a material name under any condition, and it is no less powerful than Kṛṣṇa Himself. Since Kṛṣṇa's name is not contaminated by the material qualities, there is no question of its being involved with *māyā*. Kṛṣṇa's name is always liberated and spiritual; it is never conditioned by the laws of material nature. This is because the name of Kṛṣṇa and Kṛṣṇa Himself are identical." (*Padma Purāṇa*)

Once, Satsvarūpa Mahārāja asked Śrīla Prabhupāda, "Now you are here, so we can ask you our questions directly, but what will we do when you are not here?" Śrīla Prabhupāda replied, "The holy name of Kṛṣṇa and Kṛṣṇa are the same. Do you realize this fact?"

We need do nothing else but chant the holy name—nothing. Chanting the holy name is sufficient for our own deliverance and for preaching as well. Although we speak, the actual purpose is to convince people to chant the holy name. As Śrīla Prabhupāda said, *Back to Godhead* magazine is meant simply to convince people to chant Hare Kṛṣṇa. We have so many programs, make so many arrangements, open so many centers, just to give people facility to chant.

And the more we chant, the more we relish. Any material sound or thing cannot be relished increasingly. To the contrary, when we begin to eat, the food tastes very delicious, but as we eat more and more, gradually we lose the taste, until finally we cannot take any more. As Śrīla Prabhupāda said, "When you are satiated you cannot take even one more golden sweetball."

In the early days of the Kṛṣṇa consciousness movement, sweetballs—*gulābjāmuns*, cheese balls fried in pure ghee and soaked in sugar water—were considered the ultimate experience in transcendental bliss. Even then, when someone was satiated he could not take even one more. Sweetballs were so important that Śrīla Prabhupāda used to keep a jar of them by the temple door at 26 Second Avenue. He had so much faith in Kṛṣṇa's *prasāda*—just as he did in Kṛṣṇa's name—that if the young people took *prasāda* they would become purified and satisfied. It is the devotees' only sense gratification. A person can feel so satisfied by taking *kṛṣṇa-prasāda* that he will not think of any other type of enjoyment. So in the beginning Śrīla Prabhupāda encouraged the devotees to take more and more *prasāda*. Anyone who visited him had to get a sweetball, and Śrīla Prabhupāda's were wonderful. He kept a jar of such golden balls suspended in gooey sugar water near the temple entrance, so if anyone wanted to leave Kṛṣṇa consciousness, he would first have to pass the sweetballs. And definitely the person would think, "Before I go, let me take one more—or two or three or four." Most likely, he would realize the higher taste of Kṛṣṇa consciousness and give up the idea of leaving altogether. Or he would become so full that he couldn't move. In any case, Śrīla Prabhupāda called sweetballs "ISKCON bullets—they shoot *māyā* dead."

So *kṛṣṇa-prasāda* is also Kṛṣṇa, and these two processes, chanting Kṛṣṇa's names and taking *kṛṣṇa-prasāda*, are special merciful gifts of Kṛṣṇa Caitanya—Kṛṣṇa in His most munificent form—kindly delivered to us by His Divine Grace Śrīla Prabhupāda.

Pure Servant, Pure Master

"The saint Nārada Muni continued: Although Prahlāda Mahārāja was only a boy, when he heard the benedictions offered by Lord Nṛsiṁhadeva he considered them impediments on the path of devotional service. Thus he smiled very mildly and spoke as follows.

"Prahlāda Mahārāja said: My dear Lord, O Supreme Personality of Godhead, because I was born in an atheistic family I am naturally attached to material enjoyment. Therefore, kindly do not tempt me with these illusions. I am very much afraid of material conditions, and I desire to be liberated from materialistic life. It is for this reason that I have taken shelter of Your lotus feet.

"O my worshipable Lord, because the seed of lusty desires, which is the root cause of material existence, is within the core of everyone's heart, You have sent me to this material world to exhibit the symptoms of a pure devotee.

"Otherwise, O my Lord, O supreme instructor of the entire world, You are so kind to Your devotee that You could not induce him to do something unbeneficial for him. On the other hand, one who desires some material benefit in exchange for devotional service cannot be Your pure devotee. Indeed, he is no better than a merchant who wants profit in exchange for service.

"A servant who desires material profits from his master is certainly not a qualified servant or pure devotee. Similarly, a master who bestows benedictions upon his servant because of a desire to maintain a prestigious position as master is also not a pure master."

—*Śrīmad-Bhāgavatam* 7.10.1–5

Prahlāda Mahārāja explains the pure servant and the pure master. The Lord is a pure master, the supreme master, and the unalloyed devotee with no material motives is the pure servant. One who has materialistic motivations cannot be a true servant. And one who unnecessarily bestows benedictions upon his servant to keep his own prestigious position is not a real master.

The constitutional position of the living entity is to be the eternal servant of Kṛṣṇa. But in the material world, in the bodily concept of life, we accept so many other masters. By constitution we are servants. Yet we have to see where and how we can render service to actually become happy. In the material world, the servant serves the master to get some return, generally some money or sense gratification. Although the servant appears to be serving the master, actually he is not: he is serving his own lusty desires—even though he may appear to be very devoted to his work or to his master. Today one man told me how devoted he is to his work, how much satisfaction he gets from it. But if his pay were stopped, would he continue his work? No. In spite of the pretense of service to others or job satisfaction, the gentleman is actually serving to get something, some money. In the material world, when a servant serves a master for some return, he is not really acting as a servant; he is acting as a businessman. Just as a businessman gives you some commodity in exchange for money, so the so-called servant gives service, so-called service, and takes some money in exchange. So there is no real service, no actual love.

When Lord Nṛsiṁhadeva offered a material benediction to Prahlāda Mahārāja, Prahlāda refused to be tempted, because he wanted a genuine relationship of servant and master. He didn't want to be a merchant, selling services in return for material gains. And he wanted to serve a proper master, who would not give his servant anything unbeneficial for him. The real master is the Supreme Personality of Godhead, because He will not give a devotee any benediction that is not in the devotee's best interest. Although the Lord appeared to tempt Prahlāda Mahārāja with material benefits, He really just wanted Prahlāda to demonstrate the behavior of a pure devotee, that a pure devotee does not accept any material return in exchange for devotional service.

A demigod cannot be a real master, because a demigod may offer material benefits that are not actually beneficial. Śrīla Prabhupāda cites the example of the demon Vṛkāsura, who was given the benediction that anyone whose head he touched would crack. What a horrible benediction! Demigods give such benedictions. The Supreme Lord, on the other hand, never gives such condemned benedictions. We see that Hiraṇyakaśipu was a devotee of Lord Brahmā and that Brahmā gave him such benedictions that he became encouraged to engage in all sorts of atrocious activities. Later, the Supreme Personality of Godhead chastised Brahmā for giving such boons. Similarly, Rāvaṇa and other demons obtained from Lord Śiva and other demigods material powers to be used in horrible ways. Sometimes false masters give material benefits to maintain their prestigious positions. For example, some materialistic person may approach a materialistic guru, and the so-called guru will think, "Oh! If I give him some material benefit he will become my follower and I can advertise that such-and-such big person is my disciple."

One prominent lady in Calcutta, the niece of Netaji Subhash Chandra Bose, began to associate with the ISKCON devotees there. Previously, she had been one of the leading followers and promoters of some false master, who was known for magically producing wristwatches and gold rings. When the false "God" came to Calcutta, she challenged, "Why are you giving material benefits to your followers? By giving them material benefits you are just making them more and more materialistic." Material life always ends in frustration, so to give material things is not the real magic. She told him, "Bhaktivedanta Swami Prabhupāda is doing the real magic. He is taking persons who were attached to all sorts of material activities and transforming them into pure devotees of Lord Kṛṣṇa."

The real master will not put his servant into the material darkness of sense gratification. Rather, he will try to uplift his servant from the material quagmire, and in doing so may even take away some material facility or attachment.

And the pure servant will never complain or resist if the real master takes away some false attachment. Even if the servant does protest and fight, still, the servant—the real servant—will never leave the true master.

Pṛthu Mahārāja spoke a beautiful prayer to Lord Kṛṣṇa, the Supreme Personality of Godhead. He prayed, "Please do not ask me to take some material benefits from You, but as a father, not waiting for the son's demand, does everything for the benefit of the son, please bestow upon me whatever You think best for me." (*SB* 4.20.31)

The father knows what is best for the child. The child himself may not know. Sometimes the father will hug and kiss the child; sometimes he will spank him. Sometimes the father will give sweets to the child, and sometimes he will give some bitter medicine. But whatever he does for the child is in the best interest of the child. Thus Pṛthu Mahārāja prays to the Supreme Lord, "Just as the father does whatever is best for the child, You kindly do whatever is best for me. You are my supreme father."

In other words, the devotee who is surrendered to the Lord serves the Lord without any condition.

In Vṛndāvana the devotees serve the Lord in pure love, without any condition. They do not even place the condition that Kṛṣṇa should be God. Kṛṣṇa may or may not be God. Of course, Kṛṣṇa is the Supreme Personality of Godhead. But here we are describing the mood of pure love in Vṛndāvana. There the devotees are not even concerned whether Kṛṣṇa is God or not. They simply love Kṛṣṇa and want to see that He is happy in all respects. They serve Him without any personal consideration.

Śrīmatī Rādhārāṇī addressed Lord Kṛṣṇa, apparently criticizing Him. She said, "Whoever associates with Your devotees will lose all interest in his family. Suddenly he or she may just leave the family and come to Vṛndāvana. Thus the devotee causes his family members to cry." And when the devotee comes to Vṛndāvana, is the devotee happy? Śrīmatī Rādhārāṇī says, "No. The devotee comes to Vṛndāvana and also cries: 'Where is Kṛṣṇa? Where is Kṛṣṇa?'" She says that the devotee becomes just like a bird—no fixed residence, simply wandering here and there and wondering, "Where will I get food to eat?" So those who associate with pure devotees, and by the association of the pure devotees give up their families, cause their families to suffer and "suffer" themselves when they come to Vṛndāvana in pursuit of Kṛṣṇa.

Great Vedic scholars have analyzed the words of Śrīmatī Rādhārāṇī. They say that although She was apparently criticizing Kṛṣṇa, actually She was praising Him. They ask, "Who are these birds who wander around Vṛndāvana looking for morsels of food?" They are actually great *paramahaṁsas*. *Paramahaṁsas* are liberated souls fully absorbed in relishing the mellows of Kṛṣṇa consciousness. *Haṁsa* means "swan," and the swan has the peculiar ability to extract the milk from a mixture of milk and water—and leave the water. So the *paramahaṁsa* is a swanlike man who knows the essence of life. He goes straight to the essence of life—service to Kṛṣṇa—and leaves aside everything else. Thus he is satisfied.

Only pure devotional service can satisfy the heart's innermost desire; only pure devotional service can satisfy the soul. And so pure devotees, or *paramahaṁsas*, have no desire other than to serve Kṛṣṇa, because in such service they are fully satisfied, as confirmed in *Śrīmad-Bhāgavatam* (2.8.6): "A pure devotee of the Lord whose heart has once been cleansed by the process of devotional service never relinquishes the lotus feet of Lord Kṛṣṇa, for they fully satisfy him."

If I've had a good meal and am fully satisfied, if someone offers me even one beautiful, juicy sweetball, *gulābjāmun*, I will say, "No, please excuse me; I am satisfied." The pure devotee is so satisfied in his relationship with the Lord that he doesn't want anything else. Even if the Lord offers him something, the devotee will say, "Please excuse me; I do not want anything. I am fully satisfied in my relationship with You. I simply want to be Your servant and You to be my master. I don't want anything else."

This is Prahlāda Mahārāja's prayer to Lord Nṛsiṁhadeva. And this is the prayer of any pure devotee. He wants only one benediction: that he may always remember his constitutional position as an eternal servant of the Lord. And being engaged in his constitutional position as the Lord's eternal servant, he is fully satisfied and happy. He desires nothing more.

Hare Kṛṣṇa. Are there any questions or comments?

DEVOTEE: When we come in the material world, or live in the material world, we have various obligations, and according to our circumstances we have various limitations. We want to serve Kṛṣṇa as Kṛṣṇa wants, but we also have to accept our limitations. What should we do?

GIRIRAJ SWAMI: Lord Caitanya has given the answer with reference to a verse from *Śrīmad-Bhāgavatam* (10.14.3). The verse is from the prayers of Lord Brahmā to Lord Kṛṣṇa:

jñāne prayāsam udapāsya namanta eva
jīvanti san-mukharitāṁ bhavadīya-vārtām
sthāne sthitāḥ śruti-gatāṁ tanu-vāṅ-manobhir
ye prāyaśo 'jita jito 'py asi tais tri-lokyām

Jñāne prayāsam udapāsya namanta eva means we should give up the bad habit of mental speculation and just become submissive. *Jīvanti san-mukharitāṁ bhavadīya-vārtām*: one should associate with devotees and hear the glories of the Lord. *Sthāne sthitāḥ* means that one may remain in his position. Everyone has some position in *varṇāśrama-dharma*, as a *brāhmaṇa*, *kṣatriya*, *vaiśya*, *śūdra*, or *brahmacārī*, *gṛhastha*, *vānaprastha*, or *sannyāsī*. Thus if you are a businessman, you may continue as a businessman; you don't have to become a learned scholar. If you are a householder, you may remain a householder. You may remain in your position, but *śruti-gatāṁ tanu-vāṅ-manobhir*—you hear the message of Godhead and engage in the Lord's service with body, mind, and words. Then the Supreme Lord, who is known as *ajita*, unconquerable within the three worlds, can be conquered.

You may remain in your position and follow the process of Kṛṣṇa consciousness, and in the end, when you develop pure love for Kṛṣṇa, Kṛṣṇa will be conquered.

Hare Kṛṣṇa!

Glorious Tests

We read from *Śrīmad-Bhāgavatam* Canto 8, Chapter 22: "Bali Mahārāja Surrenders His Life."

TEXT 28

eṣa dānava-daityānām
agranīḥ kīrti-vardhanaḥ
ajaiṣīd ajayāṁ māyāṁ
sīdann api na muhyati

TRANSLATION

Bali Mahārāja has become the most famous among the demons and nonbelievers, for in spite of being bereft of all material opulences, he is fixed in his devotional service.

PURPORT by Śrīla Prabhupāda

In this verse, the words *sīdann api na muhyati* are very important. A devotee is sometimes put into adversity while executing devotional service. In adversity, everyone laments and becomes aggrieved, but by the grace of the Supreme Personality of Godhead, a devotee, even in the worst condition, can understand that he is going through a severe examination by the Personality of Godhead. Bali Mahārāja passed all such examinations, as explained in the following verses.

TEXTS 29–30

kṣīṇa-rikthaś cyutaḥ sthānāt
kṣipto baddhaś ca śatrubhiḥ
jñātibhiś ca parityakto
yātanām anuyāpitaḥ

guruṇā bhartsitaḥ śapto
jahau satyaṁ na suvrataḥ
chalair ukto mayā dharmo
nāyaṁ tyajati satya-vāk

TRANSLATION

Although bereft of his riches, fallen from his original position, defeated and arrested by his enemies, rebuked and deserted by his relatives and friends, although suffering the pain of being bound, and although rebuked and cursed by his spiritual master, Bali Mahārāja, being fixed in his vow, did not give up his truthfulness. It was certainly with pretension that I spoke about religious principles, but he did not give up religious principles, for he is true to his word.

PURPORT by Śrīla Prabhupāda

Bali Mahārāja passed the severe test put before him by the Supreme Personality of Godhead. This is further proof of the Lord's mercy toward His devotee. The Supreme Personality of Godhead sometimes puts a devotee to severe tests that are almost unbearable. One could hardly even live under the conditions forced upon Bali Mahārāja. That Bali Mahārāja endured all these severe tests and austerities is the mercy of the Supreme Lord. The Lord certainly appreciates the devotee's forbearance, and it is recorded for the future glorification of the devotee. This was not an ordinary test. As described in this verse, hardly anyone could survive such a test, but for the future glorification of Bali Mahārāja, one of the Twelve Mahājanas, the Supreme Personality of Godhead not only tested him but also gave him the strength to tolerate such adversity. The Lord is so kind to His devotee that when severely testing him the Lord gives him the necessary strength to be tolerant and continue to remain a glorious devotee.

LECTURE

The present verses are spoken by the Supreme Personality of Godhead. Originally the Lord appeared as Vāmanadeva before Bali Mahārāja and asked three steps of land in charity. Bali Mahārāja agreed. Vāmanadeva expanded Himself and with one step covered the planet earth and all of space. With His second step He covered the rest of the universe. Then He arrested Bali Mahārāja and said, "You have promised three steps, but you have given only two. You have broken your promise. Now I will arrest you and punish you." Bali Mahārāja accepted the Lord's action. He did not protest. And ultimately he told the Lord, "Yes, with two steps You have covered the entire universe. Now kindly keep Your third step on my head. Thus I will fulfill my promise to You." And so Bali Mahārāja surrendered his life to Lord Kṛṣṇa.

Vāmanadeva was satisfied with Bali's surrender, and after various devotees intervened on Bali's behalf, the Lord had Bali Mahārāja released from the ropes of Varuṇa and told him, "I am going to give you your own planet, Sutala-loka, and I will personally accompany you there and serve as your doorman." Actually, the Lord never lives anywhere in the material world; He lives only in the spiritual world, Vaikuṇṭha. By accompanying Bali Mahārāja to Sutala-loka, the Lord was actually converting the place into Vaikuṇṭha-loka, which is far more opulent, more beautiful, and more desirable than any planet of the material world or all the material worlds combined.

So by surrendering to Vāmanadeva, Bali Mahārāja was not the loser; he was the gainer. One who surrenders unto the Lord never loses.

There is a story in the *Kṛṣṇa* book about a fruit vendor who came to the house of Nanda Mahārāja. As no one was tending to the vendor, baby Kṛṣṇa thought He would take some grains of rice and exchange them for some fruit. (The system of exchange then was barter, not money.) But because baby Kṛṣṇa's hands were small and He was not used to holding things, what few grains of rice He had in them fell out by the time He reached the vendor. The vendor was so enchanted by Kṛṣṇa's beauty, however, that she gave Him whatever fruits He could hold. And then, when she turned around, she saw that in place of all the fruits she had given Kṛṣṇa, her basket was filled with the most valuable gold and jewels. The purport is that one who gives to Kṛṣṇa is not the loser but is the gainer by millions of times.

Śrīla Prabhupāda made the same point about himself. When he was in India, he had five children. But when he surrendered to Kṛṣṇa, left India, and went to America to preach, Kṛṣṇa gave him five hundred children. With his family in India, there were always so many problems, but in America, in Kṛṣṇa's service, there were five hundred children but no problems. As Śrīla Prabhupāda said, "I love them, and they love me. And there are no problems."

Sometimes, because of material attachment, devotees are afraid to surrender something to Kṛṣṇa, and Kṛṣṇa, to show special favor to the devotee, will take away the thing the devotee is attached to, so the devotee ultimately comes to the point of full surrender to the Lord. And here Bali Mahārāja is the example. He had conquered the entire universe and was occupying the throne of Indra, the king of heaven. He certainly was not inclined to give up what he had worked so hard to get, but Lord Viṣṇu, in the form of Vāmanadeva, cheated him. He cheated Bali Mahārāja in the sense that when He asked for the three steps, He was very small. Thus Bali Mahārāja was surprised: "I could give You a whole planet; why are You asking for only three steps?" But Vāmanadeva replied that if He could not be satisfied with three steps, He would not be satisfied with a whole planet, or even with the three worlds. (Śrīla Prabhupāda said a similar thing, especially for *brahmacārīs*—that a *brahmacārī* is satisfied with just three steps of land—a place to lie down at night, a little *prasāda*, and some service.) On the other hand, if someone is greedy and wants more and more, he can never be satisfied, however much he gets. So Vāmanadeva's instruction is very appropriate.

Then, after Bali Mahārāja agreed to give the three steps,

Vāmanadeva expanded Himself and became so huge that with just two steps He encompassed the whole universe. And so He took everything from Bali Mahārāja.

Bali Mahārāja's spiritual master had advised him, "Don't agree. The little boy is actually Viṣṇu, and He has come to cheat you. He will take everything from you. Don't do it." But Bali Mahārāja remained true to his word, fixed in his religious principles.

Here Vāmanadeva says that when He was giving speeches about religious principles as if He were instructing Bali Mahārāja to be charitable and truthful, He was actually speaking pretentiously. He knew that Bali Mahārāja was completely truthful, but He was pretending that Bali was a criminal, an offender who broke his promise, and therefore was lecturing to him about the value of religious principles. Here Lord Viṣṇu discloses His heart: He knew that Bali Mahārāja was fully surrendered and completely truthful. He was speaking for other purposes, not to correct Bali Mahārāja.

The Lord is very merciful. We are weak. Every living entity, by nature, by constitution, is weak and does not have the strength to pass the tests that the Lord may place before him. We can pass the tests only by the Lord's mercy. And the Lord gave so much mercy to Bali Mahārāja that Bali Mahārāja was able to pass the most severe test described in the verse.

We too may face various tests—the Lord may take things from us—but we are not alone in our tests. The Lord is there to give us sufficient strength and intelligence. But He wants to see our surrender. When we surrender, the Lord reciprocates and gives us strength. He gives us sufficient strength to bear all trials and tribulations. So the tests are for our benefit, to encourage us to surrender.

And the Lord will never give us a test we are not able to pass. He gives us a test He knows we can pass—provided we surrender. And when we do surrender, He gives us the required strength and intelligence.

Once we've passed the test, the Lord accepts us as His very own, just as Lord Viṣṇu accepted Bali Mahārāja. He actually gave Himself to Bali Mahārāja. When Bali Mahārāja surrendered himself and everything he possessed to the Lord, the Lord reciprocated and gave Himself, along with all sorts of material opulence, to Bali Mahārāja. And He undertook to reinstate Bali Mahārāja as the king of heaven in the future. So although the Lord's dealings may appear harsh, actually He is merciful, and He Himself helps us pass the tests He places before us to help us surrender.

Ordinary persons, as Śrīla Prabhupāda mentions, lament and become aggrieved when they lose something. And as conditioned souls we all have the tendency to lament and grieve over losses. But Bali Mahārāja set the example for all time of how to accept the test of the Lord, how to accept being bereft of position and opulence and all the other things he lost. He set the example for us so we can learn to tolerate externally, and internally remain cheerful, fixed in our service to Lord Kṛṣṇa.

Śrīmad-Bhāgavatam mentions that when Bali Mahārāja was arrested and humiliated, he was smiling, cheerful, because he was fixed in his devotional service. Devotees, in the course of serving, preaching, may face many difficulties, and even though externally they may appear to be suffering, internally they are feeling pleasure. How are they feeling pleasure? They are feeling pleasure because they know that the Lord is pleased. Their struggle and effort and surrender please the Lord.

The *Bhāgavatam* gives the example that sometimes a man may go far from home to search for wealth for his family, and while traveling he will encounter so many difficulties. Sometimes he will travel through the jungle, sometimes through the mountains, but he does not mind. In the end he knows he will return to his family with some treasure, and thinking of the happiness he will bring to his family, he feels happy. This is *prīti*, affection. One takes pleasure in the happiness of the beloved. And even though one may undergo great difficulties in making the beloved happy, just the knowledge that the beloved is happy or will be happy is enough to make one feel happy oneself.

Śrīla Jīva Gosvāmī gives the example that even an ordinary person may undergo great personal difficulties for the sake of his family. He may be in the bodily concept of life, but for the sake of his family he will accept many austerities. For example, a man may leave his wife and children in the village and go to the city to earn for his family. In the big city he has nothing—no money, no place to stay, no food. He will search for some menial job, and from whatever little pay he gets, he will take just enough to buy some dry bread and chickpeas—simple food. The rest of his salary, ninety-five percent, he sends home to his family. He will only eat dry chapattis, but he's thinking, "Oh, my little boy is drinking milk and growing strong and healthy." And just thinking of how nicely his son will be growing, he feels happy, although externally he is undergoing austere conditions.

Devotees have the same type of relationship with the Lord. They are ready to undergo any austerity for the sake of giving pleasure to the Lord. And the knowledge that the Lord is pleased is sufficient. They are happy just to know that He is pleased. Just as the traveler takes solace that soon he will be back with his family, the devotee knows that at the end of this life, after taking so much trouble to serve the mission of the Lord, he will be back with the Lord in the spiritual world. Thus he considers the troubles he endures on the way to be insignificant.

Devotees have no fear, because whatever situation they are in, they know they can serve and please the Lord. And they know the situation is temporary. They know that in the end, simply by remaining fixed in devotional service and passing all tests, they will go back home, back to Godhead, and associate with Kṛṣṇa directly. So the Lord is very kind and merciful. Although He may appear hard and cruel, putting the devotee into some difficulty, actually He is kind and merciful. He will help the devotee pass the tests. And when the devotee does pass—when he remains fixed in devotional service despite all difficulties—the Lord will call the devotee, "All right, now you have done enough. Come back home, back to Godhead."

Śrīla Prabhupāda is the perfect example. He sacrificed everything for the service of the Lord. Sometimes he had to face very strong opposition, but he fought to the end. He fought and always remained fixed in his service to Kṛṣṇa. Therefore, although externally he may have been undergoing great difficulty, he was always relishing loving exchanges with the Lord and his spiritual master.

We should accept whatever situation the Lord ordains for us, tolerate, and continue to serve the Lord with heart and soul. After all, we are in the material world, so what can we do? Tolerate, and go on with our service. Very soon the Lord will be pleased with us, take away our miseries, and welcome us into His personal association.

Hare Kṛṣṇa.

Merciful to the Miserly

śrī-prahrāda uvāca
varaṁ varaya etat te
varadeśān maheśvara
yad anindat pitā me
tvām avidvāṁs teja aiśvaram

viddhāmarṣāśayaḥ sākṣāt
sarva-loka-guruṁ prabhum
bhrātṛ-heti mṛṣā-dṛṣṭis
tvad-bhakte mayi cāghavān

tasmāt pitā me pūyeta
durantād dustarād aghāt
pūtas te' pāṅga-saṁdṛṣṭas
tadā kṛpaṇa-vatsala

(*SB* 7.10.15–17)

TRANSLATION

Prahlāda Mahārāja said: O Supreme Lord, because You are so merciful to the fallen souls, I ask You for only one benediction. I know that my father, at the time of his death, had already been purified by Your glance upon him, but because of his ignorance of Your beautiful power and supremacy, he was unnecessarily angry at You, falsely thinking that You were the killer of his brother. Thus he directly blasphemed Your Lordship, the spiritual master of all living beings, and committed heavily sinful activities directed against me, Your devotee. I wish that he be excused for these sinful activities.

PURPORT by Śrīla Prabhupāda

Although Hiraṇyakaśipu was purified as soon as he came in contact with the Lord's lap and the Lord saw him, Prahlāda

Mahārāja still wanted to hear from the Lord's own mouth that his father had been purified by the Lord's causeless mercy. Prahlāda Mahārāja offered this prayer to the Lord for the sake of his father. As a Vaiṣṇava son, despite all the inconveniences imposed upon him by his father, he could not forget his father's affection.

LECTURE

We have been reading the history of Prahlāda Mahārāja. Prahlāda's father, Hiraṇyakaśipu, was the greatest of materialists. Although naturally affectionate toward Prahlāda, when he discovered that Prahlāda was a devotee of Viṣṇu, Hiraṇyakaśipu's "enemy," he became inimical toward Prahlāda too. In fact, he became so hostile and aggressive that he tried to kill Prahlāda in various ways. Ultimately, Nṛsiṁhadeva, the powerful half-man, half-lion incarnation of the Lord, appeared and killed Hiraṇyakaśipu.

After Prahlāda offered prayers to pacify Lord Nṛsiṁhadeva, the Lord asked Prahlāda to accept some benediction. But Prahlāda refused: "You have sent me here to the material world to exemplify the pure devotee. Why should You now tempt me with some benediction? If I accepted material benefit in exchange for my service, I would not be a servant. Rather, I would be a merchant." Prahlāda concluded, "You are my eternal master, and I am Your unmotivated servant. We have no other relationship."

Eventually, on Lord Nṛsiṁha's insistence, Prahlāda asked Him for one benediction—that his father, who had tried to kill him, be purified.

How merciful the devotee is. Without envy, he wishes well for all. No one is his enemy or special friend. The Third Canto of *Śrīmad-Bhāgavatam* describes the qualities that ornament a devotee (*sādhu*). One is *ajāta-śatravaḥ*: he has no enemies.

Even if someone becomes the *sādhu's* enemy, the *sādhu* does not become his enemy's enemy. He always remains the friend of all (*suhṛdaḥ sarva-dehinām*).

Prahlāda also prayed for the deliverance of all materialists. He told the Lord that although personally he had no problem, he did have one concern: how to bring the materialists to the shelter of the Lord's lotus feet—because without the Lord's shelter, no one can be happy.

Then he said, "There are many saintly persons who are ambitious only for their own deliverance. Not caring for others, they avoid busy cities"—like Bombay, New York, and Hong Kong. One may be concerned only with one's own liberation for two reasons, as explained by Śrīla Prabhupāda. One is that he is selfish. *Bhukti-mukti-siddhi-kāmī—sakali 'aśānta'*: those who desire material enjoyment, liberation, or mystic perfection are selfish—and they are never peaceful. Or one may feel incapable: "I am not strong enough, I do not know enough to help others. Let me take care of myself."

But Śrīla Prabhupāda has demonstrated that anyone—young or old, learned or ignorant—can preach, to his or her capacity. For example, Śrīla Prabhupāda's secretary had a three-year-old daughter named Sarasvatī. When respectable gentlemen would visit our Bombay temple, little Sarasvatī would run up and ask, "Do you know who is Kṛṣṇa? Kṛṣṇa is the Supreme Personality of Godhead!" She was preaching. As another example, Śrīla Prabhupāda cited some *brahmacārīs* who used to go to Navadvīpa to sell a devotional paper, *Dainik Nadiya Prakash*, for one paisa a copy. If a *brahmacārī* sold even a few copies, Śrīla Bhaktisiddhānta Sarasvatī Ṭhākura would take it as a very great service. So according to one's capacity, he or she should sincerely try to preach.

Prahlāda continued, "Although some saintly persons are interested only in their own deliverance, I am not like them. I do not wish to go back home, back to Godhead alone. Rather, I wish to take as many of the *kṛpaṇas* with me as possible [*naitān vihāya krpaṇān*].”

A *kṛpaṇa* (as opposed to a *brāhmaṇa*) is a miserly person who does not properly utilize his valuable human body to understand the self and permanently solve the problems of life. Because *kṛpaṇas* identify with the body, they cannot properly engage in devotional service. Even Arjuna refused to surrender to Kṛṣṇa's instructions, because of bodily affection. He frankly admitted to Lord Kṛṣṇa, “Now I am confused about my duty and have lost all composure because of miserly weakness [*kārpaṇya-doṣopahata-svabhāvaḥ*].” And immediately Lord Kṛṣṇa chided Arjuna, “The wise never lament for the body, either in the living or dead condition.”

Because of bodily identification, the *kṛpaṇas* think that sense gratification is the goal of life, that those who help them in their selfish pursuits are “friends” and that those who come in the way are “enemies.” They always try to destroy their enemies and favor their friends.

Because such materialists think that sense gratification will make them happy, they have no interest in Kṛṣṇa consciousness. Thus, to preach to such persons is extremely difficult. But the devotee, knowing the Lord's inner desire, still endeavors to bring them to the shelter of the Lord's lotus feet. And so the Lord is especially merciful to the preacher.

The desires of the Lord and the desires of the devotee are one. Lord Nṛsiṁhadeva is *kṛpaṇa-vatsala*, “merciful to the miserly.” And Prahlāda Mahārāja prays, *naitān vihāya kṛpanān*: “I do not wish to leave aside the *kṛpaṇas*. Without Kṛṣṇa consciousness they cannot be happy, so please give me Your mercy that I may deliver them.”

Here Prahlāda prays to Lord Nṛsiṁha to give mercy to the greatest of all materialists (*kṛpaṇas*), his father. Just see! The materialist is so envious; he was ready to kill his own son. And the devotee is so merciful that he prays for the deliverance of the materialist even though the materialist tried to kill him. As devotees, we should also work for everyone's spiritual benefit.

A liberal *brāhmaṇa* sees that all souls are parts and parcels of Kṛṣṇa, meant to serve Lord Kṛṣṇa, and he encourages everyone in Kṛṣṇa consciousness. When Śrīla Prabhupāda went to the West, he offered Kṛṣṇa consciousness to all who were interested. Some Indians believe that Kṛṣṇa consciousness should be given only to Hindus or *brāhmaṇas* by birth. In Hyderabad some caste *brāhmaṇas* reproached Śrīla Prabhupāda, "You are doing the greatest disservice to the Hindu religion by giving non-*brāhmaṇas* the sacred thread." Śrīla Prabhupāda had to face so much opposition simply because he wanted to deliver Kṛṣṇa consciousness.

Of course, persons became inimical to Śrīla Prabhupāda not for any fault of his; they became inimical out of their own natures. Here at Hare Krishna Land Śrīla Prabhupāda had to face so many envious parties. They thought, "Such a big property, valuable property, how can it go to some *sādhu*? It should come to us. We will use it for sense gratification." And after Śrīla Prabhupāda left, so many enemies tried to grab Hare Krishna Land. In fact, Śrīla Prabhupāda had predicted that materialists would try to capture his properties in Māyāpur, Vṛndāvana, and Bombay. And so it happened that the very first year after Śrīla Prabhupāda left there was a great attempt to take Hare Krishna Land. It even came in the newspapers that one local municipal councilor had appealed to the government to take over ISKCON from the foreigners.

But although Śrīla Prabhupāda had to face so many enemies, he never became his enemy's enemy. He always remained a friend. As Śrīla Prabhupāda himself said in one lecture, "Because we are trying to create one temple here, so many enemies are giving hindrance. Therefore we have to tolerate. We have to remain *sādhu*. We cannot become *asādhu*. The *sādhu* is friendly to all living entities."

Still, Śrīla Prabhupāda responded to his enemies accordingly. As Hiraṇyakaśipu wanted to kill Lord Nṛsiṁhadeva and Lord Nṛsiṁhadeva reciprocated by fighting and killing him, so Śrīla Prabhupāda also reciprocated with his enemies and defeated them. But he always remained their well-wisher. When the former owner of Hare Krishna Land died, some devotees thought that the envious man must have taken birth as a snake. But Śrīla Prabhupāda said no, that he had taken birth as a human because he had offered some service. Even though his intention was to cheat, still he offered Hare Krishna Land to Śrīla Prabhupāda. Pūtanā offered her poison-smeared breast to Kṛṣṇa to kill Him, but Kṛṣṇa took the bright side: "She has fed Me her breast milk. She is My mother." And He elevated her to the position of His mother in the spiritual world. Similarly, Mr. Nair offered Hare Krishna Land to Śrīla Prabhupāda, so Śrīla Prabhupāda considered that he had rendered some service—although he was envious and mischievous.

Here Lord Nṛsiṁhadeva gave *special* mercy to Hiraṇyakaśipu and purified him with His glance and nails, which pierced the demon's heart. In the next verse, the Lord tells Prahlāda, "Your father has been purified, along with twenty-one forefathers in your family. Because you were born in this family, the entire dynasty has been purified." So although a devotee is a natural well-wisher of every living being (*suhṛdaḥ sarva-dehinām*), he may have special affection and concern for his family members. He may want to know what will happen to them if he takes to Kṛṣṇa consciousness. Often when devotees come to Kṛṣṇa consciousness, their families lament, "Oh! I have lost my son." And they may even calculate, "I have lost so much income." So the devotee will consider, "If I leave my family, will they suffer? Will they lose?"

Here the Lord assures the devotee, "By your becoming Kṛṣṇa

conscious, your family will not lose. Rather, they will gain thousands and millions of times. They will get the greatest benedictions—release from the cycle of repeated birth and death, and promotion to the spiritual kingdom of God. So do not fear."

The conclusion is that we should not hesitate to surrender to Kṛṣṇa. By dedicating our lives for spreading Kṛṣṇa consciousness, we and our family members will achieve the supreme destination. Without miserly weakness we should follow Śrīla Prabhupāda and preach Kṛṣṇa consciousness for the benefit of the materialists—fools and rascals.

Hare Kṛṣṇa!

Śrīla Prabhupāda: Preaching with Patience and Tolerance

We are going back in time to 1967. Śrīla Prabhupāda had just incorporated ISKCON in New York in 1966, and in 1967 some disciples had begun a second center in San Francisco. The present discussion, as related in *Śrīla Prabhupāda-līlāmṛta*, took place in San Francisco between Śrīla Prabhupāda and Hayagrīva dāsa.

> Hayagrīva sat facing Prabhupāda, alone with Prabhupāda in his room. A few days before, Hayagrīva had shown Prabhupāda a play of Lord Caitanya he had found in the library, and Prabhupāda had said it wasn't bona fide. So Prabhupāda decided to prepare an outline for a bona fide play and have Hayagrīva write it. "I will give you the whole plot complete," Śrīla Prabhupāda said. "Then all you have to do is execute it."

Śrīla Prabhupāda continued:

> "The second scene shows Kali as decorated blackish with royal dress and very ugly features as described in the *Bhāgavatam*, and his queen is another ugly-featured lady. So they are disturbed. They will talk among themselves that, 'There is the *saṅkīrtana* movement now, so how shall we prosecute our business in this Age of Quarrel, Kali-yuga?' In that scene there will be in one corner two or three people drinking."

Śrīla Prabhupāda was giving the whole philosophy in visual images:

> "The Age of Quarrel personified and his consort are sitting in the center. In one corner someone is taking

> part in drinking, in another part someone is illicitly talking about lust and love with a woman. In another section there is slaughtering of a cow, and in another section, gambling. In this way, that scene should be adjusted. And in the middle, the ugly man, Kali, and the ugly woman will talk that, 'Now we are in danger. The *saṅkīrtana* movement has started. What to do?' In this way you have to finish the scene.
>
> "Then the third scene is very nice—*rāsa* dance."
>
> Hayagrīva interrupted. He had some of his own ideas about what he called "the dramatic point of view." "I think," Hayagrīva said, "this can apply for the whole world, in the sense that the names may be Indian but I think that the exhibition you described of the assembly of Kali and his consort Sin and the exhibition of illicit sex and the slaughterhouse can all be from Western prototypes."
>
> Śrīla Prabhupāda said that he had no objection to Hayagrīva's suggestion but [that] he didn't want people to think that he was singling out Westerners, as if they were the only ones who committed illicit sex.

This is very important. Śrīla Prabhupāda was so considerate he didn't want the Western audience to think he was criticizing just them. Similarly, when the first editor of *Back to Godhead,* Rāyarāma, asked Śrīla Prabhupāda if he could publish an article about the horrors of animal slaughter, Śrīla Prabhupāda said no. Śrīla Prabhupāda didn't want the butchers to feel they were being singled out. Śrīla Prabhupāda explained, "We are not envious of anyone. Why should we point the finger at the butchers? So many persons are involved in the slaughter of animals. He who raises the animal, he who kills the animal, he who sells the meat, he who cooks the meat, he who serves the food, he who eats such cooked animal food—in one sense all are butchers, and all are liable to be punished. If a man is murdered, not only the gunman is punished; everyone involved in the conspiracy is punished." In America now, if someone just gives another person the idea that "Oh, this man is coming in your way, why don't you remove him?" he's also punishable, because he gave the idea, or seed.

The *bhakti-latā-bīja* is the seed of devotional service—the idea or plan how to execute devotional service. And as Śrīla Prabhupāda explains, apart from the *bhakti-latā-bīja*, one may get other seeds—for fruitive activity, for mental speculation, or whatnot. The seed is the idea that may eventually germinate and bear fruit. If someone just gives a criminal suggestion, he's also a criminal.

So, Śrīla Prabhupāda was saying that everyone is involved, not just the persons who directly slaughter the animals. So why especially criticize them? Actually, the whole society must be reformed, not just one section. Here too, Śrīla Prabhupāda was very careful that the Westerners should not think that he was pointing the finger at them, that only they were sinful.

> Hayagrīva was about to reply but decided that this was no time to quibble; Swamiji was eager to go on describing the pastimes of Lord Caitanya.
>
> Prabhupāda: "*Rāsa* dance means Kṛṣṇa and Rādhārāṇī in the center and the *gopīs* are surrounding. You have seen that surrounding scene when they were dancing with us the other day in the park hand to hand?"

Śrīla Prabhupāda used to go to the park with the devotees, and the young people, hippies, used to gather around and dance in a circle during the *kīrtana*. Śrīla Prabhupāda was reminding Hayagrīva Prabhu how the young people were dancing hand-in-hand in a circle.

It is amazing how Śrīla Prabhupāda preached to people who

had no idea of Kṛṣṇa consciousness, how patient and tolerant he was. The early devotees would come to the temple with their cats and dogs. In San Francisco Śrīla Prabhupāda would sometimes look into the window of the ice-cream parlor near the temple and see so many devotees there eating. Earlier we were discussing how hard it is to change people's habits. Śrīla Prabhupāda's patience and tolerance should be a great lesson to us all.

In India too, Śrīla Prabhupāda had to patiently tolerate so many difficulties. In his last days in Juhu, in September of 1977, devotees recounted to Śrīla Prabhupāda all the difficulties he had gone through to establish the Juhu temple, while he lay on his bed listening intently. Śrīla Prabhupāda was so weak he could hardly speak, and then just one or two words, softly. But after hearing the whole narration, Śrīla Prabhupāda wanted to interject something. The devotees had missed one point. Lying on his bed, he uttered faintly, "That dog!" That dog? What did Śrīla Prabhupāda mean? "You mean Mr. Nair?" "Mr. Mhatre?" "No," Śrīla Prabhupāda said, "That dog!" Because at first there was no accommodation for Śrīla Prabhupāda at Hare Krishna Land, we had to arrange for him to stay at various friends' houses nearby. One such friend arranged for Śrīla Prabhupāda to stay next door to him, and every morning he would drive Śrīla Prabhupāda to Juhu Beach to walk.

It turned out that Śrīla Prabhupāda would have to sit in the front seat next to the man's dog. We may not be able to appreciate now how Śrīla Prabhupāda, who had descended from the spiritual world, felt, but he considered riding next to the dog to be another terrible experience he had to tolerate for the sake of Śrī Śrī Rādhā-Rāsabihārī and Hare Krishna Land. "That dog!"

Whether in America with the hippies or in India with the affluent and cultured, Śrīla Prabhupāda had to tolerate so much for Kṛṣṇa and Kṛṣṇa's mission, for reclaiming the fallen souls. Once, Śrīla Prabhupāda stayed at Hare Krishna Land for three months continuously to try and get the permission to build the temple. Yet no matter what the problems were during the day, at *ārati* time he would leave everything, go to the temple, and speak beautifully on *Śrīmad-Bhāgavatam*. Another devotee and I were working on the permission, and we had to go to the city almost every day and try to return in time for Prabhupāda's lecture. Traveling in crowded local trains, having eaten nothing except perhaps some peanuts, we would be quite exhausted—though eager to hear. One evening after a particularly discouraging day—again nobody would help us—we returned just in time for the *ārati* and *kīrtana*. And during the lecture Śrīla Prabhupāda instructed, "We have to dance in the *kīrtana*—even if we don't get the permission." Śrīla Prabhupāda was different. Whatever the difficulty was, he would just leave it behind and be completely absorbed in the *kīrtana* or lecture in the temple.

Eventually Śrīla Prabhupāda came to the verse in *Śrīmad-Bhāgavatam* that describes the qualities of a *sādhu*, and he related them to our situation. First, *titikṣavaḥ*—tolerate. "So many enemies are complaining we are creating 'nuisance.' So we are not getting the sanction. Therefore a *sādhu* is advised, *titikṣavaḥ*, tolerate! Tolerate all this nonsense! What can be done? We have no other alternative. Nobody is coming to help us. Our business is so thankless. Because we are trying to create one temple, so many enemies are giving hindrance. 'You cannot do it.' Therefore *titikṣavaḥ*. You have to tolerate. What can be done?"

And why tolerate? Because the *sādhu* is very merciful (*kāruṇikāḥ*). Śrīla Prabhupāda said we might naturally respond, "What is the use of taking so much trouble? We have so many other temples. If people here don't like us, we can go elsewhere." But "No! *Kāruṇikāḥ*—very merciful in spite of all trouble. We have come to distribute Kṛṣṇa consciousness, so we must tolerate and give this message.

"A Vaisnava is *para-duḥkha-duḥkhī*. He understands, 'People are engaged like cats and dogs in sense gratification, and they'll be punished. Let us do something for them.' This is *kāruṇikāḥ*. Just to show mercy to the suffering conditioned souls the preacher has to tolerate so many things."

It was a wonderful lecture. Śrīla Prabhupāda expressed his own feelings—how he had to tolerate so much to give mercy to the fallen souls—and now he wanted us to be merciful like him.

5

Advice

Śrīla Prabhupāda's Mission: Chant Hare Kṛṣṇa and Be Happy

An address to guests at ISKCON's new preaching center in Madrid, Spain.

We welcome you to our new center. Everything you see here, and in all our centers, is the mercy of His Divine Grace A.C. Bhaktivedanta Swami Prabhupāda, our founder and spiritual preceptor, so on this occasion we would like to say something about Śrīla Prabhupāda's mission.

For many centuries India's spiritual life was kept within India's boundaries. Orthodox Hindus believed that if one crossed the ocean one would become contaminated. But, at the age of seventy, Śrīla Prabhupāda took the risk and came to the West. Previously he had been living a simple life as a saintly person in Vṛndāvana, the holiest place of Kṛṣṇa's pastimes, chanting the holy names and relishing transcendental bliss. But in Vṛndāvana he remembered the instructions of his *guru mahārāja*—that he should go to the West and preach. So he went to Bombay to arrange for passage. One pious Vaiṣṇava lady named Sumati Morarji agreed to give him free passage on one of her steamships. At that time, one of the company's officers joked with Śrīla Prabhupāda: "Swamiji, why do you want to go to the States? You want to see the States and enjoy there." Śrīla Prabhupāda replied, "What have I got to see? My life is practically finished. But so many people there are lost in life. I want to do something good for them. I want to teach them the science of Kṛṣṇa, which will actually make them happy."

At sea, Śrīla Prabhupāda suffered two heart attacks. Finally he reached New York. He sat under a tree, chanted Hare Kṛṣṇa, and preached. After some time in America, he decided to return to India to chant and preach there as well. Then, in his last days, he returned to Bombay to his new quarters on the top floor of the ISKCON guesthouse.

In Bombay, Śrīla Prabhupāda had a staunch householder devotee named Mr. Sethi. Mr. Sethi was completely devoted to Śrīla Prabhupāda, and he loved to chant the holy names. For years, he had been associated with a group of other devoted householders who met every Sunday and did continuous Hare Kṛṣṇa *kīrtana* for twelve hours, from 6 a.m. to 6 p.m. Then from 6 to 8 they would sing songs from Vṛndāvana about Rādhā and Kṛṣṇa. One Sunday Mr. Sethi arranged for the group to do *kīrtana* at our Bombay temple, where they and the temple devotees sang together throughout the day. Śrīla Prabhupāda was in his room, listening and relishing. The devotees were very eager to have Prabhupāda's audience, but the lift in the building was not working. Śrīla Prabhupāda was too ill to go down the stairs, and the devotees were too many to climb up, and anyway, they had to be in the *kīrtana*. So they just stood beneath his window and chanted to him. Finally Śrīla Prabhupāda came to the balcony and glanced and smiled upon all the devotees, who welled up with ecstasy and love for him. Then he went inside, and the devotees continued. After 6:00 p.m., one of the ladies from the group began to sing "*Jaya Rādhe! Jaya Kṛṣṇa!*" and as Śrīla Prabhupāda was listening to her voice and appreciating, tears of ecstatic love flowed from his eyes. In the end, Śrīla Prabhupāda invited the whole group of fifty families to stay at Hare Krishna Land. He said he would build them accommodations and provide all their necessities. He wanted only one thing from them: they should chant Hare Kṛṣṇa day and night.

From the beginning to the end, Śrīla Prabhupāda's mission was to introduce and encourage the chanting of the holy names. When he went to the West and began the mission in New York, he simply chanted Hare Kṛṣṇa. He sat under a tree in Tompkins Square Park and began to chant. And in his last days and moments, he was surrounded by devotees chanting Hare Kṛṣṇa.

So although one could say many things about Śrīla Prabhupāda's mission, in the immediate sense his mission was to chant and induce others to chant.

Śrīla Prabhupāda had complete faith that by chanting one would get everything. He knew that the holy name of Kṛṣṇa is the same as Kṛṣṇa Himself. In the material world, or relative world, the name of a thing and the thing are different. For example, if I am thirsty and I chant "water, water, water," my thirst will not be quenched, because the word *water* and the substance water are different. But in the spiritual world, or absolute world, there is no difference between the name and the thing to which the name refers. When we chant "Hare Kṛṣṇa, Hare Kṛṣṇa," Kṛṣṇa is personally present, dancing on our tongue. When Śrīla Prabhupāda chanted Hare Kṛṣṇa, he knew that Kṛṣṇa was there. When he requested others to chant Hare Kṛṣṇa, he knew that they would be coming in touch with Kṛṣṇa. And when one is in touch with Kṛṣṇa, what remains for him to achieve? Kṛṣṇa is the Supreme Personality of Godhead. He is full in all opulences. He can give anything and everything to anyone who chants His holy names. And in the end He gives Himself. So Śrīla Prabhupāda knew that if people just chanted Hare Kṛṣṇa, they would get everything.

Śrīla Prabhupāda often cited the story of Ajāmila. Ajāmila was very sinful. He had married a prostitute, and for her sake he engaged in all sorts of abominable activities to get money and satisfy her by any means. At the age of eighty-eight he had a young son. In other words, even in his old age, he was attached to sex life. Then when Ajāmila was eighty-eight, the time of death came for him. As he was lying on his bed, three agents of Yamarāja, the demigod in charge of death, came to wrest his soul from his body. Seeing the horrible features of the Yamadūtas, Ajāmila became filled with fear. In complete anxiety and helplessness, he called the name of his son, who was playing nearby: "Nārāyaṇa! Nārāyaṇa!" *Nārāyaṇa* is another name of Kṛṣṇa. As soon as Ajāmila chanted the holy name of Nārāyaṇa, four beautiful persons appeared. They were representatives of Nārāyaṇa, and they immediately intervened. They told the agents of Yamarāja, "Stop! You cannot take the soul of Ajāmila! Although Ajāmila is so sinful that he deserves to die and be punished in hell, because he chanted the holy name of Nārāyaṇa at the last moment, he is freed from all sinful reactions." So the agents of Yamarāja desisted and Ajāmila was saved.

Ajāmila thought about the discussion he had heard between the Viṣṇudūtas and the Yamadūtas, during which the principles of religion were thoroughly explained. He considered, "How sinful I have been. For the sake of my sense gratification I have engaged in all abominable activities." Thinking of the instructions of the Viṣṇudūtas and of his past sinful activities, he became full of remorse and repentance. He resolved, "I must leave here. I will leave my wife and my house and even my son Nārāyaṇa, and I will go to some holy place and practice *bhakti*." Then he left and went to a temple in Hardwar and engaged in devotional service, especially in chanting the holy names of Nārāyaṇa, Kṛṣṇa. And when he became mature in devotional service, the same four glorious persons who had saved him at the time of death appeared again, to take him to the kingdom of Nārāyaṇa, to the spiritual world. Thus Ajāmila gave up his body and entered Kṛṣṇa's abode.

So we can see that just by chanting the holy name of Nārāyaṇa, or Kṛṣṇa, Ajāmila got everything: he got the association of devotees, he got instructions on the science of Kṛṣṇa consciousness, he got the chance to engage in devotional service—and in the end he achieved the highest perfection. The highest perfection is pure love of Godhead, which carries one back home, back to Godhead. Śrīla Prabhupāda knew that just by chanting the holy names of Kṛṣṇa, people would get everything. They would get the association of devotees and instructions on the science of Kṛṣṇa, and by following the instructions and continuing to chant the holy names, they would reach the highest perfection of love for Kṛṣṇa. Therefore Śrīla Prabhupāda wanted only that people should chant Hare Kṛṣṇa, and from the beginning to the end he was just trying to encourage people to chant.

The name of Śrīla Prabhupāda's project in Bombay is Hare Krishna Land. One evening Śrīla Prabhupāda was sitting in his room at the back of the property, and from the temple he heard the sound of Hare Kṛṣṇa, the sounds of *kīrtana*. He commented, "This is Hare Krishna Land. Always Hare Kṛṣṇa should be heard."

Every morning, Śrīla Prabhupāda used to walk on nearby Juhu Beach. One morning, as Śrīla Prabhupāda was walking back from the beach, some small children on the way called to him, "Hare Kṛṣṇa!" And Śrīla Prabhupāda responded, "Hare Kṛṣṇa!" Then he turned to the devotees: "Our mission is a success. They are chanting Hare Kṛṣṇa."

So we can fulfill the mission of Śrīla Prabhupāda very easily just by chanting Hare Kṛṣṇa—especially meeting together and chanting. This is the purpose of this center. People can come here and join together and chant Hare Kṛṣṇa. So we request you all to take advantage of this center and come and chant. And whatever you do here at the center you can also do at home. With your family, friends, or even by yourself, you can sit and chant Hare Kṛṣṇa. There are no hard and fast rules for chanting. One can chant anywhere, at any time, in any situation. So as far as possible you should always chant Hare Kṛṣṇa, fulfill the mission of Śrīla Prabhupāda, achieve the highest perfection of life, and go back home, back to Godhead.

Hare Kṛṣṇa!

Any questions?

DEVOTEE: You say that just by chanting Hare Kṛṣṇa one will get everything. But don't we also need association?

GIRIRAJ SWAMI: By chanting one will also get association. Ajāmila just chanted "Nārāyaṇa! Nārāyaṇa!" and he got the association of the associates of Nārāyaṇa. Then he went to a temple in Hardwar, and there he continued to chant. Because he was already eighty-eight and his family life had been so sinful, he decided to leave home. But there are also examples of persons who after chanting the holy names and getting the association of devotees stayed in family life and chanted Hare Kṛṣṇa. So each case is individual. But even if one lives at home with family and chants Hare Kṛṣṇa there, still he or she should visit the temple and have association with more advanced devotees. How many people can live in the temple? Very few. But by coming to the temple, people can get the idea how to practice Kṛṣṇa consciousness at home, and by continuing to visit the temple and associating with devotees, they can get more instruction and inspiration to continue their practice at home.

GUEST: Do we also preach to the politicians?

GIRIRAJ SWAMI: If we get the chance, we can preach to them too. But in the age of democracy, even if the president or prime minister becomes Kṛṣṇa conscious, he is not free to do as he likes. So we should make efforts on both sides—to make the leaders Kṛṣṇa conscious and to make the voters Kṛṣṇa conscious. And if the leaders become Kṛṣṇa conscious they can help make the citizens Kṛṣṇa conscious through education. Simply passing laws will not work. The people need to be educated. Governments have tried prohibition in India and in America alike. But as soon as there is prohibition there is black market, because the people are not trained properly. So just by legislation you cannot change the character of the people. There has to be education and training. If the people are educated in Kṛṣṇa consciousness, trained to be Kṛṣṇa conscious by hearing and chanting, they can leave alcohol and everything.

When Śrīla Prabhupāda first came to the United States, there was the hippie movement. Practically the whole younger generation was influenced by the hippies and was taking at least hashish and marijuana, if not other things. The government told them, "Don't do it"; their parents told them, "Don't do it"; their teachers told them, "Don't do it." But still they did it. But when Śrīla Prabhupāda came and told them, "Don't do it," they stopped. Because Śrīla Prabhupāda didn't just say, "Don't, don't, don't." He gave them a positive alternative: Chant Hare Kṛṣṇa. The young people wanted to get high. So the devotees invited them, "Stay high forever!" You want to get high, but you cannot stay high forever. You have to come down. But by Kṛṣṇa consciousness you can also get high. And you will never have to come down. In fact, you will go higher and higher. So along with the restrictions, there should be some positive inspiration. Then we can stop intoxication, meat eating, illicit sex, and other things.

GUEST: About the incident with Ajāmila—he was chanting the name of Nārāyaṇa, but he was not thinking of God. He was chanting the name of his son. So did Ajāmila have pious activities, good *karma*, and by this good *karma* and chanting attain success? To get such success, one has to chant the holy name constantly and sincerely. Otherwise, one can think that even without being Kṛṣṇa conscious one can also attain the same result. Can you explain more about this?

GIRIRAJ SWAMI: When Ajāmila chanted the holy name of Nārāyaṇa he was not thinking of God. But the holy name of God is absolute. Just like medicine. Say a child is sick and the mother wants to give some medicine. She gives some sugarcoated medicine and says, "Take this candy." The child doesn't know that he is taking medicine, but the medicine still acts. So the effect of chanting the holy name does not depend on the faith or knowledge of the chanter. Like fire. If an adult touches fire he will be burned, and if a baby touches fire he will be burned. The effect is the same whether one has knowledge or not. But the other thing you said is also true. Ajāmila did have some pious background. Therefore he named his son Nārāyaṇa. Some devotee must have come to his house, and Ajāmila must have said he had a new baby. "Oh, you should name him Nārāyaṇa." So because he had the association of some devotee and called the boy Nārāyaṇa, he benefited.

GUEST: If a person chants the holy name going deeply into it, will it not have greater effect? There must be some difference between chanting knowingly and unknowingly.

GIRIRAJ SWAMI: Absolutely right. There is one stage in chanting called *nāmābhāsa*, where one chants with or without knowledge, with or without faith. He gets a particular result: freedom from sinful reactions. But by chanting without faith or knowledge one cannot get love of Godhead. So after chanting "Nārāyaṇa" by chance at the time of death and getting the association of the associates of Nārāyaṇa, Ajāmila took to the process with faith and knowledge and thus achieved pure chanting. Then he got the result of love of God.

When we chant Hare Kṛṣṇa we are actually addressing Rādhā and Kṛṣṇa: "O Rādhe! O Kṛṣṇa!" And if They respond, "Yes, what do you want?" what will we reply? "I want a new house, a new car, a new job, a good wife?" No, we will reply, "I want only Your service." So chanting Hare Kṛṣṇa really means praying to Rādhā and Kṛṣṇa, "Please engage me in Your service." When we chant with intense desire for the service of Rādhā and Kṛṣṇa, we will get the real fruit of chanting—pure love for the Divine Couple and direct service to Them.

Yet still we can say that by chanting accidentally or negligently one can attain love of God, because by doing so one will get the mercy of some Vaiṣṇavas, learn to chant with faith and devotion, and then get love of God. So ultimately, even chanting accidentally, one will get love of God.

GUEST: Does the Hare Kṛṣṇa movement consider interfaith

activities to be important—to enter in contact with other religions?

GIRIRAJ SWAMI: There is only one God, but He is known by different names in different cultures and languages. Still, He is the same God. If someone chants "Allah, Allah" or "Jesus, Jesus," we're also very pleased because it is the same as "Kṛṣṇa, Kṛṣṇa." And the basic principles in all bona fide scriptures are the same, although the details may differ. Only due to ignorance do we think there are basic differences. So, if by coming together and discussing we can understand the basic principles of every scripture and encourage each other to follow, it is worthwhile.

Sometimes Śrīla Prabhupāda would meet Christian priests and ask them to chant the name of God, the name Christ. But he would also request them not to eat meat: "Thou shalt not kill." He had faith that if Christians would chant the holy name of Christ and give up killing and eating animals, they too would make advancement. But we don't just say, "Don't eat meat." We give a positive alternative: take *prasāda*. And that is what we are going to tell you now: "Take *prasāda*!"

Hare Kṛṣṇa!

Time for Kṛṣṇa

Time . . . "Time I am, the great destroyer of the world," says Lord Kṛṣṇa, "and I have come here to destroy all people." (*Bg* 11.32) The powerful time factor represents the Supreme Personality of Godhead. Through time the will of the Lord is manifest.

Time is of the utmost importance to all of us, because the duration of our lives is made of time. How you use your time is how you use your life.

Once, while speaking to a businessman in Bombay, Śrīla Prabhupāda quoted a verse from Cāṇakya Paṇḍita: "At the time of death one cannot purchase one more moment of life, even for all the riches in the world." Time is invaluable and must be invested carefully. "So we should utilize each moment for the greatest gain," Śrīla Prabhupāda continued. "In the ledger of your life, all time engaged in Kṛṣṇa consciousness is profit, whereas all time engaged in material activities is loss. If we want the greatest profit in life, we must use every moment in Kṛṣṇa consciousness."

What is the greatest profit? Lord Kṛṣṇa says, *yaṁ labdhvā cāparaṁ lābhaṁ manyate nādhikaṁ tataḥ*: "When one actually comes to the perfection of Kṛṣṇa consciousness, he realizes there is no greater gain." (*Bg* 6.22)

In the use of our time—our life—we should give priority to the supreme cause—Kṛṣṇa. "Things that matter most should never be at the mercy of things that matter least." (Goethe)

What could matter more than Kṛṣṇa consciousness? We are suffering repeated birth, death, old age, and disease. After so many lives we have come to the rare human form, the most valuable asset to free us from the miseries of material existence. Human intelligence is especially meant to realize God and make a permanent solution to life's problems. One who fails to use this most valuable asset for the best purpose—for Kṛṣṇa consciousness—is the greatest miser and fool.

When we plan our day, our week, and our life, we should first set aside time for the most important activities: discussing and distributing the message of Godhead in the association of pure devotees. "Both by rising and setting, the sun decreases the duration of life of everyone, except one who utilizes the time by discussing the topics of the all-good Personality of Godhead." (*SB* 2.3.17) If we first set aside time for the most important things, we'll take the less important things in proper perspective.

A teacher once brought a large open-mouthed jar into a room full of students. He filled the jar with rocks and asked the students, "Is the jar full?"

The students replied, "Yes."

The teacher then poured pebbles into the jar, filling up the spaces between the rocks. He asked again, "Is the jar full now?"

By then the students were a little wise, so they remained silent.

The teacher then poured sand between the pebbles and asked, "Is the jar full now?"

Again the students stayed silent. The teacher then poured water up to the top. Now the jar was full.

What do we learn from this? When we put the rocks in first, there is space for pebbles; after pebbles there is still space for sand, and after sand, water. If we fill our schedule with the most important activities first, with Kṛṣṇa conscious activities, we'll always be able to accommodate less important activities—if we choose to at all. But if we fill our time first with less important activities—pebbles, sand, and water—there will be no place left for the most important activities—the large rocks. So let us plan our days and weeks to include time for chanting Hare Kṛṣṇa, hearing Kṛṣṇa's glories, and serving Kṛṣṇa's devotees. Then our lives will be completely successful.

One may consider, With so many other commitments, how will I manage time for Kṛṣṇa? Let us see how the great devotee king Ambarīṣa did it. Although he was the emperor of the world, he dedicated time for Kṛṣṇa, and by the grace of the Lord his kingdom and dynasty flourished:

> Mahārāja Ambarīṣa always engaged his mind in meditating upon the lotus feet of Kṛṣṇa, his words in describing the glories of the Lord, his hands in cleansing the Lord's temple, and his ears in hearing the words spoken by Kṛṣṇa or about Kṛṣṇa. He engaged his eyes in seeing the Deity of Kṛṣṇa, Kṛṣṇa's temples, and Kṛṣṇa's places like Mathurā and Vṛndāvana, he engaged his sense of touch in touching the bodies of the Lord's devotees, he engaged his sense of smell in smelling the fragrance of *tulasī* offered to the Lord, and he engaged his tongue in tasting the Lord's *prasāda*. He engaged his legs in walking to the holy places and temples of the Lord, his head in bowing down before the Lord, and all his desires in serving the Lord, twenty-four hours a day. Indeed, Mahārāja Ambarīṣa never desired anything for his own sense gratification. He engaged all his senses in devotional service, in various engagements related to the Lord. This is the way to increase attachment for the Lord and be completely free from all material desires. (*SB* 9.4.18–21)

Mahārāja Ambarīṣa did everything without difficulty, by the grace of the Lord.

We simply need faith (*śraddhā*):

> *'śraddhā'-śabde—viśvāsa kahe sudṛḍha niścaya*
> *kṛṣṇe bhakti kaile sarva-karma kṛta haya*

"By rendering transcendental loving service to Kṛṣṇa, one automatically performs all subsidiary activities. This confident, firm faith, favorable to the discharge of devotional service, is called *śraddhā*." (Cc *Madhya* 22.62)

Now by the grace of Śrīla Prabhupāda we have come in contact with the Kṛṣṇa consciousness movement and have received a chance to realize the greatest gain in life. We can hear about Prabhupāda, follow his instructions, and serve his mission. Lord Kṛṣṇa Himself declares, *mad-bhakta-pūjābhyadhikā*: "Engaging in the service of My devotee is more profitable than trying to engage in My service directly." (*SB* 11.19.21)

So let us begin now chanting Hare Kṛṣṇa, Hare Kṛṣṇa, Kṛṣṇa Kṛṣṇa, Hare Hare/ Hare Rāma, Hare Rāma, Rāma Rāma, Hare Hare.

Now . . . Now is the time.

Our Victory

Throughout Śrīla Prabhupāda's books, we read about the transcendental glories of pure devotees. And following Śrīla Prabhupāda's teachings, we aspire to serve pure devotees, associate with pure devotees, and become pure devotees ourselves. However, as time goes by and we associate with devotees and observe their activities, we may find we are not sure who a pure devotee actually is.

We must know who a pure devotee is. We may read words in books, but because we have little realization or experience, we may imagine that a pure devotee is beyond human emotions—that heat or cold, pleasure or pain, gain or loss can never affect him. And so, out of ignorance or overfamiliarity, we could easily commit offenses.

Śrīla Prabhupāda has taught us that a pure devotee may have all the sentiments of an ordinary person—that he may on occasion feel anger or lamentation. The *Bhāgavatam* says of Dhruva Mahārāja, *after* he had realized God and spoken with Him face to face,

dhruvo bhrātṛ-vadhaṁ śrutvā
kopāmarṣa-śucārpitaḥ
jaitraṁ syandanam āsthāya
gataḥ puṇya-janālayam

"When Dhruva Mahārāja heard of the killing of his brother Uttama by the Yakṣas in the Himalaya Mountains, being overwhelmed with lamentation and anger, he got on his chariot and went out for victory over the city of the Yakṣas, Alakāpurī." (*SB* 4.10.4)

And Śrīla Prabhupāda explains in the purport, "Dhruva Mahārāja's becoming angry, overwhelmed with grief, and envious [in this verse, *amarṣa*, intolerant] of the enemies was not incompatible with his position as a great devotee. It is a misunderstanding that a devotee should not be angry, envious, or overwhelmed by lamentation. Dhruva Mahārāja was the king, and when his brother was unceremoniously killed, it was his duty to take revenge against the Yakṣas from the Himalayas."

If we look carefully into the characteristics of pure devotees, we may find that they do have the same sentiments as anyone else but that they are fixed in their duties, in their determination to serve Kṛṣṇa.

"One should therefore avoid observing a pure devotee externally, but should try to see the internal features and understand how he is engaged in the transcendental loving service of the Lord. In this way, one can avoid seeing the pure devotee from a material point of view, and thus one can gradually become a purified devotee oneself." (*NOI* 6 purport)

Śrīla Prabhupāda further explains, "One should therefore be very careful not to commit any offense against a Vaiṣṇava. . . . One is forbidden to observe the activities of a pure Vaiṣṇava from a material point of view. . . . A person cannot derive any spiritual benefit when he offends the lotus feet of a Vaiṣṇava." (*NOI* 6 purport)

So we have to be careful not to fall into the illusion of thinking that pure devotees are the same as ordinary persons. However ordinary they may appear to be, they are fixed in their resolve to serve God.

Once, after a lecture in Mauritius, the publisher and editor of a well-known weekly Mauritian newspaper asked Śrīla Prabhupāda a question:

"We have listened to you very attentively, and I have no doubt that we, the audience, have learned much which could help us in some way to realize what we are and to realize God. Now, if God Himself comes to teach someone in this world, and if the person has learned from God directly and is satisfied that he has learned and understood, can he, a few minutes later, forget that he has received instruction from God and depart in a very ridiculous way from God, from what God has taught him in person?"

Śrīla Prabhupāda replied, "Ridiculous way? What is that 'ridiculous'?"

EDITOR: "If I have read . . ."

PRABHUPĀDA: "No, no. First of all correct yourself. What is that 'ridiculous'?"

EDITOR: "If after receiving a good education you act contrary to that education."

PRABHUPĀDA: "If one has received a good education, he cannot act contradictory."

Śrīla Prabhupāda, as the external manifestation of the Supersoul, could understand the heart of the living entity and could perceive the offensive mentality in the questioner, even though the offensive thought had not yet been expressed. Thus Śrīla Prabhupāda met the gentleman's challenge even before he could ask his question. Prabhupāda said that the question itself was contradictory—that if someone is actually educated he cannot act contrary.

But the gentleman persisted, and Śrīla Prabhupāda, recognizing his impudence, countered: "If you speak ridiculously, how can I hear you? You say that a man has education and he acts ridiculously. Your statement is ridiculous."

Finally the man came out with what he wanted to say:

"Is there a passage in the *Bhagavad-gītā* where Arjuna says, 'I have heard all Your teachings; now I have understood the truth,' or not? The next day he goes on the battlefield and hears that his son has been killed. He loses all his self-control and says, 'I am going to throw myself in the fire. I have lost my son.' Is that the action of a man who has heard God Himself speak to him?"

Śrīla Prabhupāda responded: "You mean Arjuna? Of course,

theoretically we understand, *na hanyate hanyamāne śarīre.* Still, when our son dies we become affected. That is temporary. But after Arjuna heard *Bhagavad-gītā*, Kṛṣṇa gave him the freedom to choose: 'Now I have spoken to you everything. Now whatever you like you may do.' One may be affected under certain circumstances, but if one's conviction is that 'I shall act according to the order of God,' that is final. Arjuna did not act against the will of the Lord. That is his victory. Temporarily he might have been disturbed when his son was killed. That is a different thing. Everyone becomes. But that does not mean he stopped his work. What was the final conclusion? He did not leave the warfield because his son Abhimanyu was killed. 'No, I don't want to fight.' No, Arjuna did not do that. For the time being he was affected. That is natural. But finally he concluded, 'Yes—*naṣṭo mohaḥ smṛtir labdhā/ kariṣye vacanaṁ tava*—my illusion is now over. I shall fight.' That is the right conclusion."

Śrīla Prabhupāda explained that Kṛṣṇa spoke the *Bhagavad-gītā* to convince Arjuna that he should fight, and in the end Arjuna agreed to fight. And although Arjuna was temporarily affected when he heard the news of his son's death and was overwhelmed with lamentation, still he did not give up his determination to fight. He did not give up his resolution to follow the order of Kṛṣṇa. So we cannot find fault with Arjuna for having such feelings of lamentation. We should not misunderstand and think that Arjuna is not a pure devotee or that his reaction to his son's death is ridiculous or contrary to the teachings of the *Bhagavad-gītā*.

In the same way, whatever may happen to us and however we may be affected by the trials and tribulations of the world, we should remain fixed in our conviction: "Yes, I shall act only according to Śrīla Prabhupāda's order and serve Kṛṣṇa." And that will be our victory.

Never Compromise

When I was in Madras—the first time I was really on my own in India—I was meeting people and trying to preach the same way I had heard Śrīla Prabhupāda preach, declaring that Kṛṣṇa is the Supreme Personality of Godhead and criticizing demigod worshipers and impersonalists. There were many impersonalists in Madras, and many demigod worshipers too. And gradually I began to hear from some of our friends that there was an undercurrent of protest against the way I was preaching. The Śaivites didn't like it, and the Māyāvādīs also didn't like it. Hardly anyone liked it. I heard the criticism, and I was surprised, but I didn't really make any change; I just heard it.

Eventually the criticism of my criticism reached such a point that I actually began to have doubts. "So many people are saying the same thing," I thought. "Maybe I am doing something wrong." Even one of our best friends, at whose home I had been staying, echoed the others' comments. "You shouldn't criticize others," he advised. "Just say what you want about Kṛṣṇa consciousness and don't say anything negative about others. Don't criticize." And he gave the example of the Gauḍīya Maṭha: "They don't criticize others. They have a nice temple, and every year they have a big celebration of Janmāṣṭamī and thousands of people come, but they don't criticize, like you do. They just present their own activities. Why can't you be like them?"

When I thought about what he said, however, I asked myself, "Does Śrīla Prabhupāda really want us to be like the Gauḍīya Maṭha? I don't think so." So I kept going. But then another friend, whose brother had offered to sponsor Śrīla Prabhupāda's program in Madras, said the same thing: "All right, you worship Kṛṣṇa. You can worship Kṛṣṇa, but don't say that Kṛṣṇa is better than Śiva or Gaṇeśa. You do *bhakti.* That's all right, but don't say that *bhakti-yoga* is better than *karma-yoga* or *jñāna-yoga* or . . ."

I kept hearing it. Wherever I went I was hearing it. So finally I thought, "Maybe Kṛṣṇa is trying to tell me something. Maybe I should listen to what they are saying." And I made a resolution: "I am just going to present Kṛṣṇa consciousness. I'm not going to criticize; I am not going to offend people anymore."

Soon thereafter, I had an appointment with a big industrialist. Śrīla Prabhupāda had said that if we just placed his books on a person's table, the person would become a life member. So I showed him the books, showed him the pictures of our activities, took out the life membership form, explained the benefits, and asked him to sign. And he said, "What about Śaṅkarācārya? He is one of the great *ācāryas* of India. You haven't said anything about him." So I said, "Yes, he is one of the great *ācāryas* of India. Yes." "But you haven't said anything about him. What about him? What about his teachings?" I tried to avoid getting into an argument, so I said something vague and general. But he kept pushing. He kept probing. And finally it all came out. I told him that actually Śaṅkarācārya was an incarnation of Śiva and that as such we give him all respect. But he came with a special purpose: to present an imagined, monistic interpretation of the *Vedas* and thus bewilder ignorant people. I even took out the *Teachings of Lord Caitanya*—we didn't have the *Caitanya-caritāmṛta* then—and read the verses from the *Padma Purāṇa* and *Śiva Purāṇa* about Lord Śiva taking the form of a *brāhmaṇa*, preaching the false doctrine of Māyāvāda philosophy, which is covered Buddhism, and promoting atheism. Still, Śaṅkara's ultimate purpose was to bring the Buddhists, who were atheists, to accept the authority of the *Vedas*. It was a strategy. Then Lord Caitanya came and taught the proper understanding of the *Vedas*.

Things became tense. The gentleman put forward a lot of arguments, and I thought, "I really didn't want to get into an argument, but somehow I did anyway. He will never change his position, so I may as well just leave." And that was the end of the discussion. Dejected, I put away the pictures, put away the books, put away the membership form, closed my briefcase, and was ready to go. As I was just about to leave—he had quite a large compound, which included his factory, office, and residence—he said, "Before you go, I would like you to see my temple." I thought, "Oh, no. There is going to be a *śiva-liṅga*. He is going to want me to bow down, and if I don't he is going to be even more offended." I looked at him, and he looked at me, and I could see he wasn't going to take no for an answer. So I said, "All right."

He escorted me to his temple room. It was quite a large room, as personal temples go. And facing us at the opposite end was the altar. So, I walked in. It was a marble room, all white marble, with the altar on an elevated platform, and on top of the platform were large marble Deities of Rādhā and Kṛṣṇa. Boy, was I ever happy to see Rādhā and Kṛṣṇa! I hadn't seen Them for a long time, because even the Vaiṣṇava temples in Madras were almost all Viṣṇu. And there was the famous temple of Pārthasārathi, which was just Kṛṣṇa alone.

So I was delighted. I offered my obeisances and prayers, and then I looked at our friend with an expression that asked, "What is happening here?" He looked at me straight in the eyes and said, "I am a devotee of Kṛṣṇa, and all my family members are devotees of Kṛṣṇa. My family has worshiped Lord Kṛṣṇa for many generations. Actually, I was just testing you. And you did not compromise. So I am very pleased, and I will be honored to become your life member."

We went back to his office, I took out the forms, he took out his checkbook, and he paid the whole amount in one installment and became a life member.

Then I was really confused. I started thinking, "Well, maybe I haven't been doing the wrong thing after all"—but I still wasn't quite sure.

When I got back to the room where I was staying, there was a letter from Śrīla Prabhupāda. Receiving a letter from Śrīla Prabhupāda was always a great occasion. When I opened the letter, the words practically jumped out of the page: "The fact is that I am the only one in India who is openly criticizing, not only impersonalism and demigod worship, but everything that falls short of complete surrender to Kṛṣṇa." Prabhupāda's words continued: "My *guru mahārāja* never compromised in his preaching, nor will I, nor should any of my students. We are firmly convinced that Kṛṣṇa is the Supreme Personality of Godhead and that all others are His part and parcel servants. This we must declare boldly to the whole world, that they should not foolishly dream of world peace unless they are prepared to surrender fully to Kṛṣṇa as Supreme Lord."

So, I got my answer from Prabhupāda.

That was Śrīla Prabhupāda's mood—his *guru mahārāja's* mood and his mood—and that was the mood he wanted us to have. We don't compromise in our philosophy.

Śrīla Prabhupāda's Trees

Śrīla Prabhupāda had to struggle very hard to build the Juhu temple. The first struggle was to get the land, the next struggle was to get the permission to build the temple, and the last struggle was to actually build the temple and install the Deities. We worked hard to get the permission, but Indian permits often include many conditions. So although they give permission, the permission is not actually valid until one fulfills the conditions.

One of the conditions was that we had to have an internal access road of a certain width. And it just so happened that right where the access road was supposed to go, there were some palm trees. Once, when Śrīla Prabhupāda came to Juhu after being away for some time, he noticed that one or two of the trees had been cut down, and he was very concerned—I would even say upset. He asked, "Why did you cut down the trees?" We thought we had the perfect answer: we had to build the temple, and to get the permission for the temple we had to cut the trees in the way of the road. Śrīla Prabhupāda said, "No, you go to the municipality and tell them it's against our religion to cut down trees." So we had no choice, and we did it. And of course the municipal officers objected.

But one thing that really struck me about how concerned Śrīla Prabhupāda was for the trees was that the next time he came back to Juhu after a world tour, practically the first thing he said was, "I was in Tehran, and I have seen they have trees in the middle of the streets. So we can also have trees in the middle of our street." So on Śrīla Prabhupāda's order, we held our ground with the municipality, and in the end they gave us the permission to keep the tree. And even today you can see that tree, which Śrīla Prabhupāda protected, still standing there with asphalt all around it.

So I am thinking that if Śrīla Prabhupāda has so much concern and care—and even love, I would say—for a tree, then how much care and love he must have for us. And it's just because of Śrīla Prabhupāda's care and mercy and protection that we are able to stand in Kṛṣṇa consciousness—no matter what else is around us.

All glory to Śrīla Prabhupāda.

Hare Kṛṣṇa.

Service to Guru: No Higher Duty

An address at the Los Angeles ISKCON temple, delivered in 2004 on the birth anniversary of His Divine Grace A.C. Bhaktivedanta Swami Prabhupāda.

yat-sevayā bhagavataḥ
kūṭa-sthasya madhu-dviṣaḥ
rati-rāso bhavet tīvraḥ
pādayor vyasanārdanaḥ

"By serving the feet of the spiritual master, one is enabled to develop transcendental ecstasy in the service of the Personality of Godhead, who is the unchangeable enemy of the Madhu demon and whose service vanquishes one's material distresses." (*SB* 3.7.19)

PURPORT by Śrīla Prabhupāda

The association of a bona fide spiritual master like the sage Maitreya can be of absolute help in achieving transcendental attachment for the direct service of the Lord. The Lord is the enemy of the Madhu demon, or in other words He is the enemy of the suffering of His pure devotee. The word *rati-rāsaḥ* is significant in this verse. Service to the Lord is rendered in different transcendental mellows (relationships): neutral, active, friendly, parental, and nuptial. A living entity in the liberated position of transcendental service to the Lord becomes attracted to one of the above-mentioned mellows, and when one is engaged in transcendental loving service to the Lord, one's service attachment in the material world is automatically vanquished. As stated in the *Bhagavad-gītā* (2.59), *rasa-varjaṁ raso 'py asya, paraṁ dṛṣṭvā nivartate.*

LECTURE

To read Śrīla Prabhupāda's books—to study them, to try to understand them and apply them—is an important part of our spiritual development. So today, on his appearance day, I thought to discuss some of the philosophy that he has presented in his books, because the philosophy is the basis of our activities in devotional service, our activities in ISKCON.

One of the first books that Śrīla Prabhupāda translated was *The Nectar of Devotion*, a summary study of Śrīla Rūpa Gosvāmī's *Bhakti-rasāmṛta-sindhu*. There Śrīla Prabhupāda, following Śrīla Rūpa Gosvāmī, explains that there are three divisions of devotional service: *sādhana-bhakti*, *bhāva-bhakti*, and *prema-bhakti*. *Sādhana-bhakti* has been rendered by Śrīla Prabhupāda into English as "devotional service in practice," *bhāva-bhakti* as "devotional service in ecstasy," and *prema-bhakti* as "devotional service in pure love of Godhead."

For people interested in spiritual advancement, there is a great question: How do we progress? Of course, Śrīla Prabhupāda himself emphasized the chanting of the holy names, and thus we are called the Hare Kṛṣṇa movement. And we read in *Śrī Caitanya-caritāmṛta* that Śrī Caitanya Mahāprabhu also confirmed that of all the items of devotional service, the chanting of the holy names is the most important. Therefore Śrīla Prabhupāda stressed above all the chanting of the holy names, and for disciples the chanting of at least sixteen rounds daily.

Now, where does service to the spiritual master, or in our case, service to Śrīla Prabhupāda and his mission, come into the picture? Where does it fit? In the *Bhakti-sandarbha* (*Anuccheda* 237) Śrī Jīva Gosvāmī discusses the importance of serving the spiritual master, with reference to various Vedic texts. In text 237.13 he cites a verse from the *Padma Purāṇa* in which a disciple considers devotion (*bhakti*) to his spiritual master to be of paramount importance: "For me devotion to my spiritual master is more important than devotion to Lord Hari. If I am devoted to my spiritual master, then Lord Hari will personally reveal Himself to me." Śrī Jīva Gosvāmī comments, "This success does not depend even on any other practice of worshiping the Supreme Lord." (*Bs* 237.14) Later, Śrīla Jīva Gosvāmī quotes Lord Kṛṣṇa's statement in *Śrīmad-Bhāgavatam* (10.80.34):

nāham ijyā-prajātibhyāṁ
tapasopaśamena vā
tuṣyeyaṁ sarva-bhūtātmā
guru-śuśrūṣayā yathā

"I, the Soul of all beings, am not as satisfied by ritual worship, brahminical initiation, penances, or self-discipline as I am by faithful service rendered to one's spiritual master." And he remarks, "The commentary [of Śrīla Śrīdhara Svāmī] says, 'It has already been said that no one is more deserving of service than the *guru* who gives one knowledge. Consequently, there is also no higher duty than worshiping that spiritual master.'"

Śrīla Jīva Gosvāmī advises that to achieve special perfection (*vaiśiṣṭya lipsu*), one should, if one is able, constantly and specifically render service to the lotus feet of one's spiritual master(s) (*śrī-guru-caraṇaṁ nityam eva viśeṣataḥ sevaṁ kuryāt*) (*Bs* 237.3). That is the mood of service that Śrīla Prabhupāda exhibited as a disciple of Śrīla Bhaktisiddhānta Sarasvatī Ṭhākura, and that is the mood of service he instilled in us—through his example and through his words.

The verse from *Śrīmad-Bhāgavatam* that we just read states specifically that by serving the lotus feet of the spiritual master one develops ecstasy, or *rati*. *Rati* is part of that scheme of different levels of devotional service mentioned by Śrī Rūpa Gosvāmī. After *sādhana-bhakti* comes *bhāva-bhakti*, and a synonym for *bhāva* in certain contexts is *rati*. *Rati* means "attachment." As Śrīla Prabhupāda mentions in the purport and as Śrī Rūpa Gosvāmī elaborates in the *Bhakti-rasāmṛta-sindhu*, there are different *bhāvas*, or types of *rati*. There is *dāsya-rati*, attachment to Kṛṣṇa in the mood of being a servant; *sakhya-rati*, attachment to Kṛṣṇa in the mood of being a friend; *vātsalya-rati*, attachment to Kṛṣṇa in the mood of being a parent; and finally *mādhurya-rati*, attachment to Kṛṣṇa in the mood of being a lover of Kṛṣṇa.

As suggested in this verse and purport, it is by serving the lotus feet of Śrīla Prabhupāda that one can develop these *bhāvas*, these different types of attachment to Kṛṣṇa's service (*rati-rasa*). And it is by service to the lotus feet of Śrīla Prabhupāda that one develops that desire to serve Kṛṣṇa in a particular relationship. Thus, we don't have to engage in any sort of artificial esoteric practice to develop that desire for service to Kṛṣṇa in a particular relationship. That desire (*lobha*) comes by serving the lotus feet of Śrīla Prabhupāda.

Śrīla Jīva Gosvāmī also discusses today's verse in *Śrī Bhakti-sandarbha* (*Anuccheda* 244). He writes, "The word *tīvra* ('intense') hints at the special result of personal service, compared with that of mere association." Citing verse after verse, Śrīla Jīva Gosvāmī glorifies the results of associating with pure devotees (*sat-saṅga*), which is the only process that can give one the strong love that can control Kṛṣṇa. As powerful and beneficial as hearing and chanting in the association of pure devotees (*prasaṅga*) is, however, personal service rendered to pure devotees (*paricarya*), combined with chanting and hearing, brings an "exceptional result" (*vaśiṣṭaṁ phalam*): even greater love for Kṛṣṇa. I felt it appropriate on Śrīla Prabhupāda's appearance day to express our appreciation for this aspect of Śrīla Prabhupāda's mission: how he was able to present the process by which one can achieve ecstatic love of Godhead in the simplest terms—in terms of service to him. By surrendering to Śrīla Prabhupāda and developing love for him, we surrender to Kṛṣṇa and develop our love for Him. So we should serve Śrīla Prabhupāda in all respects with full faith and conviction, without reservation. The famous verse in the fourth chapter of the *Gītā* (4.34) says,

tad viddhi praṇipātena
paripraśnena sevayā
upadekṣyanti te jñānaṁ
jñāninas tattva-darśinaḥ

"One must approach a spiritual master and render service to him, inquire submissively of him, and surrender to him." And we find in the thirteenth chapter of the *Bhagavad-gītā*, as one of the items of knowledge, *ācāryopāsanaṁ*: one must approach the *ācārya*. In his purport to verses 8–12, Śrīla Prabhupāda comments that one who has approached the spiritual master with all humility and offered him all services can make advancement even if he is unable to strictly follow all the rules and regulations—or, the regulative principles will be easier for one who has served the spiritual master without reservation.

That was Śrīla Prabhupāda's spirit: he was ready to do anything to spread Kṛṣṇa consciousness. And he inspired in us the same spirit so that we were ready to do anything to assist him.

Mālatī dāsī tells a nice story about how when we first got the land in Māyāpur, Śrīla Prabhupāda invited his godbrothers to meet him there. Śrīla Prabhupāda had a small thatched hut, which is still there, although renovated. Mālatī was cooking for him. It was very difficult for her because there was almost no money. She had to struggle to get money from the treasurer, then walk with her young daughter to the boat, haggle with the boat people so they would accept the proper fare, take the boat across to Navadvīpa, haggle with rickshaw drivers so that they too would accept the right amount, ride to the fruit and vegetable markets, haggle with the vendors there to get the right price, and then return to cook on the single portable coal burner and the single portable kerosene burner on the floor in the corner of Śrīla Prabhupāda's hut, separated from him by a plain cloth curtain. As the devotees didn't have a refrigerator then, whatever she needed she had to buy fresh daily—and thus go through the same struggles every day. Mālatī was on the verge of collapsing, but then so were most of Prabhupāda's disciples, dedicated as they were to his service in spite of all material impediments and inconveniences—living in tents, eating the local food, getting dysentery, and so on.

Mālatī's constant meditation was how to make the *prasāda* come out nice so that Śrīla Prabhupāda would be pleased. And every day Prabhupāda would point out the defects in her service, so that she could improve. But she felt that he was criticizing her. And she felt that she could never get it right. Then one day she thought that she had finally managed to cook everything properly and arrange the plate just to Śrīla Prabhupāda's standard.

She brought the plate of *prasāda* to Śrīla Prabhupāda, but when she came to remove the plate he said, "There is too much salt"—not that there was too much salt in the food, but there was too much salt placed on the plate with the pepper and ginger and lemon slices.

So she concluded, "I can never get it right. I should find someone else who can do the service better." And at once she felt relieved.

So she decided, "I'll tell Śrīla Prabhupāda tomorrow."

The next day, Mālatī heard that some of Śrīla Prabhupāda's godbrothers were coming to join him for lunch, so she assumed that she would not be cooking, since Śrīla Prabhupāda had been under criticism from his godbrothers for keeping women in his ashrams and for having a woman cook. But Śrīla Prabhupāda called her to tell her what items he wanted her to cook that day, as usual.

She was dutiful, so she decided, "Well, I'll just cook today, and then I'll tell him tomorrow." So she cooked.

When the *prasāda* was ready, Mālatī lifted up the cloth that separated the work area from Śrīla Prabhupāda's room. There she saw Śrīla Prabhupāda sitting on the floor at the end of the room, with two of his godbrothers on either side. Śrīla Prabhupāda appeared to her like a diamond in a gold setting, flanked as he was by his esteemed godbrothers. And she felt intimidated by the presence of such venerable Vaiṣṇavas.

Already on her knees, she pulled her sari over her head and arms so that only her hands showed, and with her knees and elbows on the floor, she carried Śrīla Prabhupāda's plate of *prasāda* with her outstretched hands, practically crawling between the godbrothers to approach her spiritual master.

Then Śrīla Prabhupāda said to his godbrothers, "Yes, she cooks for me." He paused. "And I criticize her. But she would slit her throat for me, and I would do the same for her." When she heard that, Mālatī almost collapsed on the floor. That was more than any reciprocation she could have ever hoped for or even imagined. And what Śrīla Prabhupāda had said was true. We were ready to do anything for him—in part because we knew he would do anything for us.

So Śrīla Prabhupāda's mood was the same—toward his spiritual master and toward his disciples who were helping him in his service to his spiritual master. He would do anything for his spiritual master. He came on a steamship all the way from India to America, to New York. He lived in the Bowery. He was ready to do anything for Kṛṣṇa consciousness. And he was ready to do anything for us, really. To those devotees who gave everything to him, he was ready to give everything.

It is the love that we develop for Śrīla Prabhupāda through our surrender and service to him that becomes the basis for our developing love for Kṛṣṇa. Śrīla Prabhupāda used to say that the spiritual master is the "transparent via media" for Kṛṣṇa. We get knowledge from Kṛṣṇa through the spiritual master, and we offer service to Kṛṣṇa through the spiritual master. But more than just the mechanics of the service, it is the mood of devotion that we want to offer to Kṛṣṇa. So we develop the mood of devotion for the spiritual master, and that becomes the mood of love and devotion for Lord Kṛṣṇa—Rādhā and Kṛṣṇa.

Service to the spiritual master, to Śrīla Prabhupāda, is an extremely deep thing, and this mood of service is the very basis of the Kṛṣṇa consciousness movement. Upon that basis ISKCON was formed, and upon that basis ISKCON will grow strong. And that too is the basis on which, as Śrīla Prabhupāda said, we will have another ISKCON in the spiritual world.

Hare Kṛṣṇa.

6

Prabhupāda's Books

Thousands of Foot Soldiers

An excerpt from an arrival address given in Cape Town, South Africa, on August 28, 1995.

Śrīla Prabhupāda was especially empowered by Śrī Śrī Gaura-Nitāi to spread Kṛṣṇa consciousness all over the world, and he especially emphasized book distribution. With our limited intelligence we cannot understand what is the best way to spread Kṛṣṇa consciousness. But Śrīla Prabhupāda was given unlimited intelligence by Kṛṣṇa, and he has given us clear direction how to spread Kṛṣṇa consciousness. If we simply follow Śrīla Prabhupāda's instructions the result will be wonderful. Śrīla Prabhupāda said, "My *guru mahārāja* told me to translate, publish, and distribute books." As the *ācārya*, Śrīla Prabhupāda set the example for us. "I do not know whether my *guru mahārāja* was right or wrong, and I did not consider what the result would be, but I blindly followed his instruction, and the result has been there."

Sometimes Śrīla Prabhupāda would tell the story of Dr. Frog, Ph.D. One frog lived in a small well, and another frog, who had just visited the Atlantic Ocean, came and told him, "I've seen a very big body of water." "How big?" asked Dr. Frog—"As big as my well?" "No, much bigger than your well." "How big? Twice as big? Four times as big? Eight times as big?" He was trying to estimate the size of the Atlantic Ocean by comparing it to his little well. Similarly, our intelligence is like a little well and Śrīla Prabhupāda's is like a great ocean. We cannot even compare our intelligence with his, because his intelligence was given directly by Kṛṣṇa—unlimited intelligence. We cannot even begin to comprehend. Only by Śrīla Prabhupāda's mercy may we understand something. So we should just surrender to Śrīla Prabhupāda's plan and execute his order; then all success will be there, not only in spreading Kṛṣṇa consciousness but in developing our own Kṛṣṇa consciousness as well.

And the main program Śrīla Prabhupāda prescribed was book distribution.

Recently on the airplane, I was looking at the people. Maybe by Śrīla Prabhupāda's mercy some feelings of compassion came, and I was thinking, "What can we do for these people?" Then I thought beyond the people on the airplane to all the people in the world. So many people. How to give them Kṛṣṇa consciousness? Just on one little airplane there may be three hundred passengers. How to get the message through to them? And I thought, "The only way is through Śrīla Prabhupāda's books." Then I understood why Śrīla Prabhupāda emphasized book distribution: because through books his message or voice could reach unlimited numbers of persons. Therefore, the real way to change people's lives and reform human society is to give them the message of Kṛṣṇa through Śrīla Prabhupāda's books.

The books are so wonderful that through them Śrīla Prabhupāda's voice and message can be multiplied unlimitedly. A human being can speak only so much to so many persons, but through his books Śrīla Prabhupāda can preach to any number of persons for any amount of time and never get tired. He'll just go on and on and on. It may take thousands and millions of foot soldiers to carry Śrīla Prabhupāda's books to every house and door, but Śrīla Prabhupāda can go on speaking without limit. Like Kṛṣṇa's universal form with its unlimited heads, mouths, hands, and legs, Śrīla Prabhupāda also expands in the form of his books, goes into people's houses, and speaks to them. He stays with them all the time, all over the world. If we have to stay with one family, we might be with them from four-thirty in the morning until ten-thirty at night, but eventually we will get tired. But in the form of his books Śrīla Prabhupāda can stay with any number of families for any amount of time and never get tired. Even if someone in the house can't sleep or wakes up in the middle of the night, he can go to his shelf and Śrīla Prabhupāda will be there to talk to him. Throughout the globe it's always 6 a.m. somewhere, 7 a.m., 8 a.m., noon, 6 p.m., 7 p.m.,

8 p.m.—all at once. And Śrīla Prabhupāda is there at all times of the day and night, ready to speak to anyone who wants to hear him. So we are just aspiring to be Śrīla Prabhupāda's humble servants, his bearers, carrying him to the conditioned souls in the form of his wonderful books.

Distribute and Get Mercy

In his Concluding Words to *Śrī Caitanya-caritāmṛta*, Śrīla Prabhupāda writes: "His Divine Grace Śrīla Bhaktisiddhānta Sarasvatī Ṭhākura was very fond of seeing many books published to spread the Kṛṣṇa consciousness movement. Therefore our society, the International Society for Krishna Consciousness, has formed to execute the order of Śrī Caitanya Mahāprabhu and His Divine Grace Śrīla Bhaktisiddhānta Sarasvatī Ṭhākura. . . . On this occasion, therefore, I request my disciples who are determined to help me in this work to continue their cooperation fully, so that philosophers, scholars, religionists, and people in general all over the world will benefit by reading our transcendental literatures such as *Śrīmad-Bhāgavatam* and *Śrī Caitanya-caritāmṛta*." Now we, the members of ISKCON and followers of Śrīla Prabhupāda, must execute the order to preach and distribute books.

Śrīla Prabhupāda tells the story of the impersonalist *guru* who touched his disciple to enlighten him with spiritual knowledge. When the disciple opened his eyes, he saw his *guru* was crying. When he asked, "Master, why are you crying?" the master replied, "Because I have given all my knowledge to you and have none left."

Śrīla Prabhupāda explains that in the material concept, if you give something away, you lose it. The more you give, the less you have. But in Kṛṣṇa consciousness, the more you distribute knowledge, the more you get. And if you have spiritual knowledge and do not distribute it, you become envious. We have seen practically that the more we distribute the transcendental knowledge in Śrīla Prabhupāda's books, the more our realization increases. Thus both he who gives and he who receives transcendental knowledge benefit.

But the greatest benefit in distributing Śrīla Prabhupāda's books is that Śrīla Prabhupāda is pleased. "Go on increasing my books—go on increasing my pleasure," he wrote me.

So let us pray to Śrīla Prabhupāda and redouble our enthusiasm and determination to distribute his mercy, and surely his mercy will be upon us.

The Greatest Pain, the Greatest Gain

When Lord Caitanya was discussing with Rāmānanda Rāya, "What is the most painful experience?" the answer given was "Separation from the devotees of Kṛṣṇa." And when the question was asked, "What is the most auspicious, beneficial activity for the living entity?" the answer was "Association with the devotees of Kṛṣṇa."

To give benefit and auspiciousness to the living entities, we have to give them association. Otherwise, how will they get auspiciousness? Almost everyone in the material world is suffering. Why? They don't know, but we know they are suffering because of separation from pure devotees. Therefore, to remove their suffering and bring auspiciousness to them, we should go to them and give them Śrīla Prabhupāda's association through his words.

And in serving the mission of Śrīla Prabhupāda and Śrīmān Mahāprabhu, we bring auspiciousness not only to those we meet but also to ourselves. As Śrīla Bhaktisiddhānta Sarasvatī Ṭhākura told Śrīla Prabhupāda, "You should preach. This will be good for you as well as for your audience."

So let us deliver all souls, including ourselves, from the greatest suffering and bring them the greatest benefit—Śrīla Prabhupāda's association through his books and teachings.

Book to Godhead

A national saṅkīrtana *meeting with Giriraj Swami at the Śrī Śrī Rādhā-Rādhānātha temple in Durban, South Africa.*

BHAKTA JAMES: You were speaking yesterday about how the weeds in the heart can appear exactly like the devotional creeper and how we must learn to identify and remove them. Often I don't have anyone watching my service to see my motivations. How can we ourselves assess our motivations?

GIRIRAJ SWAMI: One successful book distributor in Europe said that if he became slack or even subtly deviated he would get feedback from the people on the street and feel that Prabhupāda or Kṛṣṇa was speaking to him. For example, someone might say, "Oh, you don't really care about us; you just want money," and he would think maybe Kṛṣṇa was telling him something, that maybe he'd lost the mood of really caring and was just thinking of money. So we can get instruction in many ways if we're open.

BHAKTA JAMES: Yesterday I met a man in the parking lot. He said, "Before you go, just one thing. You should try a little harder with each person you meet. You're giving up too easily; you should be more persistent."

BHAKTA GLEN: At the same time, nobody likes a fire-and-brimstone approach.

GIRIRAJ SWAMI: We should be enthusiastic. When the first devotees were leaving for England, Śrīla Prabhupāda told a story from a Charlie Chaplin film. Charlie Chaplin went to a formal dance party and by mistake sat on a chair with wet paint on it. His tuxedo stuck, and when he got up the tails ripped. Ordinarily one might feel embarrassed, but Charlie Chaplin began to dance so enthusiastically with his ripped tuxedo that people thought he was setting the pace with a new fashion. He was dancing like lightning all over the ballroom—up and down, up and down—and people were looking with wonder. Finally one man ripped his tuxedo like Charlie Chaplin's, then a second, and then a third. Finally all the gentlemen began to rip their tuxedos. So just by our enthusiasm we can induce people to follow us.

And Prabhupāda said that enthusiasm comes from Kṛṣṇa consciousness, and that Kṛṣṇa consciousness comes from following the regulative principles, hearing and chanting.

Bhakta James: How does the enthusiasm and desire of the devotee influence the desire of the person he approaches, and what is the role of the Supersoul?

Giriraj Swami: If the devotee is enthusiastic to engage people in devotional service and give them transcendental knowledge, and his only interest is to help people and to please Śrīla Prabhupāda and Kṛṣṇa, he can pray to the Supersoul without duplicity to kindly inspire them to take a book. He can pray with heartfelt sincerity. The person approached will respond to his sincerity, and Kṛṣṇa within the heart will also respond. But if you're not so sincere, neither your appeal to the person nor your prayer to the Supersoul will be so effective.

Mahāśṛṅga dāsa: Mahārāja, in your offering to Śrīla Prabhupāda you asked Prabhupāda's blessings to read his books, understand them, and become more convinced that they can change people's lives and change the whole world, so that we can distribute them more. Could you speak on each of these items?

Giriraj Swami: How to read Śrīla Prabhupāda's books? First we should have interest. *Jijñāsuḥ śreya uttamam*. The first qualification of the disciple is that he should be eager to inquire into the Absolute Truth. Then he will want to read. And how to understand them? If he finds some portion he cannot understand, and even after chanting and pondering over it he still can't get the answer, he may ask some senior devotee. And after hearing the answer, he may inquire further. Arjuna asked one question and Kṛṣṇa answered, but Kṛṣṇa's answer raised another question. Thus both the *Bhagavad-gītā* and *Śrīmad-Bhāgavatam* take the form of questions and answers. The sincere disciple must always inquire of the bona fide spiritual master, and the spiritual master will always be pleased to answer. Thus the reciprocation of transcendental knowledge takes place.

How can I become convinced that these books can change the world? The world will improve if the people improve, and the people will improve if they become Kṛṣṇa conscious. So people should read the books and become Kṛṣṇa conscious. If they read about the ideal life in Kṛṣṇa consciousness and then meet pure devotees who live that ideal life, they and the whole world can certainly change.

Mahāśṛṅga dāsa: How can we be so convinced that we can distribute these books and convince people to take to Kṛṣṇa consciousness?

Giriraj Swami: If we're concerned about others and convinced they can be happy only in Kṛṣṇa consciousness, we'll naturally want to give them the books. Even in material life, if we read a good book we'll tell our friends. So if you've read, appreciated, and benefited from Śrīla Prabhupāda's books, naturally you'll want to share them with others.

When I first went on *saṅkīrtana*, even before reading, I was convinced that if people didn't give their money to Kṛṣṇa they would definitely spend it on sense gratification, and I was convinced that they would benefit more by giving their money to Kṛṣṇa. So with that conviction I tried. But we should know that only by becoming Kṛṣṇa conscious can one actually be happy and solve the problems of life. And apart from everything else, if we just try to distribute these books, Śrīla Prabhupāda and Śrīla Bhaktisiddhānta will be pleased and they will shower their mercy upon us.

Mahāśṛṅga dāsa: Does one have to be convinced himself in order to convince others?

GIRIRAJ SWAMI: There are many businessmen who sell products they know are bad, but they cheat. We do not cheat. We should be genuine devotees and convince others by real concern and realization. Then people will be more inspired to actually read. We want them to take the books. That's the first priority. But if they feel that we are genuinely concerned about them and consequently decide to read, so much the better.

BHAKTA GLEN: When I was staying outside I had the attitude that "Yes, the books are wonderful to read, but practice?" How can we convince people to begin practicing?

GIRIRAJ SWAMI: Either they have to understand their miserable position and want to get out, or they have to want to improve their so-called good position—by Kṛṣṇa consciousness. And to convince them we have to be humble. Quoting Śrī Prabodhānanda Sarasvatī, Śrīla Prabhupāda taught, *dante nidhāya tṛṇakaṁ padayor nipatya*: I take the straw of the street in my mouth and bow down at your feet. *Kṛtvā ca kāku-śatam etad ahaṁ bravīmi*: And I address you with all humility—"You're so learned, intelligent, and influential. You have all good qualities." Then the person will become so eager to hear. He'll think, "Oh, this person has understood me, how nice I am. He must be very intelligent. I should hear him." He will become inquisitive. "You're appreciating me so nicely, what do you want to say?" *He sādhavaḥ sakalam eva vihāya dūrād*: Whatever you have learned, leave it far away. *Gaurāṅga-candra-caraṇe kurutānurāgam*: Just surrender unto the lotus feet of Lord Caitanya.

BHAKTA JAMES: We find that many people who read the books say, "I liked it, but I didn't understand much." Many people have difficulty understanding Prabhupāda's English. How can they benefit if they don't understand?

GIRIRAJ SWAMI: The main problem is they're not used to the subject. Otherwise, the language is quite straightforward.

BHAKTA JAMES: They say they can't understand.

GIRIRAJ SWAMI: As they become more familiar with the subject, they will understand more. And we should help them.

Śāstra is meant to be read with the help of *guru*. All of us are meant to be *gurus* and help others.

BHAKTA STEVE: Kṛṣṇa in the heart also helps. I first read the books about seven years ago, and even today I still have problems understanding, but I knew that this was it, so I kept on.

GIRIRAJ SWAMI: Yes, if the recipient is sincere, even if he can't understand intellectually, Kṛṣṇa in the heart will inspire him: "Yes, this is it. This is what you want. This is what you were looking for." The more sincere the person is, the more Kṛṣṇa helps. Śrīla Prabhupāda himself said he couldn't understand his *guru mahārāja's* language, but still he didn't go away. He used to stay and listen. Just the vibration purifies. Prabhupāda also gave the example that if you're in a foreign country and your house catches fire you will run to the neighbors. And even if you cannot speak their language, somehow, because of the urgency of the situation, you will make them understand.

BHAKTA STEVE: Do you think that the *saṅkīrtana* spirit has become watered down compared with the early days when devotees had Prabhupāda's personal presence to inspire them?

GIRIRAJ SWAMI: Does anybody want to answer?

BHAKTA GLEN: In the early days this was a sort of novelty, something fresh and new, whereas now it's established, not just another of those "cults."

GIRIRAJ SWAMI: We want people to take books and read so they will become devotees, but just reading is generally not enough. They also need association. Distributing books is like planting seeds in the field. Some will take root, some not. But when plants start to sprout they need care. They need to be watered. I think that as the movement and the devotees matured, and as the people with books started to take more interest, we saw the need to give them more association and help them nurture their devotional creepers. If we take the Bhaktivedanta College of Education and Culture here, for example—I don't think its classes are any less a service to the cause of Śrīla Prabhupāda's books than distributing them. The College teaches Śrīla Prabhupāda's books, and the students in the College, as they become convinced, in turn will also preach and distribute. So, the enthusiasm, dedication, and conviction required to teach the books is not less than that required to distribute them. The same spirit may be manifest in different ways.

It may be that in some places our service to Prabhupāda's books has been watered down by other pursuits, but it may also be that the book distribution is now being supported by other preaching activities meant to strengthen the same total effort to bring the conditioned soul back home, back to Godhead.

Saṅkīrtana Expands from Māyāpur

In *Śrī Caitanya-caritāmṛta*, Śrīla Prabhupāda explains the reasons for Śrī Kṛṣṇa Caitanya's appearance. Lord Kṛṣṇa, in His pastimes, was unable to experience the glory of Śrīmatī Rādhārāṇī's love for Him, the wonderful qualities in Kṛṣṇa that She relishes through Her love, and the indescribable happiness She feels when She realizes the sweetness of His love. Thus Lord Kṛṣṇa, assuming the guise of a devotee, adopted the mood and complexion of Śrīmatī Rādhārāṇī and descended in Navadvīpa-dhāma to fulfill His innermost desire: to experience Śrīmatī Rādhārāṇī's ecstatic love for Him.

Thus Navadvīpa-dhāma is a manifestation of Śrīmatī Rādhārāṇī's love for Kṛṣṇa. The *Purāṇas* also describe that when, in the state of *mahābhāva*, Śrīmatī Rādhārāṇī reached the extreme in ecstatic feelings of separation from Lord Kṛṣṇa, Kṛṣṇa entered into Her heart and "stole" Her feeling of *mahābhāva*. That *mahābhāva* became manifest as Navadvīpa-dhāma.

Thus, to better understand Śrī Māyāpur-dhāma and the mood of Caitanya Mahāprabhu, as well as Śrīla Prabhupāda and our own devotional service, we should understand Rādhārāṇī's mood of separation.

Once, when Kṛṣṇa left the company of the *gopīs*, Rādhārāṇī began to search for Him in one forest after another, crying in intense separation. She approached the *kadamba* tree, "Where is Kṛṣṇa?" She approached Govardhana Hill, "Where is Kṛṣṇa?" She wandered everywhere throughout Vṛndāvana crying, "Where is Kṛṣṇa? He is more dear to Me than My own life. How can I live without His service?" In divine madness, She fainted.

After some time, when Kṛṣṇa appeared, He addressed

Śrīmatī Rādhārāṇī, "I am extremely pleased with You. You may ask from Me whatever You wish." Then Śrīmatī Rādhārāṇī requested three things: "Please promise Me that You will always remain in Vraja, unseen by those without devotion. Please never disappoint the devotees who reside here, maintaining their lives by their love for You alone, hoping to attain Your lotus feet. And please always shower Your mercy on Your devotees and give them shelter at Your lotus feet."

We see that even though Śrīmatī Rādhārāṇī had been experiencing extreme separation from Kṛṣṇa, when Kṛṣṇa asked Her what She wanted She did not think of Herself. She thought of the suffering of others. This is the mood of separation. Śrīmatī Rādhārāṇī's desires to please Kṛṣṇa are so pure and so intense that She wants to engage every living entity for Kṛṣṇa's pleasure, to give them Kṛṣṇa's service and association.

Kṛṣṇa has unlimited desires to enjoy. Rādhā has the unlimited desire to fulfill Kṛṣṇa's desires. And Lord Caitanya and Śrīla Prabhupāda have the same desire to engage unlimited numbers of living entities in Kṛṣṇa's service. Like Śrīmatī Rādhārāṇī, the preacher wants to arrange for others to get Kṛṣṇa's association, to serve Him.

Śrīla Prabhupāda especially wanted unlimited numbers of books to be distributed so that unlimited numbers of persons would be engaged in devotional service. Every book distributed means another brick for the Māyāpur City temple, and as the city manifests, more and more devotees will be attracted to the *dhāma*, to develop the same mood of *saṅkīrtana*. As they become inspired to distribute more and more books, more and more people will become devotees. And thus the Vaiṣṇava's desire will be fulfilled.

7

Śrīla Prabhupāda

Studying Śrīla Prabhupāda

Śrīla Prabhupāda told me that if I simply studied the character of Lord Caitanya in *Śrī Caitanya-caritāmṛta*—as a Vaiṣṇava, even apart from His being the Supreme Personality of Godhead—I would become perfect. Similarly, if people study Śrīla Prabhupāda as a Vaiṣṇava or as a great *ācārya* or as a great personality—apart from his inner identity, which we may or may not know—they will benefit.

Exchanges and Instructions

Every Day Is a Holiday

Soon after we arrived in Bombay, we accompanied Śrīla Prabhupāda to an aristocratic gentleman's home for a program on his lawn. When we arrived, some of the respectable Hindus there told us it was a holiday. As we had never heard of the holiday and were somewhat doubtful, we asked Śrīla Prabhupāda, "Is today really a holiday?" Śrīla Prabhupāda replied, "For us, every day is a holiday: we are Kṛṣṇa's servants."

Eagerness

At one outdoor program I asked Śrīla Prabhupāda, "A devotee told me you said that just being eager to become Kṛṣṇa conscious is enough to make us Kṛṣṇa conscious. Does that mean we don't have to read books?" Śrīla Prabhupāda replied, "If you are eager, why will you not want to read books? You will want to do everything that will help you become Kṛṣṇa conscious."

Simply by Eating

In Bombay, Śrīla Prabhupāda received an invitation from Hari Krishna Das Agarwal, an industrialist who founded Prem Kutir, a religious institution where Prabhupāda had stayed for some days before going to America. Hari Krishna Das invited Prabhupāda and the devotees to attend a Vedanta Sammelan conference in Amritsar, and Śrīla Prabhupāda agreed. Thus Prabhupāda and his party of disciples went by train to Amritsar.

The conference was held at the Vedanta Ashram, which was dedicated to the propagation of impersonal Māyāvāda philosophy, and the buildings and walkways displayed signs with popular Māyāvādī slogans such as *tat tvam asi* (you are that) and *ahaṁ brahmāsmi* (I am spirit).

We had programs in the evening, and every morning we would go into Prabhupāda's room and sing the *Gurv-aṣṭaka* prayers in front of his Rādhā-Kṛṣṇa Deities, and he would speak with us. One morning he explained the different Māyāvādī slogans. And he added that the organizers knew that he did not agree with their philosophy but that they had still invited him and his disciples because they had known that the "foreign" devotees' *kīrtana* would attract people.

While discussing their philosophy, Prabhupāda commented, "They will talk and talk about *Vedānta*, but it is simply mental speculation, and they never come to any conclusion." Just then, one of the devotees brought the morning offering from Śrīla Prabhupāda's Deities to him. Śrīla Prabhupāda continued, "They will go on speculating for many lifetimes"—from the plate of *mahā-prasāda* he popped a sweet in his mouth—"but we will realize God simply by eating."

See What You Can Do

After the program in Amritsar, Śrīla Prabhupāda and his party traveled by train back to Bombay. On the way, the train stopped at the Delhi station, and a gentleman, a lawyer named D. D. Gupta, who had been corresponding with Śrīla Prabhupāda and had been informed of his stopover at the station, came to meet him. He requested Śrīla Prabhupāda to leave some disciples in Delhi to start the activities there. Prabhupāda turned to Guru dāsa, who was riding in the same compartment, and said, "This man is inviting us. Get down and see what you can do." Guru dāsa asked for some devotees, and he and Śrīla Prabhupāda agreed on a team: Yamunā-devī (Guru dāsa's wife), Gopāla dāsa, Bhakta Bruce (now Bhanu Swami), and me. And so the preaching in Delhi began.

The Glitter of Gold

After dropping us off in Delhi and spending some days in Bombay, Śrīla Prabhupāda proceeded to Indore for the Gītā Jayantī Mahotsava, and our group joined him there. When we entered his room, he looked up from his desk. Yamunā remarked, "Śrīla Prabhupāda, you look just like a picture I have seen of your *guru mahārāja* looking up from his desk." Śrīla Prabhupāda replied, with all humility, "All that glitters is not gold. My *guru mahārāja* was like gold; I am like iron."

Of course, we knew that he was pure gold—just like his *guru mahārāja.*

To Make an Old Man Happy

In Indore Śrīla Prabhupāda accepted the invitation of a wealthy gentleman related to the royal family. The gentleman received Śrīla Prabhupāda and his disciples, and Śrīla Prabhupāda spoke about the importance of Kṛṣṇa consciousness. Finally Śrīla Prabhupāda showed him his books and asked him to become a life member. The gentleman countered, "I already have these books in my own language. I don't need any more books." Śrīla Prabhupāda became very stern and replied, "I have not come here to sell you some books. I have come here begging at your doorstep." Taken aback, the man immediately volunteered, "Oh yes, I will become your member, Swamiji; I will be glad to become your member."

We proceeded to the next room for lunch. Our host seated Śrīla Prabhupāda at the head of the long banquet table, and I took my place at Śrīla Prabhupāda's right. Then we all took *prasāda.*

I was used to strict *brahmacārī* training and was particularly reserved about eating sweets. Especially being seated next to Śrīla Prabhupāda, I tried to be careful not to take too much of the more opulent preparations; I didn't want Śrīla Prabhupāda to think I was enjoying sense gratification. The elderly father of the gentleman who had invited us came around the table and repeatedly tried to give me a second *rasagullā*, but each time I staunchly refused. Prabhupāda could see that the host's father was disappointed. Finally Śrīla Prabhupāda glanced lovingly at me and said, "You can take a sweet to make an old man happy." And so I accepted another sweet.

The Spiritual Master's Pleasure in Eating

From Indore, Śrīla Prabhupāda and his party traveled to Surat, in Gujarat, where we received an extraordinary reception from the large population of pious Kṛṣṇa devotees. There, John Griesser (now Yadubara dāsa) began to stay with Śrīla Prabhupāda and his devotees. Once, John came into Śrīla Prabhupāda's room while Prabhupāda was preaching, advising a local man that the government of India should form a Department of the *Bhagavad-gītā* to present the message of the *Gītā*—as it is—all over the world.

After John had sat for some time, Prabhupāda offered him some *prasāda*. John refused to eat in Śrīla Prabhupāda's presence, but Prabhupāda insisted: "No, no. Take *prasāda*. The spiritual master is pleased when the devotees take *prasāda*." And he quoted a verse from *Śrī Gurv-aṣṭaka* (4):

catur-vidha-śrī-bhagavat-prasāda-
svādv-anna-tṛptān hari-bhakta-saṅghān
kṛtvaiva tṛptiṁ bhajataḥ sadaiva
vande guroḥ śrī-caraṇāravindam

["The spiritual master is always offering Kṛṣṇa four kinds of delicious food (analyzed as that which is licked, chewed, drunk, and sucked). When the spiritual master sees that the devotees are satisfied by eating *bhagavat-prasāda*, he is satisfied. I offer my respectful obeisances unto the lotus feet of such a spiritual master."]

Not-Liking

In Surat I asked Śrīla Prabhupāda about envy. I had on occasion been suffering from envy, and it was affecting me, disturbing my chanting and my relationships. My policy was never to ask Śrīla Prabhupāda a question if I could answer it myself. Unless I had really considered the question deeply and tried to get the answer by some other means—introspection, chanting, reading, praying, consulting with other devotees—I would not ask him. But in this case, although I had contemplated many reasons why envy served no good purpose and, to the contrary, caused difficulties and was harmful to me, I could not understand how to make the envy go away.

So I asked Śrīla Prabhupāda. First he responded, "Can you think of any reasons not to be envious?" And I had thought of many. It was disturbing to my chanting and to my relationships with devotees. Further, I had reasoned that Kṛṣṇa was unlimited and that His service was unlimited—so why be envious if someone else had some service? It was not going to deprive me of service. Kṛṣṇa can accept an unlimited quantity of service from an unlimited number of devotees. And He can give unlimited mercy to an unlimited number of devotees. So if someone has a particular service, it does not hurt my chances of getting service. And if someone gets some special mercy, it doesn't hurt my chances of getting Kṛṣṇa's mercy. Other devotees can have their service, and I can have mine, so why be envious? Thus I replied to Prabhupāda's question, "Yes."

Then he continued, "All right. Being envious means you don't like someone. Now, that not-liking should be directed against the demons, who create so much havoc in the world and cause disturbance to devotees. It should not be directed toward devotees."

Today when I think of Śrīla Prabhupāda's instruction, I think how careful we must be not to allow ourselves to "not-like" devotees. We may not-like demons, but we should remain favorably inclined to devotees, inside or outside the temple, inside or outside ISKCON, because they are all dear to Kṛṣṇa. We may deal differently with different categories of devotees, depending on their positions—and ours—but we shouldn't not-like them. Śrīla Prabhupāda wanted all devotees to cooperate to spread Kṛṣṇa consciousness. He wanted all theists to unite to fight against the atheists, the demons.

Teaching by Example

At the Ardha-kumbha-melā in Allahabad in January 1971, our program was very rigorous, because it was bitterly cold at night and we were expected to get up at four o'clock in the morning to bathe and attend *maṅgala-ārati.* A few staunch devotees like Tamal Krishna and Haṁsadūta got up early, by three or three-thirty, and walked all the way from our camp to the Ganges to take an early-morning bath. But those of us staying in the *brahmacārī* tent were not so staunch, and generally when it was time to get up at four o'clock it was so cold out that we preferred to remain in our sleeping bags.

Śrīla Prabhupāda began to notice that some of us were coming late to *maṅgala-ārati* and that some were not coming at all. He became very upset about this, because he knew how important *maṅgala-ārati* was for us. So one morning, although he was a little frail in health, he got up at four o'clock and came out in his *gamchā*, sat down under the hand pump, and took an ice-cold bath—just to encourage us to get up, bathe, and come to *maṅgala-ārati*. His action had a very profound effect on all of us, and we felt so ashamed that we just couldn't sleep late any more.

Harer Nāmaiva Kevalam

Still, the weather was freezing, and the devotees continued to struggle with rising early, taking bath with the cold water from the pumps, and reaching the *paṇḍāl* in time for *maṅgala-ārati*. And the *pūjārī*, Nanda-kumāra dāsa, struggled no less than the rest of us. He wore gloves to keep his hands from going numb, but one morning, no matter how hard he tried, he just could not light the ghee lamp to offer to the Deities. Cold gusts kept blowing out the match before it reached the wicks, and when a match finally did manage to reach the wicks, the wind would blow out either the match or the flames on some of the wicks before all the wicks were lit. Nanda-kumāra tried to shield the matches and wicks with one hand while lighting the match and the wicks with the other, but again and again he failed.

Śrīla Prabhupāda, watching the futile exercise, urged Nanda-kumāra to execute the task successfully. And one or two other devotees came forward to help him, but they, too, were unsuccessful. Finally, Śrīla Prabhupāda, in a mood of resignation born of frustration, but with profound spiritual realization, uttered,

harer nāma harer nāma
harer nāmaiva kevalam
kalau nāsty eva nāsty eva
nāsty eva gatir anyathā

["One should chant the holy names, chant the holy names, chant the holy names. There is no other way, no other way, no other way for success in the present age." (*Bṛhan-nāradīya Purāṇa* 38.126)]

We all knew how seriously Śrīla Prabhupāda took Deity worship. He understood that the Deity was Kṛṣṇa, the Supreme Personality of Godhead, Himself. And he was very strict that his followers maintain the proper standard of worship according to the injunctions of *śāstra* and *guru*. Still, in Kali-yuga, ultimately, *harer nāmaiva kevalam*.

From Indore, Śrīla Prabhupāda had been speaking on the history of Ajāmila, glorifying the holy name. Later, when his translation of the Sixth Canto was published, we found the same conclusions that he had presented to us then (reading from his volume with Sanskrit commentaries). In one purport (*SB* 6.3.26), he explained:

"Especially in this age of Kali, *saṅkīrtana* alone is sufficient. If the members of our temples in the different parts of the world simply continue *saṅkīrtana* before the Deity, especially before Śrī Caitanya Mahāprabhu, they will remain perfect. There is no need of any other performances. Nevertheless, to keep oneself clean in habits and mind, Deity worship and other regulative principles are required. Śrīla Jīva Gosvāmī says that although *saṅkīrtana* is sufficient for the perfection of life, the *arcanā*, or worship of the Deity in the temple, must continue in order that the devotees may stay clean and pure. Śrīla Bhaktisiddhānta Sarasvatī Ṭhākura therefore recommended that one follow both processes simultaneously. We strictly follow his principle of performing Deity worship and *saṅkīrtana* along parallel lines. This we should continue."

Always in Māyā

From the Ardha-kumbha-melā we traveled with Śrīla Prabhupāda to Gorakhpur. There, for the first time, I took the opportunity to go to newspapers and magazines to persuade them to publish articles—about Śrīla Prabhupāda's visit and about Kṛṣṇa consciousness in general. Enlivened in my service, I mentioned my efforts to Śrīla Prabhupāda on a morning walk. He responded, "You are a very good public relations man," which made me feel highly elated. A little later the discussion turned to humility, and I remarked that sometimes I felt I wasn't really doing anything for Kṛṣṇa or Kṛṣṇa consciousness. Śrīla Prabhupāda responded, "That is good. That feeling is humbleness." Then I added, "But sometimes that feeling is turned into *māyā*"—meaning that sometimes I felt discouraged about myself and lost my enthusiasm to preach.

Śrīla Prabhupāda stopped walking and looked me straight in the eyes. "Turned into *māyā*?" he said. "You are *always* in *māyā*."

Prabhupāda's words hit me strongly. I stopped in my tracks. As he and the other devotees continued their walk along the rural road, I placed my forehead on the ground in obeisance. By Śrīla Prabhupāda's mercy I understood my actual position—and gained a glimpse of his position as my spiritual master. He not only spoke about the importance of humility, but he also knew how to humble us—all for our benefit.

All Nectar

Also on a morning walk in Gorakhpur I asked Śrīla Prabhupāda if there was any particular order in which I should read his books. (I had heard that the sequence, in order of advancement, was *Śrī Īśopaniṣad*, the *Bhagavad-gītā*, *The Nectar of Devotion*, *Śrīmad-Bhāgavatam*, and *Śrī Caitanya-caritāmṛta*.) Śrīla Prabhupāda said, "No, they are all nectar. Wherever you have taste, you may read."

You Should Write

In Gorakhpur, Sri Hanuman Prasad Poddar, the renowned head of the Gita Press, invited Śrīla Prabhupāda and the devotees to stay at Sri Krishna Niketan, his large palatial estate and former residence.

There Śrīla Prabhupāda received the latest issue of *Back to Godhead*, which included an article I had written in Boston before leaving for India—"The Genuine Spiritual Master," the first article I had written. Śrīla Prabhupāda was very encouraged by the article and asked to see me.

"I saw your article in *Back to Godhead*. It was very nice. You should write."

The room was dimly lit—only some narrow shafts of light pierced through the slim openings in the wooden shutters along the side of the room. Śrīla Prabhupāda, sitting on his raised cushion at the far end of the temple room, was the very image of the eternal spiritual master, and his voice resonated with the truth of eternal time.

Alone with my spiritual master, I sat at his feet, eyes and ears wide open.

"You should write. This is your first business. Go on writing. We require many, many such articles about Kṛṣṇa consciousness. So you should devote yourself to writing."

"I will try. But why are you asking me? I have no qualification."

"We require many to do this work, and we need you also. So you travel with me and I will guide you. You come and stay with me."

I felt thrilled and honored. Śrīla Prabhupāda had never before given me a direct instruction. Yet I wondered how it would work. I hardly ever spoke with Śrīla Prabhupāda, and now he was inviting me to stay with him. I felt a little intimidated.

Also, I had always worked under my authorities. Who would tell them about Śrīla Prabhupāda's proposal?

So I asked, "How will we decide whether I should travel with you or what I should do?" Prabhupāda answered, "By mutual consultation."

He also instructed, "See that my books are accepted in the universities, by the scholarly class."

Then he asked, "Do you ever think of getting married?" I replied, "No, I never think of getting married," and after a moment added, "The only time I ever thought of getting married was when I saw that all the GBCs were married." Prabhupāda replied, "You will never be GBC."

"It is best to avoid marriage. Sex desire is like an itch. If you have an itch and you scratch it, it just becomes worse. Similarly, sex desire is there, and if you try to satisfy it, it becomes worse. So it is better to tolerate. Not only sex desire—all the demands of the senses—eating and sleeping also. Better to tolerate.

"So you remain *brahmacārī,* and after two or three years I will give you *sannyāsa.*"

In a matter of twenty minutes Śrīla Prabhupāda had given me my whole life's program in Kṛṣṇa consciousness.

Sri Krishna Niketan was a grand old house surrounded by fields. I was always thinking of Prabhupāda, and sometimes I couldn't sleep at night. I would just be thinking of how wonderful Prabhupāda was. I would stand at the balcony near his room and look out over the fields at the stars and the bright moon. I was in so much ecstasy that Śrīla Prabhupāda had read my article and invited me to travel with him, and I felt the awakening in my heart of a type of affection I had never felt before.

At the time, Haṁsadūta Prabhu was one of the authorities in India, and he wanted to start his world traveling *saṅkīrtana* party. Perhaps because I was submissive and responsible, he asked Śrīla Prabhupāda if I could come with him. Śrīla Prabhupāda agreed. Although I was disappointed that I could not stay with Śrīla Prabhupāda, I thought, "Prabhupāda knows best."

From Gorakhpur our *saṅkīrtana* party went by train to Agra and Aligarh. After two weeks on the road, we received a telegram from Prabhupāda calling us to Bombay for a big *paṇḍāl* program.

When we reached Bombay, Śyāmasundara dāsa, who was the temple president and in charge of the *paṇḍāl* program, instructed me, "Now we are going to have a big *paṇḍāl* and you should raise funds for it." I really had it in my mind to start writing. I had my sheets of paper and my pencils and was constantly thinking about Śrīla Prabhupāda's instruction. So I said, "Śrīla Prabhupāda told me I should write." Śyāmasundara replied, "You can write anytime, but this is the one time we can walk into the office of any big man in Bombay and ask for money. You should do it."

What he said made sense, so I agreed and became successful at raising funds by collecting advertisements for the souvenir book.

After a few weeks, Śrīla Prabhupāda came. We all sat down in his room, and Prabhupāda led a little *kīrtana*. He was radiant, beaming and smiling and casting glances everywhere. Then he said, "So, Giriraj, how is your writing going?" "Well, Śrīla Prabhupāda, I haven't done any writing." He said, "Oh, you haven't done any writing? Why not?" I was completely flustered. I didn't know what to say. So Prabhupāda said, "All right, we will speak later."

After everyone left the room I came back in. "So you are not writing?" I explained what had happened and said, "I considered that you wanted us to work cooperatively, and I thought what Śyāmasundara said made sense, so I agreed to do what he asked. Did I do the right thing?"

Śrīla Prabhupāda said, "Yes, that is all right. One may temporarily suspend the order of the spiritual master, but one should never neglect it. Just like my *guru mahārāja* gave me the order to write, but I am so busy traveling and preaching in India now, I have no time to write. But I am always thinking of his order, and when the opportunity arises, I will take it up."

Śrīla Prabhupāda was so understanding and practical. And he had confirmed that I had done the right thing. I felt relieved and satisfied.

Working like an Ass

At the Bombay *paṇḍāl*, Madhudviṣa was in charge of the stage program and Tamal Krishna in charge of the general management. So, Tamal Krishna made me the temple commander for the *paṇḍāl* and practically put all the responsibility and work on me. Thus I would be at the *paṇḍāl* all afternoon while the other devotees were enjoying at Akash Ganga with Śrīla Prabhupāda and with each other. Nobody stayed at the *paṇḍāl* to help me. I would be left alone to do all the work, and I just didn't know what to do.

Every day, Śrīla Prabhupāda would arrive at the *paṇḍāl* in the late afternoon or early evening and sit behind the stage in one of the rooms made of cloth and bamboo poles. One afternoon when he came, the room was really in a mess—the rented sofas were out of place; used, dirty cups were left here and there; the tables had not been dusted or washed—it was a mess. As I was practically the only devotee there, Śrīla Prabhupāda asked me, "What is this? Why is everything so dirty?" I replied, "I don't have anyone to help me. I have to do everything myself."

Śrīla Prabhupāda looked at me and said gently, "It is better to control five asses than to work like an ass yourself."

We Can Trick Them

After a few more days of struggle, I finally decided to take a bus to Akash Ganga to meet Śrīla Prabhupāda. Alone with Śrīla Prabhupāda in his room, I told him that Tamal Krishna wasn't giving me any help. Śrīla Prabhupāda said I should tell him that if he didn't give me help I would quit.

At the same time I asked Śrīla Prabhupāda about the use of force, as I had seen some devotees shout at the hired workers and even kick them. Śrīla Prabhupāda replied, "We cannot force them, but we can trick them." Then he told a story.

A teacher had a student who hated arithmetic. Whenever the teacher would try to tell him about arithmetic, the student would refuse to hear. Finally the teacher devised a plan. He drew three cows and one bull on the board. Then he asked the boy, "If a farmer has three cows and one bull and he gets two more bulls, how many animals will he have?" The teacher added the two bulls to the picture. "Then again, if he sells one cow and one bull, how many animals will he have?" Thus the teacher was gradually inducing the boy to learn arithmetic. Suddenly, one of the boy's friends interjected, "Don't you see what is happening? The teacher is teaching you arithmetic!" And the boy responded, "Arithmetic? I hate arithmetic!" And he refused to answer any more.

Śrīla Prabhupāda told the story to illustrate the fact that some people are just averse to service. We cannot force them to serve—but we can "trick" or induce them to serve. And everyone will benefit.

You Should Preach

The Bombay *paṇḍāl* was a great success. And almost immediately Śrīla Prabhupāda sent Tamal Krishna and me to Calcutta to organize a similar program there.

After Śrīla Prabhupāda instructed me to write, I had more questions about my service. I had other duties and also realized that I wasn't able to just sit down and write all day. I was a young *brahmacārī*.

I really wanted to understand what I should do. Although I thought about it carefully, I felt that only Śrīla Prabhupāda could answer my questions. But the devotees' mood was that one should not disturb Śrīla Prabhupāda or approach him directly. Still, many questions weighed on my mind.

Finally, one day at the site of the *paṇḍāl*, I told Yamunā dāsī that I had some questions to ask Śrīla Prabhupāda but that I didn't want to disturb him. And I told her what the questions were. "No," she replied. "You are just the type of devotee Śrīla Prabhupāda would want to spend time with, and these are just the types of questions he would want to answer."

Encouraged by Yamunā's words, I approached Śrīla Prabhupāda in his room in Calcutta and began, "Before joining the movement, I made movies, and a film I made won an award. So I was thinking maybe I should make movies about Kṛṣṇa consciousness." Prabhupāda replied, "That, others are doing."

At the time all we had were some rough movies made by Dāmodara, so I thought, "Well, if Prabhupāda thinks that's enough, making movies must not be very important."

Then Prabhupāda explained, "Our main medium is books."

"I also think of cultivating important people."

"Oh, that is very important," Prabhupāda encouraged. "You do that."

Then I asked, "Suppose in the course of time, by the gradual development of Kṛṣṇa consciousness, I become expert at everything. Suppose I become a perfect preacher and at the same time a perfect manager. What should I do?"

Śrīla Prabhupāda replied, "You should preach."

Śrīla Prabhupāda had given the clear direction I needed. And I left the room feeling much lighter.

But Don't Leave

I also asked one other important question:

"Śrīla Prabhupāda, now you are here, so everything is all right. But what if, in the course of time, when you are not here, ISKCON falls from the standard? What should I do?"

Śrīla Prabhupāda replied, "You are also one of the important members of the Society, so you work for the correction. But don't leave."

I did not consider myself an "important member of the Society." Still, I knew that Śrīla Prabhupāda had given an important instruction for the future.

The Same Message

During the course of the *paṇḍāl*, I was struck by the fact that Śrīla Prabhupāda preached in the same way to every audience. So I approached him to clarify one thought:

"Kṛṣṇa consciousness is the perfection of every discipline and endeavor. Yet I see you preach more or less the same to everyone. Why don't we explain, 'Kṛṣṇa consciousness is the perfect communism' or 'Kṛṣṇa consciousness is the perfect welfare work' or psychology or social or economic or political system? Why do we just present the same general philosophy every time?"

"Unless someone is convinced of the philosophy and has practical experience of it in his personal life, he will not feel the inspiration to apply it in his occupational duty. So we preach to convince everyone that he is not the body, that he is the eternal servant of Kṛṣṇa, and that he can realize Kṛṣṇa by chanting the holy names."

Śrīla Prabhupāda's answer made sense—and entered the heart.

The Same Result

Śrīla Prabhupāda gave us so much service we hardly had time to chant our rounds, what to speak of read his books. Although I knew that by serving Śrīla Prabhupāda I was doing the best for myself and for all living entities, I still lamented that I had so little time to read his books. Śrīla Prabhupāda must have understood my concern, so one day he spoke to me:

naṣṭa-prāyeṣv abhadreṣu
nityaṁ bhāgavata-sevayā
bhagavaty uttama-śloke
bhaktir bhavati naiṣṭhikī

"By reading the book *Bhāgavata* or by serving the person *bhāgavata*, one gets the same result. Just by serving the person *bhāgavata*, all the truths of the book *Bhāgavata* are revealed, even if you do not read the book." (*SB* 1.2.18)

Thus I continued in my service to the person *bhāgavata*, Śrīla Prabhupāda, with full conviction and enthusiasm.

The Powers That Be

There was a minister in the government of West Bengal named Tarun Kanti Ghosh, who came from a family of great devotees of Caitanya Mahāprabhu. When we greeted him with "Hare Kṛṣṇa," he would respond with "*Jaya* Gaura!" His family's daily newspaper, *Amrita Bazar Patrika*, had publicized Śrīla Bhaktivinoda Ṭhākura's efforts to build a temple in Māyāpur and later regularly featured discourses by Śrīla Bhaktisiddhānta Sarasvatī Ṭhākura and reported on his activities. Being wealthy and influential, Tarun Kanti Ghosh went into politics and became successful.

One afternoon, Tarun Kanti came to visit Śrīla Prabhupāda

at the Calcutta temple. He told Prabhupāda that he had gone to a yogi who had mystic powers and that the yogi had materialized an apple and given him a slice. Tarun Babu, as Prabhupāda called him, was quite impressed, but Prabhupāda presented a different perspective: "Yes, he can produce one apple, but what about Kṛṣṇa? Kṛṣṇa can produce an apple tree that will produce so many apples, and within every apple are so many seeds, and every seed can produce another tree that in turn can produce so many apples and so many more seeds and trees. And there are so many apple trees, not just on our planet but on so many planets. That is Kṛṣṇa's mystic power!" Then Śrīla Prabhupāda said, "If we make friends with Kṛṣṇa, Kṛṣṇa can give us any number of apples. And practically it is happening. We have so many centers all over the world, with so many devotees and so many guests coming daily, and every day we are offering and distributing so many apples. Where are the apples coming from? Our devotees are not going to the factory or the office to work. Where are all the apples coming from? Kṛṣṇa is supplying them. So we are not so interested in making friends with some yogi who can give us one slice of apple. We are interested in becoming friends with Kṛṣṇa, who can give us any number of apples."

After the discussion in his room, Prabhupāda was going to a program to give a lecture, and Tarun Kanti wanted to accompany him. So we all went in the same car, Śrīla Prabhupāda in the front with the driver, and I in the back with Tarun Babu. He asked, "I don't know what to do about my political career. Sometimes I think I should just get out of politics and concentrate more on devotion, and sometimes I think I can use my position in politics to serve Caitanya Mahāprabhu and His devotees. What should I do?"

I was just a young man and really didn't know what to say. So I began, "It could be good if you can use your position to serve Kṛṣṇa, but then again . . ."

Śrīla Prabhupāda overheard us, turned around, and said, "No. Politics is a dirty game. You should get out."

The Marginal Position

After I joined in Boston, Śrīla Prabhupāda formed the GBC, and somehow I thought the GBC members were in a different category from the rest of us. Then one of the GBC members fell down. Still, I thought it was a fluke and tried to discount it. Later, when another GBC member fell, I had some doubt. So I asked Śrīla Prabhupāda:

"Śrīla Prabhupāda, you know everything about us—you know us better than we know ourselves—yet sometimes we see you put someone in an exalted position, and then he falls down. How is that?"

Śrīla Prabhupāda replied, "The living entity is always marginal, so whatever position he is in, he can use it either for Kṛṣṇa's service or for personal sense gratification."

Thus the spiritual master places the disciple in the best position for devotional service, but the disciple can always misuse the position for personal gratification and fall down.

What Pleases You Most

One day, while Śrīla Prabhupāda was taking his massage on the balcony in Calcutta, I humbly approached him: "Śrīla Prabhupāda, I have been trying to understand what you want of us, what your desire is." Śrīla Prabhupāda was so pure he took every word into his heart. "Yes?"

"Two things seem to please you the most," I offered. "Distributing your books and building the big temple in Māyāpur."

Prabhupāda's face lit up, his eyes opened wide, and he smiled. "Yes, you have understood."

"And I want you to know I am ready to give my life to help fulfill your desires."

Prabhupāda smiled and said, "Thank you."

I felt so satisfied, by his divine grace. I had understood what Śrīla Prabhupāda desired.

The Greatest

rādhā kṛṣṇa-praṇaya-vikṛtir hlādinī śaktir asmād
ekātmānāv api bhuvi purā deha-bhedaṁ gatau tau
caitanyākhyaṁ prakaṭam adhunā tad-dvayaṁ caikyam āptaṁ
rādhā-bhāva-dyuti-suvalitaṁ naumi kṛṣṇa-svarūpam

"The loving affairs of Śrī Rādhā and Kṛṣṇa are transcendental manifestations of the Lord's internal pleasure-giving potency. Although Rādhā and Kṛṣṇa are one in Their identity, They separated Themselves eternally. Now these two transcendental identities have again united, in the form of Śrī Kṛṣṇa Caitanya. I bow down to Him, who has manifested Himself with the sentiment and complexion of Śrīmatī Rādhārāṇī although He is Kṛṣṇa Himself."

—*Śrī Caitanya-caritāmṛta, Ādi-līlā* 1.5

Once, in Calcutta, Acyutānanda Swami had a conversation with our landlord, a Bengali gentleman named Mr. Ray. The landlord had told Acyutānanda his version of Rādhā and Kṛṣṇa and Lord Caitanya. He said that Lord Caitanya is the original and that Rādhā and Kṛṣṇa come from Him. And he said that Lord Caitanya is even greater or more beautiful than Rādhā and Kṛṣṇa, as *rasagullā* is better than milk and sugar. Acyutānanda was somewhat confused by the landlord's philosophy, so he approached Śrīla Prabhupāda to understand the truth.

Acyutānanda Swami presented the whole discussion to Śrīla Prabhupāda. Then he asked, "Who comes first?" Śrīla

Prabhupāda replied that Rādhā and Kṛṣṇa come first, and that when They combine together, the combination is Lord Caitanya. "The same example: first milk and sugar exist separately, and then they combine together to make *rasagullā*." Then Acyutānanda asked, "Well, who is greater?" Śrīla Prabhupāda paused for some moments, closed his eyes, and then answered, "Rādhārāṇī is greater." Then he pointed to a picture on the wall, where Śrīmatī Rādhārāṇī was sitting on a raised platform and Kṛṣṇa was kneeling at Her feet, trying to please Her. And Śrīla Prabhupāda said, "Śrīmatī Rādhārāṇī is the greatest." Then he pointed to another picture, where baby Kṛṣṇa was carrying the shoes of Nanda Mahārāja on His head, and said, "Nanda Mahārāja is the greatest." Then there was even a picture of Mother Yaśodā with a stick and little Kṛṣṇa cowering in fear.

Śrīla Prabhupāda concluded, "The devotee is the greatest."

The Process of Knowledge

After the *paṇḍāl* program in Calcutta, Śrīla Prabhupāda celebrated another huge Hare Kṛṣṇa festival, at Connaught Place, in the center of New Delhi. And there he staged a most dramatic display.

Perhaps twenty thousand people came daily, and every night a prominent leader from some field was invited as chief guest. The whole event was very glamorous. One evening while Śrīla Prabhupāda was giving his lecture, a wild-looking young man—a Westerner—approached the stage. He had long hair, big tattoos all over his torso, an open vest on his bare chest, large leather boots, and an iron chain around his neck; he was what in the West we would call a "hood." As he approached the stage, the devotees rushed forward to keep him away. But Śrīla Prabhupāda, interrupting the lecture, told the devotees to let him come on stage. So he came on the stage, and Śrīla

Prabhupāda said, "Give him *āsana*." The devotees gave him an *āsana*. Then Śrīla Prabhupāda said, "Give him a microphone." They gave him a microphone. Then Śrīla Prabhupāda addressed him, "So? You want to say something?"

In a very challenging tone, the boy said to Śrīla Prabhupāda, "Have you really realized yourself within yourself?" Śrīla Prabhupāda very matter-of-factly replied, "Yes." The boy was taken aback. Then he asked, "According to you, when did Kṛṣṇa speak the *Bhagavad-gītā?*" Śrīla Prabhupāda replied, "Five thousand years ago." The boy started to argue that according to So-and-So and Such-and-Such, the *Bhagavad-gītā* was spoken only two thousand years ago. Prabhupāda replied, "That's nonsense." Then the boy started arguing. He quoted all sorts of people and kept pursuing his question. Finally, Śrīla Prabhupāda said, "All right, now you answer my question. What is the process for understanding the *Bhagavad-gītā?*" "No," snapped the boy. "First you answer my question." Prabhupāda insisted, "No, you answer my question." "No," the boy shot back. "First you answer my question. I asked first." Śrīla Prabhupāda responded, "I am not your servant. I am not obliged to answer your question."

It turned into a big fight. Then Śrīla Prabhupāda motioned to the devotees, and they removed the young man from the stage.

I had been distributing books in the audience, but I moved near the stage. I was watching what was happening—everyone was watching. As soon as the encounter ended, the audience broke into pandemonium. People surrounded us, the devotees on the floor; and most of the people—at least those who approached us—sided with the young man. "Your *guru mahārāja* lost his temper. He should have answered his question. Why didn't he answer his question?" The situation was very tense, and I started feeling that I didn't want to be alone in this mob of angry people. So I made my way to the stage.

Behind the stage, some of the organizers surrounded Mālatī, and one told her, "We put so much money into this program, we put our names behind it, and now your *guru mahārāja* has spoiled everything. He lost his temper. He didn't answer the boy's question. He's spoiled everything." But Mālatī retorted, "My *guru mahārāja* didn't spoil anything." And, displaying transcendental indignation, she slapped the man on the cheek.

So, what did Śrīla Prabhupāda actually do, and why? He was demonstrating, through the wild young man, just what the process of knowledge is and is not. The process of knowledge is not to challenge. Therefore the *Bhagavad-gītā* (4.34) says that one should inquire submissively. The boy was inquiring, but not submissively. He was challenging. He wanted to prove Śrīla Prabhupāda wrong. He wanted to trap Śrīla Prabhupāda by his questions and expose him—or maybe just present himself as better than Śrīla Prabhupāda. And the audience became polarized. Some people were sympathetic to Śrīla Prabhupāda and some to the boy. The ones who were sympathetic to Śrīla Prabhupāda most likely remained in their seats to hear the rest of the lecture. But many, many others were sympathetic to the boy.

So, to get knowledge we need two things. We have to approach a proper authority, a *tattva-darśī*, and we have to approach him in the right way—with submissive inquiries and service:

tad viddhi praṇipātena
paripraśnena sevayā
upadekṣyanti te jñānaṁ
jñāninas tattva-darśinaḥ

"Just try to learn the truth by approaching a spiritual master. Inquire from him submissively and render service unto him. The self-realized souls can impart knowledge unto you because they have seen the truth." (*Bg* 4.34)

What's Wrong with Anger?

One young American who attended the *paṇḍāl* program became so inspired by Śrīla Prabhupāda and the devotees that he came to meet Prabhupāda after the program ended. In a heartfelt display of eloquence, he expressed his appreciation to Śrīla Prabhupāda: "If the world could just become Kṛṣṇa conscious, there could be peace and happiness. People would learn to love each other and give up their hatred and anger." Śrīla Prabhupāda replied, "Anger? Is there something wrong with anger? Did someone tell you that anger is wrong?" The young man didn't know what to say. Then Śrīla Prabhupāda explained, "Kṛṣṇa spoke the whole *Bhagavad-gītā* just to make Arjuna angry. He wanted to convince Arjuna to fight and kill the enemy, and how can you fight and kill unless you are angry? He spoke the whole *Bhagavad-gītā* just to make Arjuna angry, so how can you say that anger is wrong?" Śrīla Prabhupāda explained that anything can be used in the service of the Lord—including anger.

Special Mercy

During the same period, the father of Rajiv Gupta, a young student who was translating Prabhupāda's books into Hindi, came to visit. The father was also sort of a devotee, but he did have one bad habit—smoking. So, Śrīla Prabhupāda asked the father, "Have you given up smoking?" The father looked down and said, "No. But isn't there special mercy? Can't I get some special mercy to give up smoking?" And Śrīla Prabhupāda replied, "Special mercy? Yes, there is special mercy: *yasyāham anugṛhṇāmi hariṣye tad-dhanaṁ śanaiḥ*. The Lord can give special mercy, and when He does, the first thing He does is He takes away the devotee's material opulence. Then, when the devotee becomes poverty-stricken, his friends and relatives reject him. So he suffers doubly—because he has lost his opulence and because his so-called friends and family rebuke and neglect him. So yes, there is special mercy. Do you want some special mercy?"

"No, no," Mr. Gupta replied. "That's all right. I don't want any special mercy. I'll make my own efforts."

Pūjā and Bhakti

From Delhi I went to Madras to arrange a public program for Śrīla Prabhupāda. There I met many so-called intellectuals who tended toward impersonalism. They thought, "Oh, how silly. You are saying that Kṛṣṇa is supreme, and someone else is saying that Śiva is supreme." These impersonalists considered themselves to be more intelligent than the naive sentimentalists who worship particular deities, and they considered us, Śrīla Prabhupāda's followers, to be naive sentimentalists because we worshiped Kṛṣṇa, chanted Kṛṣṇa's name, and preached Kṛṣṇa's supremacy. (And in Madras, there are many Śaivites, and they argue that Śiva is supreme.)

As the first ISKCON devotee to visit Madras, I became quite a sensation—an American Vaiṣṇava. Most people there had never seen a Western *sādhu*, and they wanted to help. Several suggested that I meet a Mr. Ramakrishna, who they said was pious and religious and would be happy to hear of our activities. So I met him, and he turned out to be one of those people who thought that Śiva was supreme. Very quickly we came to blows—verbal blows. He had a volatile nature, and he became very angry. He became red in the face, and he raised his voice. And the meeting ended quite abruptly. But as I kept preaching, I kept meeting people who suggested, "You have to meet Mr. Ramakrishna. He is a very pious man. He is a very religious man." And I imagine that he was meeting people who were saying, "Oh, you should meet the Hare Kṛṣṇa devotees. They are very good people. They are doing excellent work."

After a few weeks I thought, "Maybe I should give it another try. This time I will be more careful." So I phoned him, and he immediately agreed to meet me. That made me think that people were speaking favorably about us to him and that it was embarrassing for him as well that we had disagreed so vehemently. We met, and I tried to restrain myself, and he tried to restrain himself, but eventually we came to the same point: Who is supreme—Kṛṣṇa (Viṣṇu) or Śiva? The argument escalated, but neither of us wanted it to end the same way as the last time. Then I got an inspiration and suggested, "In two weeks my spiritual master, His Divine Grace A. C. Bhaktivedanta Swami Prabhupāda, is coming to Madras. So instead of us discussing, why don't I invite you to meet him, and you can discuss with him directly." He liked the idea. It was a way out for both of us. And ultimately, what could be better than to meet a pure devotee of Kṛṣṇa?

After Śrīla Prabhupāda arrived, Mr. Ramakrishna came to see him. "I met your disciple Giriraj," Mr. Ramakrishna said, "and I argued that Śiva is supreme, and he argued that Kṛṣṇa is supreme. So, who is supreme?" Śrīla Prabhupāda took a completely different approach. He didn't enter into the polemics about who was supreme. Rather, he said, "There are two words in Sanskrit—*pūjā* and *bhakti*. In *pūjā* one worships the deity to get some material benefit, and in *bhakti* one worships only to give pleasure to the deity, without expectation of personal return." Then Śrīla Prabhupāda said, "Generally the worshipers of Śiva engage in *pūjā*—they worship to get some material benefit—whereas in *bhakti* we worship Kṛṣṇa for the sake of Kṛṣṇa's pleasure, just to please Him."

"Is it not possible," Mr. Ramakrishna asked, "to worship Śiva in the mood of *bhakti*?" And Śrīla Prabhupāda replied, "It is possible, but it would be exceptional. For example, generally people go to a liquor shop to buy liquor. Now, one could go for another purpose, but that would be an exception. Generally people go to buy liquor." Śrīla Prabhupāda did not enter into the controversy over which deity was supreme; rather, he explained the different moods in the worship of different deities. And Mr. Ramakrishna was satisfied with the answer.

Real Nectar

Sitting in his room in Madras, Śrīla Prabhupāda suddenly gave me a brief description of each of his books, in just one or two sentences. Concluding, he said, "*The Nectar of Devotion* is real nectar" and "The *Kṛṣṇa* book is pastimes and philosophy woven together in such a way that while reading it you don't even realize that you're getting the philosophy."

Govinda and Govinda's Organization

In Madras, I arranged for Prabhupāda to meet many prominent citizens—K. K. Shah, the governor; Dr. S. Radhakrishnan, author and former president of India; and C. Rajagopalachari (Rajaji), the first chief executive of independent India and author of a well-known English translation of the *Mahābhārata*.

Rajaji, a venerable gentleman at the age of ninety-three, was highly appreciative and respectful of Śrīla Prabhupāda. Still, he expressed his apprehension that one would become attached to the organization, ISKCON, rather than to Kṛṣṇa, Govinda. And Śrīla Prabhupāda replied, "No. Govinda is absolute. Govinda and Govinda's organization—the same."

(Of course, as followers of Śrīla Prabhupāda we must be ever alert and active to keep ISKCON as Govinda's and Prabhupāda's in truth. As Śrīla Prabhupāda said, "It is not automatic.")

Which Do You Want?

From Madras I returned to Calcutta and Māyāpur for the first Gaura-pūrṇimā festival and the cornerstone-laying ceremony for the Māyāpur temple.

At the time in Māyāpur, Śrīla Prabhupāda was living in a straw hut near the entrance of the property. When I entered his room he was in a very grave mood. With a choked voice he said, "Kṛṣṇa is giving us everything now. Everything is the mercy of Kṛṣṇa." He had tears in his eyes.

Soon Śrīla Prabhupāda called me to his room again. After offering obeisances on the cow-dung floor, I sat on a grass mat at Śrīla Prabhupāda's lotus feet. Śrīla Prabhupāda explained that when the British were ruling India they divided the country into three provinces—Bombay, Madras, and Calcutta—each ruled by one governor.

"Which one do you want?" Prabhupāda asked.

Prabhupāda's words left me speechless. I had never made an independent decision about my service. I told Śrīla Prabhupāda that I would do whatever he wanted me to do. But Prabhupāda did not accept my answer; he wanted me to decide. So I asked if I could have time to think about it, and he agreed.

I thought and thought but could not decide. The preaching in Calcutta was good, but Madras also had potential. And I already knew people in both places. Then again, Bombay was the biggest field. Actually, all I really wanted to do was please Śrīla Prabhupāda. But how?

After Māyāpur we came to Calcutta. There I would stand before the beautiful Deities of Śrī Śrī Rādhā-Govinda and chant and pray to Them for guidance.

Soon I realized that Śrīla Prabhupāda was forcing me to come to a higher level of Kṛṣṇa consciousness. To obey the order of the spiritual master requires some basic submission, but to know the desire of the spiritual master without being told requires much more spiritual advancement. I was being compelled to become sincere enough and pure enough to hear the *guru* in the heart.

Although I thought and thought and prayed and prayed, still no answer came. Where did Prabhupāda want me to serve? Finally I decided to "trick" Śrīla Prabhupāda into revealing his desire. Sitting before him in his room in Calcutta, I ventured that I had decided to go to Bombay. Prabhupāda's response was noncommittal: "That's all right." His face was inscrutable. "But then again, the preaching potential in Madras is very good," I continued, hoping that either by word or gesture or facial expression Prabhupāda would indicate his approval or disapproval. But again he simply replied, "That's all right." "But then again," I said, "I was thinking of staying in Calcutta." "That's all right."

How could I try to trick Śrīla Prabhupāda? I felt so ashamed, trying to cheat my spiritual master. But I also felt exhilarated: my spiritual master was so great and perfect that he could not be tricked.

Soon Śrīla Prabhupāda left Calcutta for Bombay. While I was preaching and making life members in Calcutta, and training Mādhavānanda, I thought, "Well, if I go back to Madras, I can preach on my own, but if I stay in Calcutta, I can help teach others to preach also." That was better. So I crossed Madras off the list.

After many days of thought and prayer, the answer finally came: I should go to Bombay. The most important program in India was life membership. Śrīla Prabhupāda had written, "If you all get me at least two life members daily, I shall do the rest." And he was pleased that I was making so many life members. But the life members were up in arms against us because we had not given them everything we had promised.

I reasoned, "Yes, we are making life members, but are we

taking care of them? If we take nice care of them, they will be so pleased they themselves will make more members. But if we neglect them, they will feel cheated and speak ill of us. Then even when we ourselves approach people they will not agree." I felt I should go to Bombay and organize the life membership on an all-India basis. So I wrote Śrīla Prabhupāda my conclusion: "Since Bombay has the most life members and is our head office, I should come and take care of the life members as Membership Secretary."

Śrīla Prabhupāda seemed pleased and immediately cabled: COME BOMBAY IMMEDIATELY. LETTER FOLLOWS.

Spontaneous Vaiṣṇavism

When I arrived in Juhu from Calcutta, Śrīla Prabhupāda was holding a *paṇḍāl* program at Hare Krishna Land to draw people's attention to the project there. After preaching at Hare Krishna Land for about two weeks, Śrīla Prabhupāda left for Australia, and soon thereafter one couple, Dr. and Mrs. Singhal, who had attended the program, invited us to their home for a small program of *kīrtana* and *prasāda*—our first invitation after the *paṇḍāl* program.

Dr. and Mrs. Singhal were among our first friends in Juhu. As the days and weeks went by, Dr. and Mrs. Singhal became closer and closer to the devotees and offered more and more service. Dr. Singhal offered free medical treatment, while Mrs. Singhal took care of the devotees and sometimes sewed for the Deities. They introduced us to their friends, and through Dr. Singhal we met Mr. Kejriwal, who was later initiated by Śrīla Prabhupāda as Man Mohan dāsa, as well as Mr. Pandiya and Mr. Bhatia. They all became life members and in turn helped us enroll other members. Subsequently Mr. Pandiya and Mr. Bhatia also took initiation.

One day, Mrs. Singhal invited Śrīla Prabhupāda for lunch, and Śrīla Prabhupāda, Tamal Krishna Goswami, and I drove together to their small apartment in Vile Parle. Dr. and Mrs. Singhal received us warmly, led us to the next room, seated us on the floor on cushions, and affectionately served us *prasāda*. Toward the end of the meal, Mrs. Singhal and one of her lady friends suddenly burst through the door into the room. They were singing Hare Kṛṣṇa while Mrs. Singhal played on her violin. Goswami Mahārāja turned and gave a look as if to say, "What on earth is going on here?" Śrīla Prabhupāda turned to Tamal Krishna and said, "This is spontaneous Vaiṣṇavism. You have to learn to be a Vaiṣṇava. They are naturally Vaiṣṇavas."

Kṛṣṇa Will Be Satisfied

For some time we did not have any proper place for Śrīla Prabhupāda to stay at Hare Krishna Land, so we often arranged for him to stay with some friend in Bombay.

When Śrīla Prabhupāda was staying at Kartikeya Mahadevia's apartment at Sea Face Park in 1973, I used to go to the city every day to meet people. If someone didn't want to become a life member, I would ask him to place an advertisement in a publication. If he didn't want to place an ad, I would ask him to buy a set of books. If he didn't buy a set of books, I would ask him to give a donation, or at least buy one book, or at least give something, anything, to help. And at the end of the day, I would report to Śrīla Prabhupāda.

One day I met many men and not one contributed in any way. So in the evening when I came back and gave the report to Śrīla Prabhupāda, I felt somewhat disappointed. But Śrīla Prabhupāda instructed, "If you sincerely try your best to please Kṛṣṇa, Kṛṣṇa will be satisfied—even if others are not."

When Two Are Better than One

Tamal Krishna Goswami and I formed a team to collect for Vṛndāvana, and later the same team continued to collect for Juhu. Because both he and I were powerful preachers, some devotees questioned the need for us to go and preach together, and they raised the issue with Śrīla Prabhupāda.

"If by going together they can collect more than the combined total of what they can collect separately," he replied, "they should go together."

Our Duty is to Engage Everyone

Soon after entering the agreement to purchase the Juhu land in February of 1972, Śrīla Prabhupāda left on a world tour. We, his followers, were living in tents on the land, but he instructed us to build a *chāṭāi* hut with a tarpaulin roof, which we did. Somehow, Dr. C. P. Patel, a medical doctor from nearby Andheri, heard about us and came to the land to meet us. At that time, we did not have even the hut. And it was so hot that we often just slept outdoors, mainly on the flat roofs of the tenement buildings that came with the land. There were a lot of mosquitoes, and many of the devotees got sick, some with malaria. The circumstances were quite difficult.

Dr. Patel took a liking to the "foreign" devotees, and he got inspired to take up a collection to help them. He went to a huge cloth market in Bombay, MJ Market, Mulji Jetha Market, and he moved from stall to stall to beg cotton and cloth—to get the cotton stuffed into the cloth to make pillows and mattresses—and to obtain blankets, sheets, and mosquito nets as well. Because he was a little proud, it was a big thing for him to beg; he had never begged in his life. Still, he did it, and he came and presented each devotee with a set of items—a simple mattress, pillow, sheet, blanket, and mosquito net.

When Śrīla Prabhupāda returned to Bombay, Dr. Patel came to meet him, and soon he became Śrīla Prabhupāda's constant companion on his morning walks. He would usually come to Prabhupāda's room at about six and either walk with Prabhupāda to Juhu Beach or drive him there. Then they would walk and talk for about an hour.

Dr. Patel was also a little proud because he was born in a Vaiṣṇava family and followed the Vaiṣṇava principles of purity. He had gone to London to study medicine—quite a big thing then—and even there he never ate meat, smoked, or drank. So he considered himself to be a Vaiṣṇava, although he often spoke like an impersonalist. And when Prabhupāda would call him a Māyāvādī, he would beg to differ: "No, Sir. I am a Vaiṣṇava."

I appreciated Dr. Patel and the service he did for us, and I liked his discussions with Śrīla Prabhupāda. Still, some devotees found him to be annoying at times. He knew Sanskrit—that was another factor that contributed to his pride—and he knew a lot of verses. And the way he spoke, it was hard to figure him out.

On their walks, Prabhupāda would come to the point of calling people, even reputed ones, *mūḍhas*—fools, or asses. The *Bhagavad-gītā* says,

na māṁ duṣkṛtino mūḍhāḥ
prapadyante narādhamāḥ
māyayāpahṛta-jñānā
āsuraṁ bhāvam āśritāḥ

"Those miscreants who are grossly foolish, who are lowest among mankind, whose knowledge is stolen by illusion, and who partake of the atheistic nature of demons do not surrender unto Me." (*Bg* 7.15) Prabhupāda would say, "Anyone who doesn't surrender to Kṛṣṇa is a *duṣkṛtina*, miscreant." He is either a *mūḍha*—"fool," "rascal," or, in stronger language, "ass"; *narādhama*—"the lowest among mankind"; *māyayāpahṛta-jñānā*—someone who may be very knowledgeable or intelligent but whose knowledge has been taken away, stolen away, by *māyā*; or *āsuraṁ bhāvam*—one who has the nature of demons. Prabhupāda would say, "Anyone who is not surrendered to Kṛṣṇa falls in one of these four categories: fool, rascal, demon," and so on. And sometimes Dr. Patel would become very upset. But Śrīla Prabhupāda would counter, "I am not saying; Kṛṣṇa is saying. I am only repeating what Kṛṣṇa says."

Still, Śrīla Prabhupāda and Dr. Patel had an affectionate relationship, and after Śrīla Prabhupāda left this world, Dr. Patel was inspired to write his memories of him, and they were quite touching. His article was published in *Back to Godhead* as "My Life's Most Precious Moments" with the subtitle "A Bombay doctor wins the title 'big fool' and loves it." So he relished, at least in retrospect, being called a *mūḍha* by Prabhupāda.

In a way Dr. Patel was a Māyāvādī, but he thought he was a Vaiṣṇava. He accepted Kṛṣṇa and the *Bhagavad-gītā*, but it wasn't quite clear how he accepted Kṛṣṇa—as the person Kṛṣṇa or as something impersonal speaking through Kṛṣṇa. His position was always a little ambiguous. But he would always insist that he was a Vaiṣṇava, a *pure* Vaiṣṇava.

One day, Śrīla Prabhupāda criticized one of the revered so-called spiritual leaders of India, and Dr. Patel became livid. He was shaking, he was so angry. He shouted at Prabhupāda, "You cannot criticize like this!" And Prabhupāda shouted back, "I am not saying! Kṛṣṇa is saying—*na māṁ duṣkṛtino mūḍhāḥ* . . ." They were shouting back and forth. This was one time when Dr. Patel's friends—he had his group of cronies, and he was their leader, perhaps because he was a little intellectual and outspoken—tried to drag him away, saying, "Swamiji has a heart condition. Don't upset him so." Yet Dr. Patel persisted. He was shouting at Prabhupāda, and Prabhupāda was shouting at him. Finally they pulled Dr. Patel away.

Afterwards, back at the temple, Tamal Krishna Goswami went into Prabhupāda's room and asked, "Śrīla Prabhupāda, why do you do it? Why do you put up with him? He is so offensive." And Prabhupāda said, "It is our duty to engage everyone." Then Tamal Krishna asked, "But what is his actual position? Is he a Vaiṣṇava? Is he a Māyāvādī? What is he?" In response, Prabhupāda told a story about a man who could expertly speak many languages—in whatever language people addressed him, he immediately responded perfectly in the same language. So no one could figure out where he was actually from. People were talking: "Where is he from? In whatever language we speak to him, he answers in the same language perfectly, immediately." Finally one man said, "I will find out."

One day, when the speaker of many languages was preoccupied, that man came up behind him and gave him a big whack. Then the linguist started to curse in his native tongue, and so his real identity was disclosed. Prabhupāda said, "Dr. Patel is like that. He can speak very expertly. He can sound like a devotee, sound like a Vaiṣṇava, sound like a Māyāvādī, sound like anything. But when I gave a slap where it really hurt—this so-called saintly person that he revered—his real language came out."

Thereafter Prabhupāda said, "Now no more discussion. We will only read *Kṛṣṇa* book." And for the first time in years, Dr. Patel avoided Śrīla Prabhupāda.

Finally one day, as Dr. Patel described it, he felt pulled back to Śrīla Prabhupāda as if by force. He was walking on one side of the beach, and Prabhupāda was walking on the other, but something made Dr. Patel change his course and he walked toward Śrīla Prabhupāda and bowed at his feet—he came back.

He said, "Swamiji, we have been taught to respect all the saints of India." And Śrīla Prabhupāda replied, "And our business is to point out who is not a saint."

They Are Liberated

In their own way, Śrīla Prabhupāda and Dr. Patel remained friends, and they resumed their walks and talks.

On one morning walk Dr. Patel brought up the topic of his gift of the twelve sets of bedding, complaining to Śrīla Prabhupāda that the devotees hadn't taken care of them. At first there were twelve sets; then, after a while, there was one less blanket and two fewer pillows. In time, there were only about seven sets, then three sets, and then, in the end, there was nothing left of the gift at all. So Dr. Patel complained that he had gone and begged and organized the gift and now there was nothing left. There was not even a trace—not a single thread. Prabhupāda said, "These boys and girls from Europe and America who have come to serve me, they don't care for their bodies. They know, 'I am not this body,' so why should they care? As long as they can serve their spiritual master and chant Hare Kṛṣṇa, they are happy. They don't mind if they have to sleep on the floor or get bitten by mosquitoes. They are detached from the body. All they care about is devotional service."

Śrīla Prabhupāda concluded, "They are already liberated. That *mokṣa* that you so much want, that *mokṣa* they already have. That is why there is nothing left of your gift—they don't care for the body or the comforts of the body. They are liberated, which you so much want to become."

Śrīla Prabhupāda's answer was profound, expressed with a wry twist. And it is true that devotees are liberated. Pure devotional service begins on the liberated platform:

brahma-bhūtaḥ prasannātmā
na śocati na kāṅkṣati
samaḥ sarveṣu bhūteṣu
mad-bhaktiṁ labhate parām

"One who is thus transcendentally situated at once realizes the

Supreme Brahman and becomes fully joyful. He never laments or desires to have anything. He is equally disposed toward every living entity. In that state he attains pure devotional service unto Me." (*Bg* 18.54) According to authorities, even a neophyte devotee is beyond a Māyāvādī who desires only to become liberated. So in a subtle, tactful way (this time), Śrīla Prabhupāda put Dr. Patel in his place and exalted the devotees in comparison.

Still, even liberated devotees may take care of so-called material possessions, knowing them to be Kṛṣṇa's property, to be used in Kṛṣṇa's service. The highest conception of renunciation, or detachment, is *yukta-vairāgya*, defined by Śrīla Rūpa Gosvāmī:

anāsaktasya viṣayān
yathārham upayuñjataḥ
nirbandhaḥ kṛṣṇa-sambandhe
yuktaṁ vairāgyam ucyate

"Things should be accepted for the Lord's service and not for one's personal sense gratification. If one accepts something without attachment and accepts it because it is related to Kṛṣṇa, one's renunciation is called *yukta-vairāgya*, befitting renunciation." (*Bhakti-rasāmṛta-sindhu* 1.2.255)

Śrīla Prabhupāda himself perfectly demonstrated the principle of *yukta-vairāgya*. He carefully maintained whatever Kṛṣṇa sent him. And he engaged not only anything and everything in Kṛṣṇa's service, but he also engaged everyone—even Dr. Patel.

Enjoyment and Renunciation—and Service

In the winter of 1972 in Bombay, Śrīla Prabhupāda spoke to his disciples on *The Nectar of Devotion*. His Sanskrit editor, Pradyumna dāsa, read a section in the Preface that led to a most interesting discussion:

"The relish or taste of the mundane *rasa* does not long endure, and therefore mundane workers are always apt to change their position . . . Material engagement means accepting a particular status for some time and then changing it. This position of changing back and forth is technically known as *bhoga-tyāga*, which means a position of alternating sense enjoyment and renunciation."

Śrīla Prabhupāda told us that he had asked his *guru mahārāja* about *bhoga-tyāga*. Rūpa Gosvāmī, he had understood, left everything for the service of Caitanya Mahāprabhu: his lucrative service, his post as minister—*tyāga*. And Rāmānanda Rāya, who was a governor and a householder, lived in great material opulence—*bhoga*. Both were accepted equally by Lord Caitanya. "So," Śrīla Prabhupāda had asked, "what is the difference? Both were devotees of Caitanya Mahāprabhu." Thus he had raised the question of *bhoga* and *tyāga*—enjoyment and renunciation.

Śrīla Bhaktisiddhānta Sarasvatī Ṭhākura had given a striking answer. He had invoked the term *proṣita-bhartṛkā*, which refers to a wife when her husband is away. In Vedic culture, when the husband was away, the wife would wear very plain clothes. She wouldn't decorate herself or comb her hair. She would lie down and sleep on the floor—live in a very austere and renounced way. And the same woman, when her husband was home, would bathe twice daily, apply oil to her body, wear beautiful clothing, and decorate herself in a very attractive way. But in both cases the central point was the husband. When the husband was away she lived in that renounced way, and when the husband was present she acted in that more spirited way, but in both situations the central point was the husband—to please the husband—and so there was no difference. Thus Śrīla Bhaktisiddhānta had explained that as devotees we are interested neither in *bhoga* nor in *tyāga*. We are interested only in Kṛṣṇa and Kṛṣṇa's service. For Kṛṣṇa's service we can give up everything, like the Gosvāmīs. And for the sake of Kṛṣṇa's service we can accept any opulent position, like that of Rāmānanda Rāya, who was a governor. And either—or both—will please Śrī Caitanya Mahāprabhu.

Śrīla Prabhupāda concluded, "Our policy is not *bhoga-tyāga*. Our policy is satisfaction of Kṛṣṇa. That is pure *bhakti*." And pure *bhakti* is the subject of *The Nectar of Devotion*—and the purpose of the Kṛṣṇa consciousness movement.

A Good Fight

Finally, after months and years of struggle, Mrs. Nair signed the conveyance to transfer the Juhu land to "His Divine Grace A. C. Bhaktivedanta Swami Prabhupāda, founder-*ācārya* of the International Society for Krishna Consciousness." It was a momentous occasion, as if two powerful parties had come together to sign a peace treaty.

At the time, Śrīla Prabhupāda was staying in the Khatau's vacation house, a thatched cottage near Juhu Beach. Many wealthy and aristocratic gentlemen from Bombay had bungalows in Juhu, where they would come and spend weekends and holidays near the seaside. They also used their Juhu bungalows as guesthouses.

After the signing, Śrīla Prabhupāda said we should have a feast. There were fireworks, and after the event was over and all the guests had left, Śrīla Prabhupāda leaned back on his *āsana* with his legs up and exclaimed, "It was a good fight!"

(Then he added, "Someone should write a book about it.")

"But You Are Discouraging Me"

For some time Śrīla Prabhupāda continued to stay in the Khatau's hut, near Sumati Morarji's bungalow. Mahāṁsa Prabhu,

Dr. Patel, and I sat in the room with Śrīla Prabhupāda the day after the conveyance was signed. Now Śrīla Prabhupāda was anxious to begin construction and said he needed one crore of rupees. Dr. Patel ventured, "Prabhupāda, you should bring the money from America." Śrīla Prabhupāda, disturbed by Dr. Patel's suggestion, replied, "I could bring the money from America, but then what will be your credit?" Prabhupāda said that Bombay was such a place that if people were willing, we could collect one crore in one day. Dr. Patel countered, "But people are not willing." Dr. Patel went on insisting that people wouldn't give. "Of course, I don't want to discourage you, but . . ." "But," Śrīla Prabhupāda interjected, "you are discouraging me."

So although Śrīla Prabhupāda was superhuman, in another sense he was also very human, and he could also feel discouraged.

I Always Got What I Wanted

Mr. Ratnaparkhi owned a dilapidated old dwelling at the corner of Hare Krishna Land, right where Śrīla Prabhupāda wanted to construct the Deity rooms, and Mr. Ratnaparkhi knew we needed to demolish his structure in order to build the temple.

Although Mr. Ratnaparkhi had agreed to give us the house for Rs. 8,000, he later intimated that he wanted Rs. 20,000. Even then, we could not finalize the transaction. Finally, when Śrīla Prabhupāda returned to Juhu for the conveyance, Mr. Ratnaparkhi revealed that he wanted to negotiate with Śrīla Prabhupāda directly and have Śrīla Prabhupāda meet with him at his residence nearby on Juhu Road.

Śrīla Prabhupāda agreed.

Mr. Ratnaparkhi was a volatile person who we feared could become violent. Now, with Śrīla Prabhupāda in his home, he asked Śrīla Prabhupāda, "How much will you give?" Immediately Prabhupāda countered, "How much do you want?" Ratnaparkhi insisted, "No, how much will you give?" Prabhupāda repeated,

"No, how much do you want?" The situation was tense. Finally Mr. Ratnaparkhi said, "Thirty thousand rupees"—an outrageous amount. And Śrīla Prabhupāda immediately agreed, "Yes."

On the way back to the *chātāi* house, Śrīla Prabhupāda commented, "Whenever I really wanted something, I always got it. I didn't care how much I had to spend, but I always got what I wanted."

Inside Is Freedom

After acquiring the Juhu land, Śrīla Prabhupāda instructed Mr. Sethi to construct a compound wall around the property. One morning, as we approached the temple on our way back from Prabhupāda's morning walk, Śrīla Prabhupāda's friend and constant companion on his walks, Dr. C. P. Patel, pointed to the new, five-foot–high wall and told Śrīla Prabhupāda, "Seeing this wall, people are saying you have made a prison inside."

Śrīla Prabhupāda immediately responded, "Nooo," elongating the "o" sound. "The prison is outside. Inside is freedom."

You Can Never Be Cured

After serving in India for two and a half years, I contracted jaundice. With great patience and care I was able to overcome my condition, but within two weeks I had a relapse. Then no matter what I did I could not recover. Finally Śrīla Prabhupāda said that as long as I remained in Bombay I would not get better.

With great difficulty I got the necessary stamps in my passport to leave the country and undertook the arduous flight from Bombay to Chicago. In Chicago my parents received me at the airport and took me to their home, where I had lived from the age of eight. One day an old family friend who was a psychologist came to meet me. She came in my room and began to inquire: "Tell me, Glenn, did you feel that your parents didn't love you?" "Which parents?" I asked. "I have passed so many lifetimes, and in every lifetime I have had different parents." In this way, whatever questions she asked, I answered with Kṛṣṇa consciousness. After some time she left my room, and I could overhear her speaking with my parents. "I am sorry, I did whatever I could. But I don't think I can help him." Then I realized my parents had sent her to "cure" me.

After three days I began to feel uncomfortable at home and went to the Chicago temple. And a few days later I flew to Los Angeles to recuperate at the temple there. Soon Śrīla Prabhupāda also arrived from India. He inquired about my health and my stay in Chicago, and I told him how the psychologist had come to cure me. "You have been infected permanently," Śrīla Prabhupāda remarked. "You can never be cured."

Until Then, Worship Kṛṣṇa

When I became well enough, I began to accompany Śrīla Prabhupāda on his morning walks. On one, I asked, "We say that Kṛṣṇa is the original cause of all causes, but some people question, 'Then who is the cause of Kṛṣṇa?' How do we answer them?" Śrīla Prabhupāda replied, "According to our information, Kṛṣṇa is the first cause. If you do research and find someone who is the cause of Kṛṣṇa, we will worship him. But until then, you should worship Kṛṣṇa."

Speak like a Gentleman

In his talks, Śrīla Prabhupāda often took the opportunity to smash the mundane scientists and inspire his devotee scientist

Svarūpa Dāmodara dāsa (Dr. Thoudam Singh, an organic chemist) to form the Bhaktivedanta Institute to preach the principles of the *Bhagavad-gītā* in scientific language and establish that Kṛṣṇa is the origin of everything, both matter and spirit. I also became inspired by the idea of scientific preaching, and although I was not qualified like Svarūpa Dāmodara, I did have some desire to participate.

One day I approached Śrīla Prabhupāda in his room, during his massage, and told him that I was willing to join in the scientific preaching. He simply smiled and said, "Your field is psychology." (He knew I had been a psychology major.) Still, he said I could apply that knowledge in the work of the Bhaktivedanta Institute. Then I told him that I had noticed that when he spoke about the scientists he used words such as "nonsense," "rascals," "bluffers," and "cheaters," and that he often said we should "kick them in the face with boots." So I asked whether when we preached or met with scientists we should use such language. And Śrīla Prabhupāda replied, "No. You should speak like a gentleman."

The Art of Listening

When I returned to America after three years away, it was such a major event for my family that even my uncle, my father's brother, came from Chicago, and I arranged for him to meet Śrīla Prabhupāda in his quarters. My uncle was a doctor with high ideals, and he opened his heart to Śrīla Prabhupāda about how disillusioned and disappointed he was with the state of the medical profession. He felt that doctors had become too materialistic and were more interested in money than in the welfare of their patients. As he went on sharing his chagrin, Śrīla Prabhupāda simply listened, intently and with sympathy. In the entire half hour of the conversation, Śrīla Prabhupāda didn't say more than a few sentences. He just listened with tremendous sympathy. And at the end, as we were leaving the room, my uncle turned to me and said, "My God! I've never met anyone like him. I must get a picture of him. I have never seen a face like his."

Because I Like Everyone

It was said of the Six Gosvāmīs: *dhīrādhīra-jana-priyau priya-karau nirmatsarau pūjitau*—they are popular both with the gentle and with the ruffians, because they are not envious of anyone; whatever they do, they are all-pleasing to everyone.

On a morning walk in Los Angeles in 1973, Śrīla Prabhupāda demonstrated the same qualities. He reciprocated with scientists, preachers, managers, book distributors, and even my parents so perfectly that they all were pleased and satisfied.

Śrīla Prabhupāda was gracious with everyone. One morning, when my parents were visiting me from Chicago, they joined us for a walk at Cheviot Hills Park. Prabhupāda greeted my mother, "Oh, Mrs. Teton, you look so young." She was pleased—and everyone was pleased. At the end of the walk we came to the parking lot, and my father began to eye the Rolls Royce the devotees had arranged for Prabhupāda. Śrīla Prabhupāda, ever so humbly, almost diffidently, responded, "My disciples got this for me." And my father immediately replied, "Oh, no, you deserve it. You deserve it." Then Śrīla Prabhupāda invited him, "You can come and ride with me." But my father replied, "No, no, we have our own car."

After we left (as related to me later), Śrīla Prabhupāda's servant said to His Divine Grace, "Śrīla Prabhupāda, everyone likes you so much." And Śrīla Prabhupāda replied, "Yes, because I like everyone."

A Pure Devotee's Longing

One afternoon, after dealing with various managerial problems, Śrīla Prabhupāda leaned back on the bolsters of his *āsana* and quoted a verse from Narottama dāsa Ṭhākura: *viṣaya chāḍiyā kabe śuddha ha'be mana, kabe hāma herabo śrī-vṛndāvana*—"When will I give up material sense objects? When will my mind become purified? When will I be able to behold Vṛndāvana?" He said, "Of course, it is not *viṣaya*, material; it is Kṛṣṇa's service. But still, I wish to be freed. I am hankering for Vṛndāvana."

Back to Bombay

Śrīla Prabhupāda, responding to appeals from India for me to return, encouraged me, in his words, to go "back home, back to Bombay." I got the impression that he was telling me that if I went back and served him in Bombay, I would go back to Godhead. And in time, when I was well enough, I returned "back home, back to Bombay."

Gosvāmī

While Śrīla Prabhupāda was in America, Tamal Krishna Goswami and the other devotees had secured one of the apartments on Hare Krishna Land for his use. Somehow one of the tenants had vacated the flat and moved elsewhere. Finally Śrīla Prabhupāda had his own place on his own land. And as always, he was concerned that his property be managed properly.

I was always attracted to the Six Gosvāmīs of Vṛndāvana, and I imagined that one day I would be like them, roaming the forests of Vṛndāvana, chanting "Kṛṣṇa! Kṛṣṇa!"

Śrīla Prabhupāda knew my mind, and one day he spoke to me:

"Raghunātha dāsa managed his father's estate just like an expert businessman. Similarly, you should also manage your father's estate. Then you go to Vṛndāvana and become a Gosvāmī."

Not "Like," but "Life"

Flushed with enthusiasm after a day of meeting people in Bombay, I went to see Śrīla Prabhupāda in his room in Juhu. "I like preaching very much," I said. He replied, "Not 'I *like* preaching,' but 'preaching is my *life*.'"

Sweet Grapes

One evening I came to Śrīla Prabhupāda's room after a long day in Bombay. As usual, I had traveled to and from the city in the crowded trains, and to and from the train station in a crowded bus. And as usual, I had not taken any *prasāda* from the morning until the time I returned. Śrīla Prabhupāda looked at me and asked, "How are you feeling?" I then noticed how weak and sick I was. "Well, frankly speaking, Śrīla Prabhupāda, I feel a little tired." Anyway, Śrīla Prabhupāda already knew.

Immediately Śrīla Prabhupāda ordered grapes for me. He said that grapes were very good for strength and energy. Then he insisted that I eat the grapes in his presence, and soon he asked if I was feeling stronger. And yes, I was.

Finally he concluded: "To work very hard for Kṛṣṇa for two days, and then to recuperate for three days—that is not a very good proposal."

Oh, Kṛṣṇa, Where Are You?

In Bombay, a recording of a song written by George Harrison arrived. The devotees wanted to play it for Śrīla Prabhupāda, and he agreed. The song was written and arranged by George to be sung by Lakshmi Shankar, Ravi Shankar's sister. The refrain goes, "I am missing you/ Oh, Kṛṣṇa, where are you?" and the whole piece is in the mood of separation from Kṛṣṇa. Later, devotees told me that Śrīla Prabhupāda had said that the song was in the mood of the Six Gosvāmīs of Vṛndāvana, who were always searching for Kṛṣṇa.

Selling Books, Not Tickets

One life member in Juhu suggested to Śrīla Prabhupāda, "If you have a charity benefit performance with some famous artists, you can make a lot of money for the temple." Śrīla Prabhupāda replied, "You can do." Then the life member said, "Only, Prabhupāda, we will need some devotees to sell tickets." Śrīla Prabhupāda replied, "Our devotees cannot sell tickets. They are meant for selling books."

Śrīla Prabhupāda reiterated that if the member and his friends promoted the program and gave the profit to the temple, he had no objection, but that the devotees could not be directly involved.

Why We Are Successful

One of our best life members in Bombay was Sri Biharilal Khandelwal. He was a very pious man from a prominent industrial family. In fact, he was the first life member in India to pledge one lakh (one hundred thousand) rupees for any of Śrīla Prabhupāda's projects. One day his secretary phoned and gave us the bad news: Sri Biharilal Khandelwal had passed away. We were requested to come and perform *kīrtana* in the presence of his widow and other family members. So I organized whatever devotees I could, and we went to the widow's residence to chant and try to console her with some words from the *Bhagavad-gītā*.

One devotee we could not inform was Haridāsa Prabhu. That evening Haridāsa was fanning Śrīla Prabhupāda on the terrace on top of his apartment. At seven o'clock Śrīla Prabhupāda noticed that there was no sound of *kīrtana* from the temple. So he asked Haridāsa why. "The devotees must have gone to the city to collect and not yet returned," Haridāsa replied. Prabhupāda said, "This was not my idea, that they should go to the city and collect all day and night. Our process is to please Kṛṣṇa. They may go at nine and return by five, and then chant and dance in front of the Deities. Otherwise they will become like *karmīs*.

"We are successful because we try to please Kṛṣṇa and Kṛṣṇa is merciful and reciprocates with us. Otherwise Mr. Nair was much more powerful than we. He had money, influence—his own daily newspaper—he had contacts, so many politicians and government officers. And who were we? We had no money, no influence, and no support. Yet we were successful—by Kṛṣṇa's grace.

"So we should come and sing and dance in front of the Deities and please Them, and by Their grace we will get all success. We are not successful by our own strength; we are successful by Kṛṣṇa's grace."

Never Forget God

Another time, Śrīla Prabhupāda explained to me the purpose of *gurukula* in Kṛṣṇa conscious children's education. He said,

"We cannot expect that many of the students will stay in the temple. But they should be so nicely trained that no matter what they do later in life, they will never forget Kṛṣṇa." Then Śrīla Prabhupāda told how he and his sister used to fly kites and pray to God to make their kites fly higher. "They should be trained in such a nice way that no matter what they do in life, they will never forget God."

Keep It Simple

Once, when I happened to be in Śrīla Prabhupāda's room during the Māyāpur festival, one of Śrīla Prabhupāda's disciples came to discuss the Arcanā-paddhati, the rules and regulations for Deity worship, which he was compiling for the Society. Śrīla Prabhupāda instructed, "Keep it simple. In Kali-yuga, our main process is *harer-nāma*. We should always remember that."

Rooms in Vaikuṇṭha

Eventually, Śrīla Prabhupāda's great friend and staunch devotee Sri P. L. Sethi obtained permission to build one story on top of the apartments at the rear of Hare Krishna Land, to serve as residential quarters for the devotees. Mr. Sethi also arranged for the workers and the purchase of building materials, and he personally oversaw the construction.

When the first rooms were almost ready, Mr. Sethi took Śrīla Prabhupāda up to the additional floor to see the new quarters. Śrīla Prabhupāda instructed us that every day the *brahmacārīs* should lift everything off the floor and wash the floor with water. Then, with great affection and appreciation, Śrīla Prabhupāda said to Mr. Sethi, "Just as you are building these rooms for my disciples here, Lord Kṛṣṇa is building your rooms for you in Vaikuṇṭha."

Service Is Important

Thereafter, from time to time Śrīla Prabhupāda would ask me how each room at Juhu was being used, and I would explain. Thus we would proceed building by building, room by room.

Once, when we came to the B-block, I mentioned that Bilvamaṅgala and his wife were staying in one room. Śrīla Prabhupāda replied, "Oh, you have given a room to Bilvamaṅgala and his wife?" "Yes." "Why?"

"Because he was staying away from the temple in some apartment and sleeping late, and he wasn't coming to the morning program and was hardly coming to the temple at all. So I wanted to save him."

"That way if you offer a room with fan and electricity and all facilities and food, the whole of Bombay will come to be saved. And how many will you be able to save like that?"

Some months later Śrīla Prabhupāda again asked how the rooms were being used. When we came to the A-block, I mentioned that the ladies were staying there. Again Śrīla Prabhupāda asked who was staying in which room and what she was doing. (Śrīla Prabhupāda had instructed that in Juhu we should keep only those ladies who were doing essential service.) When I mentioned that one lady was sewing for the Deities, Śrīla Prabhupāda remarked, "That is not very essential," meaning it was not essential that the lady be in Juhu to do the service. Still, I was not quite sure what Śrīla Prabhupāda intended, so I asked, "But Śrīla Prabhupāda, there are so many ladies in Los Angeles who distribute books." He replied, "Oh, book distribution. Book distribution is very important service."

"You should never underestimate the value of service," Śrīla Prabhupāda stated. "Service is very important."

Bus Stop

Even after Prabhupāda got the permit to build the residences for the devotees, he still had to get permission to build the temple. And the government seemed determined not to give it. Sometimes, when things looked really bad, Śrīla Prabhupāda almost appeared to become hopeless. But even when he seemed hopeless, he would always see the positive side. One day he said, "Even if we don't get permission and build the temple, never mind. We'll make Hare Krishna Land into a bus stop. We will have many buses, and we'll send devotees out to do *saṅkīrtana* and distribute books, and every now and then they can come back and refuel."

Śrīla Prabhupāda had an amazing way of turning something that appeared to be negative into something positive.

Śrīla Prabhupāda was always a fighter, always a hero.

Still You Must Dance

After serving Śrīla Prabhupāda as zonal secretary for India for more than three years, Tamal Krishna Goswami returned to America to preach, and soon Goswami Mahārāja formed the Radha-Damodara Traveling Sankirtana Party, which made devotees, distributed books, and sent money to India. In the meantime, Bhagavān dāsa, who was GBC for France, came to spend some time as GBC in Bombay, and almost every day he and I would go to the city to work on the permission for the temple. In fact, Śrīla Prabhupāda did not want to leave Bombay until he got the permit. During this time, he was lecturing every evening on the teachings of Lord Kapila to Devahūti, and Bhagavān and I would usually return just in time to take some *prasāda* and attend the class and *kīrtana*. Śrīla Prabhupāda was so concerned about the work that sometimes he would call us to the *vyāsāsana* during the program and ask for the news.

Still, Śrīla Prabhupāda wanted us to be happy in Kṛṣṇa consciousness. So one evening during the program he announced from the *vyāsāsana*, "You must always dance in *kīrtana*—even if you don't get the permission."

Patience and Tolerance

Almost every day, Haridāsa Prabhu too would go to the city to make members and collect donations. One evening, after a long, hard day in the city, Haridāsa returned to Juhu. Unfortunately, nobody had saved *prasāda* for him.

Frustrated and upset, Haridāsa went upstairs to see Śrīla Prabhupāda. He went into Śrīla Prabhupāda's room, threw his beads on Śrīla Prabhupāda's desk, and told him, "I quit."

"What happened?"

"I went out all day to make life members and no one was interested."

"Don't worry," Śrīla Prabhupāda replied. "Just be patient. When the new temple opens, people will stand in queue to become life members."

Then Haridāsa began to complain about the foreign devotees, how he was going out to preach all day and they didn't even save *prasāda* for him. Prabhupāda replied, "Practically only they have come forward to help me. They are giving service, so we have to tolerate. Sometimes when you go to milk a cow, the cow kicks you—but you tolerate, because you want the milk."

The Same ABC

Once, Mr. Sethi approached Śrīla Prabhupāda in his quarters in Juhu and told him that he had some ideas for devotees to make money for the temple. Śrīla Prabhupāda replied, "Your ideas may be good, but if I tell my disciples, they will think, 'I have come for *bhajana*, and now he wants me to do the same business again.'"

Then Śrīla Prabhupāda told a story. Once, a boy was learning algebra and his mother saw him write A + B = C. Seeing the letters A, B, and C, she exclaimed, "Oh, you have grown so much, and still you are doing the same ABC?" She could not understand there was a gulf of difference between this ABC and that ABC, between a child's learning to write the alphabet—ABC—and an adult's doing algebra—ABC.

Prabhupāda continued, "I can give my disciples so many ideas, but they will think, 'I have come for *bhajana*, and again I am doing the same business?' They cannot understand there is a gulf of difference between this business and that business—between working for Kṛṣṇa and working for *māyā*."

Śrīla Prabhupāda was so intelligent and kind. He knew our consciousness; he knew our understanding was wrong. But he did not disturb us. He allowed us to continue in our devotional service, and he maintained faith that the process of hearing and chanting about Kṛṣṇa and serving Kṛṣṇa's pure devotee would purify us and enlighten us in the proper understanding of Kṛṣṇa consciousness.

Line the Walls with Books

Once, when we were discussing with Śrīla Prabhupāda the decor for the restaurant, he said, "You should line the walls of the restaurant with my books. That way we will call people's attention to my books and at the same time save storage space."

Why We Protect Cows

Once, Haṁsadūta dāsa came to meet Śrīla Prabhupāda in Juhu. He had been having difficulties with the other leaders of the

ISKCON Hyderabad farm project, and he wanted to share his grief with Śrīla Prabhupāda, who listened patiently and with sympathy. I was struck not only by how kind and compassionate Prabhupāda was, but also by how much time he had to spend with us to smooth our rough relationships and heal our hurt hearts.

As I sat there listening, and marveling at Śrīla Prabhupāda's deep care and expertise, the topic turned to cows on the farm. Haṁsadūta explained his strategy, that the devotees would create such a superior breed of cow that produced such large quantities of milk, that they would have more than enough milk for their own needs and would be able to sell the surplus for a good profit. This way, he reasoned, people would see that keeping cows was profitable and they wouldn't kill them.

Having listened carefully, Śrīla Prabhupāda responded: "This is not the idea, to keep cows and get milk and produce yogurt and cheese and ghee and by selling them to become fat, rich capitalists. The idea is to please Kṛṣṇa. That is *bhakti.* In the *Bhagavad-gītā* (18.44) Kṛṣṇa says, *kṛṣi-go-rakṣya*: 'agriculture and cow protection.' We protect the cows because Kṛṣṇa wants it, for Kṛṣṇa's pleasure—whether we make money or not. Even if we lose money, we will still protect the cows—and depend on Kṛṣṇa. Our interest is to please Kṛṣṇa. That is *bhakti.*"

To Remember Means to Remember to Write It Down

One day I sat before Śrīla Prabhupāda in his room in Juhu, and he was ready to give me some important instructions. As usual when Śrīla Prabhupāda would instruct me, I would concentrate with my full attention and try to remember everything he said. He began, "To remember means to remember to write it down." And he added, "You should always carry a pen and paper."

Then he gave me the other important instructions he wanted me to remember.

Chant Loudly

Riding next to Śrīla Prabhupāda in a car, I asked him, "What do I do when my mind wanders, when I cannot fix my mind on the sound of the holy name?" He replied, "Chant loudly."

Why Are You Attracted?

One morning on his walk on Juhu Beach, Śrīla Prabhupāda challenged us, "Why are you attracted by sex?" Different devotees fumbled for words. Finally Śrīla Prabhupāda gave the answer. "You are attracted to sex . . ." Our suspense mounted. "You are attracted to sex because you want to be."

Bluffing Others and Bluffing Themselves

On another morning walk, Śrīla Prabhupāda was vehemently criticizing the politicians for bluffing the people with false propaganda about birth control. Knowing some politicians myself, I felt they actually believed what they were saying, so I asked Śrīla Prabhupāda, "When you say the politicians are bluffing the people, are they consciously bluffing them or do they actually believe they are doing good?" Śrīla Prabhupāda replied with great force, "They are bluffing the people—and they have also bluffed themselves."

Nonviolent

Once, as we were walking from Juhu Beach back to the temple, Śrīla Prabhupāda continued to speak to the devotees. He said, "When we take charge of the government, we will go to the people and tell them, 'Either you chant Hare Kṛṣṇa or we will kill you.'" Responding to Śrīla Prabhupāda's playful remark, all the devotees laughed heartily, except, perhaps, for me.

Śrīla Prabhupāda turned to me and said, "What do you think, Giriraj?" With as much conviction as I could muster, I said, "Yes, very good, Śrīla Prabhupāda." Then Śrīla Prabhupāda turned to the other devotees and announced, "Our Giriraj is nonviolent."

Then we all laughed.

Association while Working

In November 1975, when Śrīla Prabhupāda arrived from the airport at the Juhu temple, I saw a new *brahmacārī*, dressed in saffron robes, opening the trunk of the car and carrying the bags. When I inquired who he was, I was told, "Oh, that's Ambarīṣa dāsa—Alfred Ford, great-grandson of Henry Ford, who invented the automobile and founded the Ford Motor Company."

Later, Ambarīṣa told me, "I spent so much money in so many ways to become happy, but nothing actually made me happy. But when I started to give my money to Kṛṣṇa, through Śrīla Prabhupāda, I actually became happy."

Before leaving Bombay, Ambarīṣa came to meet Śrīla Prabhupāda and ask him what he should do with his future. Śrīla Prabhupāda said that he should work and at the same time be Kṛṣṇa conscious. Ambarīṣa asked whether he had to work with the Ford Motor Company, and Prabhupāda replied, "No, you can do any work that suits you. I want people to understand that one can be a devotee and still work like any gentleman." Then Ambarīṣa asked, "But what will I do for association?" And Śrīla Prabhupāda responded, "If while you work you think, 'I am working for Kṛṣṇa'—that will be your association."

Why Sixteen?

On a morning walk on Juhu Beach, Lokanath Swami asked Śrīla Prabhupāda why he had prescribed sixteen as the number of rounds to chant. "Why not less or more?"

"No," Śrīla Prabhupāda replied, "We say 'minimum sixteen.' Minimum. If you can chant sixteen thousand, you can do. That is welcome. Haridāsa Ṭhākura was engaged in chanting, and a prostitute came and offered, 'Let us enjoy.' 'Yes, let me finish. Let me finish this chanting.' He refused to have sex with a beautiful young girl, because he had engagement: 'First of all let me finish my engagement.' And we say we have no engagement. How unfortunate we are. Caitanya Mahāprabhu says, *kīrtanīyaḥ sadā hariḥ*. Twenty-four-hours engagement He has given."

Lokanath continued, "Some devotees have fixed different numbers than sixteen. Some are chanting twenty minimum or twenty-five."

"Yes," Śrīla Prabhupāda said, "It should be increased. But don't decrease; increase. Therefore a number is fixed: 'At least this much I shall do.' That is sixteen rounds."

Still, Lokanath persisted, "But you are recommending sixteen as a minimum, and some devotees are choosing twenty as a minimum."

And Prabhupāda responded, "So, who forbids? Who says, 'Don't do it'?"

Lokanath: "They can chant?"

Prabhupāda: "Yes. That is wanted. But because you cannot do it, therefore we have fixed up this minimum. *Saṅkhyāta asaṅkhyāta. Saṅkhyāta* means with vow, numerical strength. And *asaṅkhyāta* means there is no limit."

Lokanath: "Prabhupāda, if we chant more than sixteen

rounds, how can we know whether we are imitating Haridāsa Ṭhākura or following in his footsteps?"

Prabhupāda: "Imitation is also good. If you imitate Haridāsa Ṭhākura, that is also your great fortune. Imitating does not mean you are condemned. Even if you imitate, that is also good. But if you have some other business and you say, 'Now I am imitating Haridāsa Ṭhākura; I cannot do it,' that is very bad. 'I am busy in imitating Haridāsa Ṭhākura.' That is not good."

Brahmānanda added, "If the devotees are asked for service, they say, 'Oh, I have to chant.'"

Prabhupāda responded, "Yes, 'I am imitating Haridāsa. This is my first business.' That is very bad."

Everything Will Be Revealed

In a room conversation in Juhu in August of 1976, some disciples raised the question of other disciples going to Rādhā-kuṇḍa. In response, Śrīla Prabhupāda discussed the whole process of advancement in Kṛṣṇa consciousness.

These devotees going to Rādhā-kuṇḍa were supporting their actions by citing Śrīla Rūpa Gosvāmī's advice in the last verses of the *Upadeśāmṛta* (9–11) that one should bathe in and reside at Rādhā-kuṇḍa. Śrīla Prabhupāda challenged whether they had followed the other instructions, beginning with the first verse: *vāco vegaṁ manasaḥ krodha-vegaṁ/ jihvā-vegam udaropastha-vegam etān vegān yo viṣaheta dhīraḥ sarvām apīmāṁ pṛthivīṁ sa śiṣyāt*: "A sober person who can tolerate the urge to speak, the mind's demands, the actions of anger, and the urges of the tongue, belly, and genitals is qualified to make disciples all over the world." He said that there is a test—whether one is sober and can tolerate these urges (*etān vegān yo viṣaheta dhīraḥ*). If so, then Rādhā-kuṇḍa is for him—not that someone keeps "three dozen *sevā-dāsīs* [maidservants, mistresses] and is living in Rādhā-kuṇḍa."

He said that his *guru mahārāja* had wanted to publish the confidential scripture *Govinda-līlāmṛta* and asked Bhaktivinoda Ṭhākura's permission. First Bhaktivinoda Ṭhākura said, 'I'll tell you one day.' And when Bhaktisiddhānta reminded him, he said, 'Yes, you can print one copy—for you. Not for distribution.' Śrīla Prabhupāda explained, "So, we are printing all these books for understanding properly—not that 'Here is Rādhā-kuṇḍa. Let us go.' Jump over like monkey. 'Here is *rāsa-līlā*.'"

When Acyutānanda added, "Even in *Kṛṣṇa* book, *rāsa-līlā* should not be told in public," Śrīla Prabhupāda responded, "No, why? *Kṛṣṇa* book must be there, in the book it must be there. But you should go gradually. First of all understand Kṛṣṇa, then *kṛṣṇa-līlā*. If you have not understood Kṛṣṇa, you'll think Kṛṣṇa's *rāsa-līlā* is just like our mixing with young women. And then it becomes polluted—because you have not understood Kṛṣṇa. The *Bhagavad-gītā* (7.3) says, *manuṣyāṇāṁ sahasreṣu kaścid yatati siddhaye/ yatatām api siddhānāṁ*—'Out of many thousands among men, one may endeavor for perfection, and of those who have achieved perfection, hardly one knows Me in truth.' Kṛṣṇa understanding is so easy? If you do not understand Kṛṣṇa, how can you go to Kṛṣṇa's confidential activities? . . . You read all the books first of all. Then you'll be able to understand. . . . Kṛṣṇa lifted a hill. Now, how you can become equal with Kṛṣṇa?"

Acyutānanda continued, "They also wear the Rādhā-kuṇḍa *māṭi, tilaka*." And Śrīla Prabhupāda replied, "There is no harm, but they should understand what is Rādhā-kuṇḍa and how to deal with Rādhā-kuṇḍa. Raghunātha dāsa Gosvāmī showed how to live in Rādhā-kuṇḍa. *Saṅkhyā-pūrvaka-nāma-gāna-natibhiḥ kālāvasānī-kṛtau*. He was circumambulating Rādhā-kuṇḍa, falling down, making a mark. That is Rādhā-kuṇḍa *vāsī* [resident]. He not only counted holy names but also offered obeisances so many hundred times. That is Rādhā-kuṇḍa. So much *vairāgya* [detachment] he showed. He can take bath in Rādhā-kuṇḍa. First of all, do this like Raghunātha dāsa

Gosvāmī: *saṅkhyā-pūrvaka-nāma-gāna-natibhiḥ kālāvasānī-kṛtau nidrāhāra-vihārakādi-vijitau cātyanta-dīnau ca yau*. ['The Six Gosvāmīs were engaged in chanting the holy names of the Lord and bowing down in a scheduled measurement. In this way they utilized their valuable lives, and in executing these devotional activities they conquered over eating and sleeping and were always meek and humble.' (*Ṣaḍ-gosvāmy-aṣṭaka* 6)]

"The *Bhagavad-gītā* is the entrance. Then the *Bhāgavata* is graduate, and then *Caitanya-caritāmṛta*. This is the step-by-step. But if one is sincere, everything becomes revealed. He does not commit mistake."

The conclusion, then, apart from the various arguments, is that we must be sincere. But how do we demonstrate that we are sincere—or become sincere?

Śrīla Prabhupāda said, "You see, you can become independent; nobody can check you. Everyone is independent (*yathecchasi tathā kuru* [*Bg* 18.63]). But one who wants to be regulated, he has to surrender. That is voluntary. Otherwise, everyone is free to do whatever he likes. And those who are surrendered souls, they will wait for the instruction of *guru* and do accordingly. That is the proper . . . *Guru-mukha-padma-vākya, cittete kariyā aikya, āra nā kariha*. ['Make the teachings from the lotus mouth of the spiritual master one with your heart, and do not desire anything else.' (*Śrī-guru-vandanā 2*)] That is wanted. Otherwise, all living beings are independent. Even if I say that you do not do it, you are independent, you can do it. Even Kṛṣṇa gives independence to Arjuna: *yathecchasi tathā kuru*—'I have told you everything. Now you do whatever you like.' So, that depends on the candidate. Everyone is free to do anything, but if he's actually serious then he has to do *guru-mukha-padma-vākya, cittete kariyā aikya, āra nā kariha*."

To be sincere, serious, surrendered—that is our challenge. But if we are, we will be saved from mistakes, and everything will be revealed, step-by-step.

The Solution Is to Follow

Śrīla Prabhupāda had a disciple named Amoghalīlā dāsa, who was assisting in Juhu. Amoghalīlā did not have so much personal association with Śrīla Prabhupāda, but one morning, in December 1976, he joined him for his morning walk. Śrīla Prabhupāda wasn't feeling well, so instead of walking on Juhu Beach as usual, he was walking on the rooftop of one of the old buildings at the back of the property, above his quarters. Amoghalīlā took the opportunity to join Śrīla Prabhupāda.

Now, in the temples in America, the devotees would do all the services. There was no question of hiring someone or paying someone to do work in the temple. The devotees would do everything: cut the vegetables, cook the *prasāda*, wash the pots, clean the kitchen, do the laundry, clean the bathrooms—everything, from top to bottom. In India, maybe because there were so few devotees, or because the labor was so cheap, we began to hire people to clean the toilets and wash the pots and even cook.

On the rooftop walk, Amoghalīlā said to Śrīla Prabhupāda, "I heard that you quoted a saying that anyone who goes to Laṅkā becomes a Rāvaṇa and that similarly, when devotees come to India they become Rāvaṇa. Can you explain what you meant and how we can avoid that happening?" Śrīla Prabhupāda responded immediately, "Ask the leaders!" Then he explained that he was saying that in all our other branches our devotees managed the cooking and kitchen but that as soon as they came to India they became *baḍā sāb*, big masters. "That is Rāvaṇa. Why do they not do here? Here we have to keep some cook who is neither initiated nor very clean. In all other branches the boys and girls manage everything."

"So the solution," Amoghalīlā proposed, "is to follow your instructions, to chant the holy names and follow the regulations more strictly?"

Śrīla Prabhupāda replied, "That means Rāvaṇa. He's asking. I am repeatedly saying to follow, and he's asking. That means he's a Rāvaṇa. Why you are inquiring? If you know this is the solution, why don't you do it? Therefore I say, *yāya sei laṅkā sei haya rāvaṇa*: 'Anyone who comes to Laṅkā, he becomes Rāvaṇa.'"

So Amoghalīlā started going around saying, "Śrīla Prabhupāda wants us to do all the cooking ourselves. We should get rid of the hired people." The next morning, the local GBC told Amoghalīlā that he had informed Prabhupāda how Amoghalīlā was telling devotees that we should get rid of all the hired help, and that Śrīla Prabhupāda had said, "Who is this Amoghalīlā? Why is he creating a disturbance?"

In any case, Śrīla Prabhupāda wanted us to know, be convinced, that if we just followed his instructions, the process that he had given, all the problems would be solved. And we should apply such instructions intelligently, according to time, place, and circumstances—as Śrīla Prabhupāda did.

Future Hope

At Juhu we were under constant attack from all sides, and I hesitated to leave the land for long, lest some unfortunate occurrence should take place. But sometimes I thought, "Am I imagining the threat? Am I overestimating the need for my presence?"

After almost five years in India, I had still not been in Vṛndāvana with Śrīla Prabhupāda. In fact, I had hardly left Bombay at all. Finally I decided to go to Vṛndāvana and spend a few days with Śrīla Prabhupāda.

As soon as I got there, Śrīla Prabhupāda inquired of his secretary. "Oh, Giriraj is here? What is he doing here?" Śrīla

Prabhupāda also said, "Giriraj can never leave Bombay for more than three days." When I heard what Śrīla Prabhupāda had said, I decided to return to Bombay the next day. Somehow in the end I stayed for two days.

Still, Śrīla Prabhupāda was very kind to me.

One day, two other devotees and I were sitting in the intimacy of Śrīla Prabhupāda's room, at his lotus feet. Śrīla Prabhupāda spoke about the importance of management. He said that the American Express Corporation had made millions of dollars just from management. "They give you a piece of paper and tell you, 'If you lose this piece of paper, we will give you another piece of paper.' Nothing! Just management."

After some time, Śrīla Prabhupāda said, "If a girl comes, you should not think, 'Oh, this girl has come; let me exploit her.' Rather, you should think, 'Oh, this girl has come to serve Kṛṣṇa; let me help her.'"

Then Śrīla Prabhupāda spoke each of our names and concluded: "Future hopes of the world."

Mystery Solved

Months after the struggles to get the land and permits to build had ended, Śrīla Prabhupāda sat in his room, deep in thought. Suddenly he looked up at me, shook his head, and said, almost with wonder, "I thought Diwanji [our lawyer] was our friend. I could not know that he was implicated with Nair." He paused for a minute, and then he added, "Or, Kṛṣṇa did not want me to know"—as if he had just solved the mystery.

(Lord Kṛṣṇa says in the *Bhagavad-gītā* [15.15], *mattaḥ smṛtir jñānam apohanaṁ ca:* "From Me come remembrance, knowledge, and forgetfulness.")

Presenting the Gītā As It Is

In May of 1976 a prominent industrialist named Ramkrishna Bajaj (almost everyone in India knows Bajaj Autos and Bajaj Electricals) wrote Śrīla Prabhupāda that he was organizing a conference under the banner of the Gita Pratishthan (Gita Foundation), to promote the preaching of the *Bhagavad-gītā*, and that he wanted Śrīla Prabhupāda, as the world's foremost preacher of the *Gītā*, to attend. Śrīla Prabhupāda, however, did not want to join, because although the purpose of the conference was to discuss how to preach the message of the *Gītā*, he was concerned that different participants would have different ideas of what the message of the *Gītā* was. The meeting would host many Māyāvādīs (impersonal speculators) who preach in the name of the *Bhagavad-gītā* that people can become Kṛṣṇa, that they can merge and become one with God. Who would decide what the actual message of the *Gītā* was? So, Prabhupāda considered, "What is the use of my going and wasting time, with no conclusion?" Instead, he asked me to go on his behalf.

In his letter to me, Śrīla Prabhupāda wrote that we must insist that the *Bhagavad-gītā* be presented as it is and that people not use the words of Kṛṣṇa simply to make money or to promote their own philosophies. "If they have got their own philosophy, then let them preach their own philosophy," he said, "but not in the name of the *Gītā*." And he gave an example: "Suppose a man wants to smoke ganja [marijuana], but he does not want to be caught. So he takes a friend's hand and smokes it in his hand, and then when the authorities come he says, 'Oh, I have not smoked ganja. See, my hands are clean!' The idea is that if one wants to preach the *Gītā*, then he must preach it as it is. Otherwise, don't use the *Gītā*." In other words, don't preach your own concocted philosophy and present it as Lord Kṛṣṇa's.

Eventually, Mr. Bajaj came in person to appeal to Śrīla Prabhupāda to attend, and Prabhupāda finally agreed. And so, in

December, we went to Wardha, near Nagpur, in Maharashtra, in the center of India.

Most of the Bajaj family members were followers of Vinoba Bhave, a prominent freedom fighter under Mahatma Gandhi. And Ramkrishna's father, Jamnalal Bajaj, had been Gandhi's treasurer. So, every day Śrīla Prabhupāda and his party would take *prasāda* on the veranda of the house where Mahatma Gandhi, Jawaharlal Nehru, Sardar Vallabhai Patel, and Jamnalal Bajaj all used to take their meals. And Mr. Bajaj would point out where each of them had sat, as we sat in the very same places.

On the main day of the conference all the participants went to Vinoba Bhave's Paunar ashram. When Śrīla Prabhupāda addressed them, his argument was clear and simple: Kṛṣṇa preached the *Bhagavad-gītā* to instruct people to become devotees (*man-manā bhava mad-bhakto*). And how do people become devotees? By chanting the Hare Kṛṣṇa *mahā-mantra* (*harer nāmaiva kevalam*). Therefore, those who want to preach the message of the *Bhagavad-gītā* should propagate the chanting of the holy names of Kṛṣṇa—Hare Kṛṣṇa, Hare Kṛṣṇa, Kṛṣṇa Kṛṣṇa, Hare Hare/ Hare Rāma, Hare Rāma, Rāma Rāma, Hare Hare—because that will fulfill the Lord's purpose in the *Bhagavad-gītā*.

Then Śrīla Prabhupāda took his *karatālas* and began to chant Hare Kṛṣṇa, which infused the meeting with tremendous spiritual energy, especially after so many impersonal speculators had just spoken. The *kīrtana* wasn't in the schedule, and Śrīla Prabhupāda didn't take anyone's permission (not that he had to); still, he was very tactful, and before the audience could become impatient, he stopped the *kīrtana*—and what had been a most dramatic interlude.

On the last day, there was to be a meeting of all the invitees to discuss practical programs for promoting the teachings of the *Gītā*, and the organizers told Prabhupāda that they would invite him when they were ready to present their proposals to him. Later than expected, they finally invited him to come.

When he entered the meeting room, everyone had to take heed of him, because he was the foremost preacher of the *Gītā* in the world and because from every point of view—age, learning, success in preaching—he was the natural leader. When he spoke, he stuck to one point: *paramparā*. Unless you follow the disciplic succession and present the *Bhagavad-gītā* as it is, without personal interpretation, you have no right to preach the *Bhagavad-gītā*. "You can preach any philosophy you like," he told them, "but don't take the name of *Bhagavad-gītā*." And he explained his success: "There is no interpretation. Kṛṣṇa says, 'I am the Supreme.' *Mattaḥ parataraṁ nānyat*. We are presenting, 'Here is God.' You are searching after God, Kṛṣṇa, and they [foreign devotees] are accepting. . . . How they are accepting? Because it is the real thing, there is no interpretation."

Of course, no one could really refute what he was saying.

Then Śrīla Prabhupāda agreed to hear the group's proposals. The committee wanted to agree on a list of specific initiatives to promote the teachings of the *Gītā*. As soon as they presented their first proposal, Śrīla Prabhupāda again insisted on the point of *paramparā*—and surrender: first you must surrender in *paramparā*, as Arjuna surrendered to Kṛṣṇa as *guru*, and then you can preach the *Bhagavad-gītā*. And Śrīla Prabhupāda was not ready to proceed to the next proposal until the group accepted the basic principle for understanding—and thus properly presenting—the actual teaching of the *Bhagavad-gītā*. Śrīla Prabhupāda was so heavy—truly powerful.

After the meeting, he commented in confidence, "We have injected our poison, and now it will act." Of course, he actually meant, "We have injected our nectar, or medicine," but as a sort of poetic device he said, "We have injected our 'poison,' and now it will act."

Although Śrīla Prabhupāda was bold and forceful when he

preached, and sometimes blunt in private, he was most polite and tactful otherwise. Even though he argued on philosophical principles in debate, he was always cordial in personal dealings. And because Śrīla Prabhupāda was so genuine, Mr. Bajaj remained friendly even after Prabhupāda took such a strong position, and later Mr. Bajaj gave quite a large donation to one of Śrīla Prabhupāda's farm projects. And, out of respect for Śrīla Prabhupāda, he held the next *Gītā* conference at the Kṛṣṇa-Balarāma temple in Vṛndāvana, in Śrīla Prabhupāda's last days.

Even then, Śrīla Prabhupāda repeated the same message to Mr. Bajaj—one can lead others only if he follows the supreme leadership of the Supreme Lord Śrī Kṛṣṇa, through *paramparā.*

Increasing Enthusiasm

In Wardha, before the conference began, Śrīla Prabhupāda told me, "When I see you all enthusiastic to distribute my books, my enthusiasm increases." I was surprised, because Śrīla Prabhupāda was always unlimitedly eager to distribute Lord Kṛṣṇa's message. Still, the *Vedānta-sūtra* says that Brahman [Kṛṣṇa, or Kṛṣṇa consciousness] is unlimitedly great and always expanding. And by Prabhupāda's mercy, our little enthusiasm was able to contribute to his great enthusiasm.

Kīrtana—Quiet and Serene

While in Wardha, after the meetings one day, Śrīla Prabhupāda visited Gandhi's ashram Sevagram. There, as the sun was setting and stars were appearing in the sky, we chanted Hare Kṛṣṇa. And Prabhupāda wrote in the guest book, "I was fortunate to come to the Gandhi Ashram Sevagram today. It is so quiet and serene. I have requested them to chant the Hare Kṛṣṇa *mahā-mantra.*"

Organization and Intelligence

In Kārtika of 1977 Śrīla Prabhupāda was in Vṛndāvana, during his last days. He was so weak that he would just lie on his bed, and when he did speak, it was only with great difficulty. We did not know how long he would be with us.

One night—maybe midnight or one in the morning—I was sleeping on the roof of the *gurukula* building when a devotee woke me up and said that Prabhupāda wanted to see me. "Prabhupāda is calling you!" he said. "Prabhupāda is calling!"

I rushed to Prabhupāda's room. The silent intensity in there heightened my anticipation. I didn't know what to expect. Why had Prabhupāda called me? What did he want to say? His health was so delicate we thought that any word he uttered might be his last.

Śrīla Prabhupāda was lying silently in an internal state of consciousness. I offered my obeisances, sat close beside him, and waited in the silence. Then, in a very soft voice, Prabhupāda asked, "So, do you think this movement will go on after I leave?" I was surprised that he had called me in the middle of the night to ask me this question, but I replied, "Yes, as long as the devotees are sincere and go on chanting Hare Kṛṣṇa and following the regulative principles, the movement will be successful."

Śrīla Prabhupāda was silent for a moment. Especially considering that whatever he said might be his last words, I strained intently to hear. He uttered one word: "Organization." He paused and then whispered, "Organization and intelligence."

I was startled. Prabhupāda's words were full of meaning, and they had a profound effect on me. Yes, I realized, we must be sincere and chant our sixteen rounds and follow the regulative principles, but we are meant to do more than just maintain our own spiritual lives. We are meant to preach, to expand the movement, increase the number of devotees, and to do that requires organization—and intelligence. The endeavor to spread Kṛṣṇa consciousness in an intelligent, organized way is real service to

Śrīla Prabhupāda and Śrī Caitanya Mahāprabhu. It is as much service as chanting the holy names and following the regulative principles.

Then Śrīla Prabhupāda said, "Is there anything else?"—was there anything else I wanted to say? Within my heart I was crying out, "Śrīla Prabhupāda, please stay with us; don't leave us." My heart was screaming, but in the prevalent mood of not wanting to impose our will on Śrīla Prabhupāda, I simply said, "No," offered my obeisances, and left.

Sannyāsa

Around 1971 Tamal Krishna Goswami asked Śrīla Prabhupāda about my taking *sannyāsa*. Śrīla Prabhupāda said yes, that I should take *sannyāsa*.

* * *

At Juhu, in 1975, a wave of devotees wanted to take *sannyāsa*—Nava Yogendra Swami, Lokanath Swami, Sridhar Swami. I was actually senior to them, and so devotees suggested that I should take *sannyāsa* too. Somehow, within my heart, I felt reluctant. But Gopal Krishna dāsa, the GBC for Bombay at the time, mentioned the idea to me and then took the initiative to speak to Prabhupāda.

Śrīla Prabhupāda called for me.

"So, you want to take *sannyāsa*? Gopal Krishna says you want to take *sannyāsa*."

I was stunned. I had never said I wanted to take *sannyāsa*. And I never expected that Gopal Krishna would ask him. But I didn't want to contradict my authority, so I said, "Yes."

"Why?"

I knew the answer. "So I can have more facility to preach."

I looked at Śrīla Prabhupāda with nervous anticipation. Śrīla Prabhupāda asked, "You cannot preach as a *brahmacārī*?"

"I can."

Śrīla Prabhupāda peered back at me. "Is there any other reason you want to take *sannyāsa*?"

The only other reasons that passed through my mind were that devotees would offer me obeisances and that I would get *mahā-prasāda*, but I could not present those reasons to Śrīla Prabhupāda.

"No."

Somehow Śrīla Prabhupāda did not seem to want me to take *sannyāsa*. I left to go to the city to preach.

In the evening, when I returned to Juhu and went upstairs to Śrīla Prabhupāda's quarters, one of Prabhupāda's servants approached me, "Boy! Śrīla Prabhupāda really didn't like your idea of taking *sannyāsa*! He said, 'What does Giriraj think, that by taking *sannyāsa* he will sprout four arms for preaching?' Then Prabhupāda said, 'Giriraj can never leave Bombay.'"

I could understand that Śrīla Prabhupāda was concerned that if I took *sannyāsa* I might prefer to travel and preach and leave the management in Bombay.

I wondered why I had gone along with Gopal Krishna's proposal. Within my heart I didn't even really want to ask for *sannyāsa*. I vowed never to bring up the subject again.

* * *

On November 14, 1977, at 7:26 p.m., in his room at the Kṛṣṇa-Balarāma temple in Vṛndāvana, Śrīla Prabhupāda left this mortal world to go back to Godhead. Before he left, Śrīla Prabhupāda had expressed his desire to go to Govardhana, but his loving disciples, fearful for his health and of his imminent departure, appealed to him not to go. "First recover and become a little stronger. Then you can go." Śrīla Prabhupāda submitted to the love of his disciples. "I shall not put you in anxiety." And Śrīla Prabhupāda commented, "Just see how much affection they have for me."

Still, as Śrīla Prabhupāda's devoted servants, we wanted to fulfill his last desire to go to Govardhana Hill, so Tamal Krishna

Goswami and the other leaders arranged for a small deity of Śrīla Prabhupāda to be taken on *parikramā* to Govardhana after Śrīla Prabhupāda's disappearance.

The day before the Govardhana *parikramā* was Ekādaśī, and the devotees did Vṛndāvana *parikramā*, joining thousands of other pilgrims on the auspicious day, walking together barefoot around Vṛndavāna. As usual, I walked near Tamal Krishna Goswami and the other *sannyāsīs* who were close to Śrīla Prabhupāda. At one point, Acyutānanda turned to the others and spoke in such a way as if for me to hear. "So, when will our Giriraj take *sannyāsa*?" Because of Śrīla Prabhupāda's previous instruction to me, I had decided never to even think of the idea of *sannyāsa*, but somehow, when Acyutānanda asked his question, something within my heart inspired me to reply, "Maybe quite soon." I was surprised at myself. I looked at the faces of the others for their response and they too were taken aback. One of them said, "But Giriraj, Śrīla Prabhupāda didn't want you to take *sannyāsa*."

Later, another *sannyāsī* made the same point. "Prabhupāda didn't want you to take *sannyāsa*. Why are you so eager?" Although I had never expected the desire to take *sannyāsa* to manifest in my heart, even when the senior devotees discouraged the idea, the desire still remained.

Then one devotee approached me in confidence. "Actually, it is the tradition that when a disciple asks a *guru* for *sannyāsa*, the *guru* will refuse three times—to test the disciple." Then I understood what was happening. The *sannyāsīs* were discouraging me, not really to change my determination, but to test me. So the third time when one of the *sannyāsīs* attempted to dissuade me, I confidently upheld my determination. And somehow or other, the idea of my taking *sannyāsa* was accepted.

From Vṛndāvana, Tamal Krishna Goswami, Bhavānanda Mahārāja, and some other devotees and I went to Māyāpur for the *puṣpa-samādhi* ceremony. We carried flowers from Śrīla Prabhupāda's *samādhi* in Vṛndāvana to be placed in the earth under the site of the *puṣpa-samādhi.* Śrīla Prabhupāda had asked that the *puṣpa-samādhi* be built near the *pukkur,* or pond, where his Māyāpur house was to have been constructed.

On the way to and from Māyāpur we stopped in Calcutta. There Śrīla Prabhupāda's former family members came to meet us. One of them inquired, "Now that Prabhupāda is gone, who will speak to people about Kṛṣṇa?" Tamal Krishna Goswami looked at me and in a telling way said, "That is the question."

From Calcutta we proceeded to Bombay to prepare for the grand opening of the Śrī Śrī Rādhā-Rāsabihārī temple and international cultural center. After the grand opening in January, as Śrīla Prabhupāda had desired, we all returned to Māyāpur for the annual GBC meetings and Gaura-pūrṇimā festival. There, on the auspicious day of Gaura-pūrṇimā, His Holiness Tamal Krishna Goswami gave me my *sannyāsa daṇḍa* and name, "Giriraj Swami." The next to take *sannyāsa* was Jayādvaita. After Goswami Mahārāja gave me my *daṇḍa,* Satsvarūpa Mahārāja gave Jayādvaita his. And Tamal Krishna Goswami commented, "An era has ended. Giriraj and Jayādvaita were known as the original *brahmacārīs* in ISKCON. Now they have taken *sannyāsa.*"

As is the custom, after the ceremony I happily went from door to door, person to person, to beg donations to give to my *sannyāsa-guru.* And the devotees I approached, who had been waiting so long for me to take *sannyāsa,* were happy to give.

Initially I felt some regret that Śrīla Prabhupāda had not personally given me my *daṇḍa* and name, but I felt happy that my relationship with Goswami Mahārāja had been solidified by my accepting him as *sannyāsa-guru.*

Although Tamal Krishna Goswami Mahārāja gave me my name and *daṇḍa,* the original instruction for me to take *sannyāsa* had come from Śrīla Prabhupāda. Still, Prabhupāda's desire was fulfilled through his beloved son and my dear godbrother Tamal Krishna Goswami.

Śrīla Prabhupāda's Faith in the Holy Name

A talk by Giriraj Swami delivered at a japa *retreat in Śrīla Prabhupāda's Palace, New Vrindaban, West Virginia, on April 9, 2009.*

As we were chanting, I looked at the picture of Śrīla Prabhupāda on the wall, painted from a photograph of him from early 1967, and I thought of how he came to the Western world to give us the holy name. He did so on the order of his spiritual master, with full faith in the holy name, that if people like us would just chant the holy name everything else would follow.

Śrīla Prabhupāda had a godbrother named Akiñcana Kṛṣṇadāsa Bābājī, who Prabhupāda said was a *paramahaṁsa*, a liberated soul. I heard that Bābājī Mahārāja approached another godbrother of Prabhupāda's, who had been sent by Śrīla Bhaktisiddhānta Sarasvatī Ṭhākura to England to preach but who didn't really have much effect and then came back to India, and said to him, "You went to the West, and Swami Mahārāja [Bhaktivedanta Swami—because Śrīla Bhaktisiddhānta's disciples also refer to their *guru mahārāja* as "Śrīla Prabhupāda"] went to the West. You presented the teachings of Lord Caitanya, and Swami Mahārāja presented the teachings of Lord Caitanya. You introduced the Hare Kṛṣṇa *mahā-mantra*, and Swami Mahārāja introduced the *mahā-mantra*. But Swami Mahārāja was tremendously successful, and you hardly achieved anything. What is the reason?" Then Bābājī Mahārāja himself gave the answer: "Because Swami Mahārāja had full faith in the holy name of Kṛṣṇa, and you didn't."

This is a very powerful statement, a most significant point. Prabhupāda had full faith in the holy name, and with that conviction he came to the West, gave us the holy name, and encouraged us to chant.

Earlier, another godbrother, Dr. Oudh Bihari Lal (O. B. L.) Kapoor, initiated as Ādi Keśava dāsa, had met Prabhupāda in Mathurā. In *gṛhastha-āśrama* Śrīla Prabhupāda had been a chemist, or pharmacist. Dr. Kapoor asked him, "You are a chemist; you know many formulas. Do you know the formula for developing love of God?" Śrīla Prabhupāda answered, "Yes, I do." Dr. Kapoor replied, "Can you tell me what it is?" And Prabhupāda said, "Yes. *Tṛṇād api su-nīcena, taror iva sahiṣṇunā/ amāninā māna-dena, kīrtanīyaḥ sadā hariḥ.*" ["One should chant the holy name of the Lord in a humble state of mind, thinking oneself lower than the straw in the street; one should be more tolerant than a tree, devoid of all sense of false prestige and ready to offer all respect to others. In such a state of mind one can chant the holy name of the Lord constantly." (*Śikṣāṣṭaka* 3)] Śrīla Prabhupāda's faith in the holy name was there from the beginning. It formed the basis of his journey to the West and his service to his spiritual master and to all of us.

At Śrīla Prabhupāda's *sannyāsa* initiation ceremony in Mathurā, while the priest was conducting the fire sacrifice and reciting various *mantras*, Akiñcana Kṛṣṇadāsa Bābājī was chanting the holy name. And when there was an interlude in the ceremony, he led *kīrtana*. Bābājī Mahārāja really relished the holy name and always chanted with full absorption, tasting, savoring its nectar. When the time came to resume the ceremony with the recitation of *mantras*, the priest requested that he end the *kīrtana*. But when the priest returned to the ceremony, Prabhupada discreetly gestured to Bābājī Mahārāja, "Keep chanting. Keep chanting." Later, recounting the incident, Bābājī Mahārāja commented, "Then I knew he would be the world leader of the *Hare Kṛṣṇa* movement." Śrīla Prabhupāda had that deep faith in the holy name.

Soon after I joined the Boston temple, the devotees there faced a financial crisis. At that time the devotees didn't regularly perform *hari-nāma-saṅkīrtana* or distribute books in the streets. They just had evening programs in the temple on Mondays, Wednesdays, and Fridays, and the love feast on Sunday afternoons. Prabhupāda had said that if the devotees needed to, they could get jobs. Satsvarūpa dāsa, the temple president, was a social worker, and his paycheck from the welfare department was the only income the temple had. But as the art department grew and more devotees joined, that income became insufficient.

The devotees, who were very surrendered, had a meeting. One devotee, Patita-pāvana, said that he had worked for the post office before he joined and so he could get a job with the post office. Another said that he knew the grocer down the street and might be able to get a job in the grocery store. Devotees volunteered to help in whatever ways they could. Then one devotee, Nanda-kiśora, raised his hand. He was very humble—all the devotees were, but he was really very humble. He recalled a letter from Śrīla Prabhupāda. All of Prabhupāda's letters were taken as important documents, instructive for everyone. Whenever a letter came, all the devotees would gather round, the addressee would open and read it, and everyone would listen. So, Nanda-kiśora quoted a letter from Śrīla Prabhupāda: "If you just go on *saṅkīrtana*, all of your problems will be solved—spiritually and materially." And everyone agreed: "Yes, this is what we should do."

The next day we went out on the streets. We chanted—we didn't even have copies of *Back to Godhead* to distribute—and asked people for donations. Then we came back, counted up the *lakṣmī*, and found that we had collected seven dollars. In those days, seven dollars was something. The prospects looked promising, and we decided to try the same process the next day. So, we went out, perhaps with even more enthusiasm and conviction, came back, and counted up: twelve dollars. I thought, "This is getting good. What Prabhupāda said is true." We went out the third day, came back and counted up nineteen dollars. Then we had no doubt, and we would go out every day. What Prabhupāda had said was true: "If you chant Hare Kṛṣṇa, all your problems will be solved—materially and spiritually." He had that faith.

Eventually we moved from the small storefront at 95 Glenville Avenue to a big mansion, 40 North Beacon Street. It was the first property that ISKCON owned, that the devotees purchased. Śrīla Prabhupāda was very enthusiastic and said that the press should move from New York to Boston. The devotees began to print Prabhupāda's books, and one of the first was *Easy Journey to Other Planets*. He guided every aspect of publication, including the presentation of the books. He gave the titles and at least in this case told us what he wanted on the cover: One part was to be the material universe—outer space with different stars and planets—and the other part was to be the spiritual sky, with some Vaikuṇṭha planets, mainly Goloka Vṛndāvana with Rādhā and Kṛṣṇa. And he wanted a devotee flying through space from the material universe into the spiritual sky, with dhoti, *kurtā*, *śikhā*, and *japa-mālā*. The cover was meant to depict the theme of the book, that by *bhakti-yoga*, by chanting *japa*, one can travel beyond the material universe to the spiritual sky, to Goloka Vṛndāvana. The chanting is our ticket back to Godhead. Later, when the devotees showed Prabhupāda the cover, he was pleased and said, "Yes, by the beads." Chanting the holy name has such potency. Śrīla Prabhupāda had that faith.

Then Śrīla Prabhupāda and some disciples went to India, and there he surprised us. We began doing *hari-nāma-saṅkīrtana*, as we did in the West, but eventually Śrīla Prabhupāda stopped us. He said that we should not do street *saṅkīrtana* too much because in India beggars take to the streets and chant to solicit money, and he didn't want people to think we were beggars. He introduced the life membership program, which he said was designed to distribute his books. And he encouraged big *paṇḍāl* programs, which he called "Hare Krishna Festivals." The first was held in Bombay, and the second was to be in Calcutta. Calcutta then was under the sway of the Communist Party and a group of communist youth called Naxalites, whose program was to terrorize rich people. They would kidnap the sons of rich families and demand large ransoms. Sometimes they would just shoot rich people dead in the street. It was a terrible situation, and at that time many of the wealthier people actually left Calcutta and moved to Delhi and other places.

In this climate Śrīla Prabhupāda wanted us to organize a big *paṇḍāl*, and he sent Tamal Krishna Goswami and me from Bombay. Before the program began, Prabhupāda received a letter, "Fly or die." It sounds overdramatic, but whoever sent the note cut the letters out of the newspaper so no one could trace the typewriter, pasted them on paper, and sent it. The day before the program there was a press conference. The mood of many of the reporters was aggressive. One reporter challenged Prabhupāda, "What is this *paṇḍāl* program going to accomplish? You could spend the money to help poor people." Prabhupāda replied, "What will it accomplish? It will accomplish hearing. People will get a chance to hear." Then he said, "This whole huge arrangement has come from hearing. I went to the West and spoke, and some young people heard me, and because they heard me, now they have come and arranged this big program." Śrīla Prabhupāda, always fearless, persisted in his mission.

It was the tradition in *paṇḍāls* that most of the ground was covered with *darīs* (Indian carpets), with chairs for special guests on the side. In our *paṇḍāl* the chairs were reserved for invited VIPs, life members, and anyone who paid a rupee. So, on the first night, just as the program was beginning, a group of Naxalites raised a big ruckus: "Why do some people get to sit on chairs and other people have to sit on the ground? Everyone should sit on the ground." They were looking for an excuse to pick a fight. While Prabhupāda was on the stage with the Deities and disciples, these Naxalites began shouting and hollering, deliberately making a disturbance. Then they took some of the folding chairs we had set up and began to clap them together, to make noise and disrupt the program. The situation was really tense, because these Naxalites could do anything; they could become violent. We didn't want to provoke them further, but at the same time, unless they stopped, Śrīla Prabhupāda wouldn't be able to speak, because they were making such a commotion.

We all were looking to Prabhupāda—What would he do? Suddenly he bent forward toward the microphone, and . . . he began to sing: "*Govindam ādi-puruṣaṁ tam ahaṁ bhajāmi.*" He sang the *Govindam* prayers, and somehow the whole disturbance subsided. The young men put down the chairs and quietly left. It seemed miraculous.

The next *paṇḍāl* program was in Delhi, and there Śrīla Prabhupāda got an invitation to go to Madras. But he was planning to go to Vṛndāvana, taking his disciples there for the first time. Still, he wanted someone to go to Madras. No one wanted to go; everyone wanted to go with Prabhupāda to Vṛndāvana. Somehow I had the idea that the secret of success in Kṛṣṇa consciousness was to follow the order of the spiritual master and please him, so I volunteered.

In Madras I was alone for much of the time. I kept asking for help, but it was hard to get devotees. In any case, while I was there a song came out. In Śrīla Prabhupāda's purports he sometimes mentions cinema songs, which are the most popular in India. The refrain of this song (I don't know all the words) was "*Dam maro dam . . . Hare Kṛṣṇa Hare Rāma. Hare Kṛṣṇa Hare Rāma. Hare Kṛṣṇa Hare Rāma.*" We didn't have a center in Madras then; I was just staying with different people. Because I kept hearing the song, I finally asked my host what the translation was. I don't know if he misunderstood the actual meaning or was just being polite, but what he said was, "With every breath that I take, Hare Kṛṣṇa Hare Rāma"—which sounded very nice. So for a while we were in the illusion that that was what the song meant. Eventually we found out what it really meant: "With every puff that I take, Hare Kṛṣṇa Hare Rāma."

From Madras we went to Calcutta, and there the movie that featured this song was playing. We didn't really know what the movie was, but in those days in America whenever the musical or the movie *Hair* would show, devotees would do *hari-nāma-saṅkīrtana* in front of the theater and distribute books, because *Hair* featured a song with the full Hare Kṛṣṇa *mahā-mantra*. So we thought, "Oh, the movie *Hare Rama Hare Krishna* will be a great opportunity." So we had *hari-nāma* and distributed books outside the theater. But when most of the customers had entered the theater, I thought, "Let me steal a peek. Let me see what this movie is." So I went inside, just as it was about to begin. It was very impressive on a big screen, with loud amplifiers. The film began with shots of the ocean, the waves of the ocean on the shore. The narrator, with a deep, resonant voice, intoned, "For centuries India's spiritual culture remained within the shores of India, but one man . . ." —then it showed a picture of Śrīla Prabhupāda—"took India's spiritual culture across the ocean." Then it showed the London Ratha-yātrā, so dramatic on the big screen, and I thought, "Wow! This is amazing!" And then it showed a bunch of hippies smoking ganja and hashish and chanting Hare Kṛṣṇa Hare Rāma. They were dressed just like hippies, with boys and girls mixing. It was really bad—the theme of the movie was that Śrīla Prabhupāda was degrading the sacred Indian culture by giving it to hippies who were just misusing it, chanting Hare Kṛṣṇa Hare Rāma and smoking dope and indulging in free sex and everything else.

That was a blow. Later, Śrīla Prabhupāda said the government was behind the film, because they were afraid that our movement would become too popular and they wanted to turn people away from it. Communists in the government also started rumors that we were CIA. It was the same type of thing.

They knew we weren't CIA, but they spread rumors about us because they didn't want people to take to Kṛṣṇa consciousness. They thought that spiritual life would keep the people down. Actually, they wanted to keep the people down.

Anyway, now we come to the point—Śrīla Prabhupāda's faith in the holy name. Prabhupāda said, "In the long run the film will actually help us, because eventually people will forget the *dam maro dam* and just remember the Hare Kṛṣṇa Hare Rāma." And it came true. From Calcutta I went to Bombay, and especially the street urchins there—so many street urchins stand at corners and beg or sell magazines—whenever they saw us they would gather around us and put their hands to their mouths, as if they were smoking chillums with charas (hashish), and sing, in a mocking way, "*Dam maro dam, dam maro dam* . . ." Most of the time they wouldn't even get to the "Hare Kṛṣṇa Hare Rāma"—just "*Dam maro dam.*" It was like a plague. Wherever we went these little kids would surround us and taunt us: "*Dam maro dam.*"

It went on like that for some time, and it was difficult. Then after maybe a year of the song playing—it was extraordinarily popular—the emphasis shifted. The two parts—the "*Dam maro dam*" and the "Hare Kṛṣṇa Hare Rāma"— became equal. And eventually, just as Prabhupāda had predicted, the "*Dam maro dam*" dropped out altogether. It was a mundane sound vibration and had no real attraction. But the "Hare Kṛṣṇa Hare Rāma" was transcendental and ever fresh. After the "*Dam maro dam*" dropped out, when people saw us they would simply smile and say, "Hare Kṛṣṇa Hare Rāma." That came to pass.

Soon, Śrīla Prabhupāda took up the Juhu project. That's a whole history, but after Śrīla Prabhupāda's first stay and public program there, while he and the devotees waited in the exclusive VIP lounge at the airport before Prabhupāda's departure, there was an uproarious *kīrtana*, ecstatic chanting and dancing.

And Prabhupāda said, "If you go on having *kīrtanas* like this, our project will be successful."

Śrīla Prabhupāda named the project Hare Krishna Land. Once, he was in his room at the back of the property, and he was hearing the *kīrtana* from the small temple at the front, and he said, "This is Hare Krishna Land. We should always hear the sounds of Hare Kṛṣṇa."

Later, some devotees printed postage-style stamps (without postal value) with a picture of Rādhā-Kṛṣṇa and "Hare Kṛṣṇa," to be pasted on envelopes, and Śrīla Prabhupāda wrote me, "These two words, 'Hare Kṛṣṇa,' must appear everywhere."

Another time, Śrīla Prabhupāda was on the terrace of one of the old tenement buildings that came with the land, and a devotee named Haridāsa was fanning him. At seven o'clock Prabhupāda looked at his watch and said, "Haridāsa, do you hear the sound of *kīrtana* in the temple?" Haridāsa strained to hear but couldn't. "No, Śrīla Prabhupāda." "You don't hear *kīrtana* coming from the temple?" "No." "That is the point," Śrīla Prabhupāda said. "There is no *kīrtana* in the temple, and there should be." Then he asked Haridāsa, "Where are all the devotees?" Haridāsa ventured that they must have gone to the city to collect and had not yet returned. Prabhupāda said, "That was not my idea, that the devotees should go and collect all day and night. They may go at nine and return at five, and then chant and dance in front of the Deities. Otherwise they will become like *karmīs*."

Then he asked Haridāsa, "Do you know why we were successful and Mr. Nair wasn't? Nair was well established in Bombay, whereas we were completely new. He was very wealthy, whereas we had no money or regular income. As the owner of the *Free Press Journal*, one of three English dailies in Bombay, and the former sheriff, he knew many people and was very influential, whereas we hardly knew anyone and had practically no influence. But we were successful and he was not. Why?" Then Śrīla Prabhupāda gave the answer: "We were acting to please Kṛṣṇa, and he was acting for his personal gain. And because we tried to please Kṛṣṇa, Kṛṣṇa mercifully reciprocated and we were successful—by His grace.

"So the devotees should come and sing and dance before the Deities, for Their pleasure. By pleasing the Deities, by Their mercy, by Kṛṣṇa's mercy, we will be successful—not by our independent strength and endeavor." Śrīla Prabhupāda really had that faith in Kṛṣṇa, in the holy name, in the Deities—that if we sincerely chant to please Kṛṣṇa, Kṛṣṇa will be satisfied and we will be successful.

The last incident I shall relate came toward the end, in 1977, when Śrīla Prabhupāda was already quite ill. Śrīla Prabhupāda had a dear devotee, Sri P. L. Sethi, who was so staunch and had so much faith in Prabhupāda that his devotion for him reminded me of Hanumān's for Rāma. From before he met Prabhupāda he was associated with a group called the Radha Madhava Prema Sudha Sankirtana Mandala. Their *guru* was based in Vṛndāvana, and they chanted the Hare Kṛṣṇa *mahā-mantra*. In Bombay, they were all householders. Every Sunday they would have a twelve-hour *akhaṇḍa-hari-nāma-saṅkīrtana*, unbroken, continuous *kīrtana*, from six in the morning to six in the evening, followed by two hours of Vraja songs.

So, Mr. Sethi had the idea that instead of having the *kīrtana* in one of their devotees' homes, as they usually did, they could have it at Hare Krishna Land. So we arranged it, before the Deities in the small temple, beside the new complex that was nearing completion, just beneath Śrīla Prabhupāda's new quarters. Although the construction wasn't finished and the lift wasn't working, Śrīla Prabhupāda insisted on staying there. And ill as he was, he was listening to the *kīrtana*, reclining or lying down. These devotees in the temple really wanted to see him, but they were too many to come up, Prabhupāda was not able to come down, and anyway it would have been too taxing for him to meet them all.

At one stage they were so eager that they came out of the temple and were doing *kīrtana* beneath Śrīla Prabhupāda's balcony. Eventually Mr. Sethi helped Prabhupāda walk to the balcony. Prabhupāda glanced down upon them. They were in ecstasy. He stayed for a little while and then went back in. One highlight came at the end when a lady devotee sang, "*Jaya rādhe jaya rādhe rādhe, jaya rādhe jaya śrī rādhe. Jaya kṛṣṇa . . .*" Later, Mr. Sethi told us that when Prabhupāda was listening to that song, tears were streaming down his cheeks.

The next day, I went up to see Śrīla Prabhupāda. "That *kīrtana* was wonderful," he said. "We should invite the whole group to stay at Hare Krishna Land. Tell them that we will maintain them. They won't have to work. All they have to do is continuous *kīrtana*." I wasn't sure what to do about that—I just heard it. But I think Prabhupāda knew that that might take some time. [laughter] Then he said, "At least our devotees, they should do the twelve-hour *kīrtana* every day, from 6:00 a.m. to 6:00 p.m." Now, we had been taught by Prabhupāda that we have to serve and spread the mission, and in Juhu we were especially busy, finishing the temple and getting it ready to open. I didn't see how all the devotees could spend twelve hours a day in the temple chanting. So I said, "Śrīla Prabhupāda, we have so much service to do. How will we be able to do it all?" Then Prabhupāda said, "All right, then one day a week, on Sunday." And when Prabhupāda said that, I said, "Yes," because I felt relieved—only one day, twelve hours. Later, Tamal Krishna Goswami commented that Prabhupāda had done some transcendental bargaining. If he had begun, "Twelve hours every Sunday," I might have said, "Oh, that's too much. Maybe four hours." But because he began with twelve hours a day seven days a week, when he finally said twelve hours, one day a week, I was relieved. "Oh yes, we can do that." [laughter]

So every Sunday we did twelve hours' continuous *kīrtana*. And it was just as Prabhupāda had said—that all problems would be solved, materially and spiritually. I was the temple president and had to deal with many problems. We had to construct the temple complex, deal with the civic authorities, organize the temple programs, deal with the devotees, and just survive in India, with all the disease and other hardships. So, devotees would come to me, and on Monday, Tuesday, maybe Wednesday, I would deal with the problems. But by Thursday we were getting close to the twelve-hour *hari-nāma*, and I knew—it happened every time, without fail—all the problems would be solved. Either the problem would solve itself or the devotee would realize that the problem wasn't really a problem after all or we would get some insight into and inspiration about how to deal with it. So from Thursday I would say, "Well, just give me a few days to think about it," but I knew, "Let Sunday come—let us do the twelve-hour *kīrtana*—and it will be solved." And it happened every time. It was really wonderful.

So, by sincerely chanting Hare Kṛṣṇa, Kṛṣṇa is satisfied, and by Kṛṣṇa's pleasure and mercy, we are successful in all respects. This was Śrīla Prabhupāda's mood, his conviction. So we should give ourselves fully to that process, to pleasing Kṛṣṇa by our chanting. In fact, whatever we do should be in the mood of pleasing *guru* and Kṛṣṇa. From the beginning, I would think, "Prabhupāda is hearing my chanting, so I should chant nicely, to please him." On the Radha-Damodara party, Viṣṇujana had a large photo of Śrīla Prabhupāda's ear, and he would chant with that idea, that Prabhupāda was hearing his *japa*; he would chant to please Śrīla Prabhupāda. So it all goes together: service to *guru*, service to the holy name, chanting the holy name, pleasing Kṛṣṇa, pleasing Śrīla Prabhupāda, and being successful—materially and spiritually.

Hare Kṛṣṇa.

Śrīla Prabhupāda—Dear to Kṛṣṇa

After discussing a verse from the Bhagavad-gītā, *Chapter 12, at a Sunday program at Chowpatty, Mumbai, Giriraj Swami invited questions and comments, and a senior* brahmacārī *preacher responded:*

GAURĀṆGA DĀSA: Thank you for a wonderful class. In this same *Bhagavad-gītā* chapter, entitled "Devotional Service," in the thirteenth verse, Kṛṣṇa speaks about the qualities of pure devotees, thus establishing how pure devotional service is the highest. Could you please explain how Śrīla Prabhupāda demonstrated some of these qualities?

GIRIRAJ SWAMI: All right. We shall read from *Bhagavad-gītā As It Is*, Chapter Twelve, "Devotional Service," texts 13–14:

adveṣṭā sarva-bhūtānāṁ
maitraḥ karuṇa eva ca
nirmamo nirahaṅkāraḥ
sama-duḥkha-sukhaḥ kṣamī

santuṣṭaḥ satataṁ yogī
yatātmā dṛḍha-niścayaḥ
mayy arpita-mano-buddhir
yo mad-bhaktaḥ sa me priyaḥ

"One who is not envious but is a kind friend to all living entities, who does not think himself a proprietor and is free from false ego, who is equal in both happiness and distress, who is tolerant, always satisfied, self-controlled, and engaged in devotional service with determination, his mind and intelligence fixed on Me—such a devotee of Mine is very dear to Me."

Adveṣṭā—nonenvious. There are many examples of Śrīla

Prabhupāda's nonenvious nature, but one that comes to mind relates to a disciple of Śrīla Prabhupāda's in a country where Prabhupāda didn't spend much time. He was being accepted and worshiped like a *guru* by the other devotees there, and when some devotees informed Śrīla Prabhupāda, he said, "That's all right. If they are getting instruction and inspiration from him, it is all right if they worship him like a *guru*." Śrīla Prabhupāda wasn't envious. He wanted everyone to advance in Kṛṣṇa consciousness. That's really all he wanted—whatever would help people to advance in Kṛṣṇa consciousness. As long as in the end it wouldn't harm them, he was happy.

Sarva-bhūtānāṁ maitraḥ—friendly towards all living entities. A devotee is *suhṛdaṁ sarva-bhūtānāṁ*, "the benefactor and well-wisher of all living entities." (*Bg* 5.29) Śrīla Prabhupāda saw the soul within every body, and he didn't want to cause any pain to any living entity. We have the example of Mṛgāri the hunter, who in the jungle didn't want to even step on an ant. Although he was so eager to meet his *guru mahārāja*, he checked himself because he didn't want to step on the ants. Likewise, Śrīla Prabhupāda said that we shouldn't walk on the grass, because the grass has consciousness—the living entities in the bodies of grass—and that if somehow we can't avoid it, we should chant the holy names while walking.

Śrīla Prabhupāda wanted to deliver all living entities from the pangs of material existence. In *Śrī Caitanya-caritāmṛta*, Haridāsa Ṭhākura assured Lord Caitanya that any living entity, moving or nonmoving, who hears the holy name can be delivered. And Śrīla Prabhupāda wanted us to chant everywhere—anywhere and everywhere—loudly. He said that if we chant loudly even the ants will hear, the cockroaches will hear, the mosquitoes will hear, the trees will hear, the grass will hear—all living entities will hear and benefit.

When Śrīla Prabhupāda first came to America and was staying in an apartment in New York (before he established

ISKCON), the landlord brought an exterminator to kill all the "pests," the insects, in the building, but Śrīla Prabhupāda wouldn't let them do it in his apartment. So all the insects from the other apartments came to Śrīla Prabhupāda's, and Śrīla Prabhupāda commented, "Just see, they are taking shelter of Kṛṣṇa consciousness." He was the friend of all living entities.

Karuṇaḥ—kindly. A *sādhu*, devotee, is *kāruṇikāḥ suhṛdaḥ sarva-dehinām*, "merciful and friendly to all living entities." (*SB* 3.25.21) Śrīla Prabhupāda exhibited his kindness by preaching Kṛṣṇa consciousness. He came to the West, befriended the hippies, and made them devotees. He traveled all over the world to deliver the message of Kṛṣṇa. And he wrote books about the science of Kṛṣṇa consciousness. While the world was sleeping, he stayed awake at night to translate and comment upon Vedic literature. That was his kindness, his compassion, his mercy. He slept only two hours at night. He would take rest at about ten and awake at about twelve and translate and write. He was *karuṇa*, kind, merciful.

Nirmamaḥ—no sense of proprietorship. Although Śrīla Prabhupāda had so many temples, residences, vehicles, and other facilities, he didn't feel himself to be the proprietor. He was always detached and equal in all circumstances.

Śrīla Prabhupāda had a very staunch devotee friend named P. L. Sethi who lived near Juhu. Now, in the Juhu temple complex there are two towers, and on the top of the one facing the ocean are Śrīla Prabhupāda's quarters. They were done very nicely, with marble floors, carved-wood ceilings with chandeliers, and carved-wood furniture. Mr. Sethi was a contractor; he helped with the construction at Juhu and in many other ways. And Śrīla Prabhupāda always encouraged him to live with the devotees, but he never did. So, when Śrīla Prabhupāda's quarters were ready, he invited Mr. Sethi to see them. He showed him around, pointing out the bedroom; the drawing room, a spacious hall with facilities for meeting people, for writing, and for honoring *prasāda*; the servants' quarters; the kitchen; the foyer; and the waiting room and library—all very beautifully done. Then Śrīla Prabhupāda told Mr. Sethi, "You always said that you couldn't adjust to ashram life, so come and stay here, and I will stay somewhere else. I am a *sannyāsī*; I can stay anywhere. You stay here." That is *nirmamaḥ*, no sense of proprietorship. Whatever is there is Kṛṣṇa's and is meant to be used for Kṛṣṇa's service—no personal attachment or false proprietorship.

Nirahaṅkāraḥ—without false ego. Once, Śrīla Prabhupāda was giving a talk about *varṇāśrama-dharma*—*brāhmaṇas, kṣatriyas, vaiśyas, śūdras*—and a newspaper reporter challenged him, "You mentioned all these different orders of life; which are you in?" thinking that Śrīla Prabhupāda was implying that he was the highest. Prabhupāda paused for a moment. He didn't answer. He looked down, and with genuine humility said, "I am the lowest. I am the servant of everyone." And he meant it.

In the Vṛndāvana temple, when the devotees were originally planning to make the deities of Śrīla Prabhupāda and Śrīla Bhaktisiddhānta Sarasvatī Ṭhākura, Śrīla Prabhupāda said that his deity should show him with folded palms, offering respect to all. And he said, "I am the servant of everyone." *Nirahaṅkāraḥ*—no false ego. He considered himself *dāsa-dāsā-anudāsa*—servant of the servant of the servant of Kṛṣṇa. He even felt that he was the servant of his disciples. He felt that his *guru mahārāja* had sent him disciples to help him in his mission and that his disciples were representatives of his *guru mahārāja* and he was their servant. And he served them by training them in Kṛṣṇa consciousness and engaging them in devotional service. So, *nirahaṅkāraḥ*—no false ego.

"No false ego" doesn't mean that we merge and become one with the impersonal Brahman; "without false ego" means that we are established in our real identities as Kṛṣṇa's eternal servants (*jīvera 'svarūpa' haya—kṛṣṇera 'nitya-dāsa'*), and in particular as servants of the servants of the servants of the servants of Kṛṣṇa (*gopī-bhartuḥ pada-kamalayor dāsa-dāsānudāsaḥ*). (Cc *Madhya* 13.80) *Muktir hitvānyathā rūpaṁ sva-rūpeṇa vyavasthitiḥ*: "Liberation means being situated in one's eternal, original form after giving up the changeable gross and subtle bodies." (*SB* 2.10.6, Cc *Madhya* 24.135)

Sometimes when Śrīla Prabhupāda had to chastise disciples he felt bad. He did it as a service, but he felt bad. He said that one thing about being a spiritual master that was hard for him was that he sometimes had to chastise his disciples. He felt that they were Vaiṣṇavas and that he was their servant. But as duty he did it, following Cāṇakya Paṇḍita's maxim: *lālane bahavo doṣās tāḍane bahavo guṇāḥ/ tasmāt putraṁ ca śiṣyaṁ ca tāḍayen na tu lālayet*: "Pampering increases faulty habits, and chastisement increases good qualities. Therefore, you should always chastise your sons and disciples. Never give them lenience." So as a duty he did it, but within his heart he wasn't happy.

Sama-duḥkha-sukhaḥ—equal in happiness and distress. Śrīla Prabhupāda was always fixed in Kṛṣṇa consciousness. Sometimes he would be having a discussion in his room about some difficult problem, but when it was time to give class he would drop everything, walk into the temple room, and give the most perfect lecture. All the heavy topics from the meeting were forgotten—at least temporarily. He did what he had to do as the *ācārya*, but he was always fixed on Kṛṣṇa.

Being equal in all circumstances doesn't mean being artificially detached. When one is attached to Kṛṣṇa, he is naturally detached from *māyā*. The *Bhagavad-gītā* (14.24–25) says,

sama-duḥkha-sukhaḥ sva-sthaḥ
sama-loṣṭāśma-kāñcanaḥ
tulya-priyāpriyo dhīras
tulya-nindātma-saṁstutiḥ

mānāpamānayos tulyas
tulyo mitrāri-pakṣayoḥ
sarvārambha-parityāgī
guṇātītaḥ sa ucyate

"He who is situated in the self and regards alike happiness and distress; who looks upon a lump of earth, a stone, and a piece of gold with an equal eye; who is equal toward the desirable and the undesirable; who is steady, situated equally well in praise and blame, honor and dishonor; who treats alike both friend and enemy; and who has renounced all material activities—such a person is said to have transcended the modes of nature." Such a position is possible when one is completely dedicated to Kṛṣṇa. The Lord is *sac-cid-ānanda-vigraha*, the form of eternity, knowledge, and bliss, and when one is attached to Him, anything material—pebbles or gold—is merely dead matter. It has no importance or value to him (unless it can be used in Kṛṣṇa's service).

Santuṣṭaḥ satataṁ—always satisfied. When Śrīla Prabhupāda first stayed in Māyāpur, he lived in a thatched hut. After some time, the devotees built what he called a "marble palace"—the first temple and guesthouse—but Prabhupāda didn't want to move. He said, "This grass hut is in the mode of goodness, but modern technology is in the mode of passion. Living in a grass hut—in the mode of goodness—is more conducive for spiritual advancement." "But Śrīla Prabhupāda," the devotees protested, "if you stay in the grass hut, people won't come and hear your message. For the sake of preaching, you should move into the marble palace." Then Prabhupāda agreed.

Personally, Śrīla Prabhupāda was always satisfied. He didn't mind where he was.

Once, when some disciples were planning his travel schedule, they asked him where he would like to go and which programs he would like to accept. And Śrīla Prabhupāda replied, "I am like a cow. You can put me anywhere and I will give milk." Cows by nature are satisfied. If they just get a little grass to eat, they don't mind where they are—and they give milk, nectar. So, Śrīla Prabhupāda was satisfied.

Yata-ātmā—self-controlled. Śrīla Prabhupāda was completely self-controlled—he engaged everything in Kṛṣṇa's service. Being self-controlled doesn't mean sitting and endeavoring to control the mind and senses in an impersonal way. In a more advanced stage, it means engaging in Kṛṣṇa's service. Śrīla Prabhupāda gave the example that in a classroom if a child misbehaves, the teacher may discipline him or her by ordering, "Just stand in the corner and look at the wall. Don't say or do anything else." That kind of discipline is like the *yoga* process. People who misbehave—who cannot engage their mind and senses in devotional service—must restrain their mind and senses. "Don't look at anything, and don't say anything." But those who are more mature and behave nicely don't have to restrain their mind and senses; they naturally engage them in Kṛṣṇa's service. Śrīla Prabhupāda's self-control was that he was always engaged in Kṛṣṇa consciousness.

Dṛḍha-niścayaḥ—with determination. Śrīla Prabhupāda demonstrated his fierce determination in the great struggle to get the Juhu land and build a temple for Śrī Śrī Rādhā-Rāsabihārī. He was determined, but not for himself—for the Deities. He said that he did not care so much for the land but that because he had invited the Deities to stay there, it would be a great insult if They were driven away. Some people said, "There are so many other pieces of land; why fight so hard for this one?" But because he had invited Śrī Śrī Rādhā-Rāsabihārī, he didn't want Them to be insulted and sent away. As he later explained, he had told the Deities, "You just come and stay here, and I will build You a nice temple." And by his determined, selfless service, he was successful.

•

Mayy arpita-mano-buddhir—with mind and intelligence fixed on Kṛṣṇa. That was always there. When Śrīla Prabhupāda first came to America, he was exposed to concerts and other events with young people—hippies—who were engaged in free sex, drugs, crass music, nudity, and whatnot, but he always remained fixed in his determination to serve Kṛṣṇa and prosecute his mission. He wasn't affected by attacks on his senses, because his mind and intelligence were always fixed on Kṛṣṇa. And thus he was always in a completely pure state.

oṁ apavitraḥ pavitro vā
sarvāvasthāṁ gato 'pi vā
yaḥ smaret puṇḍarīkākṣaṁ
sa bahyābhyantara-śuciḥ

"Unpurified or purified, or even having passed through all situations, one who remembers the lotus-eyed Supreme Personality of Godhead is cleansed without and within." (*Garuḍa Purāṇa*, quoted as *Hari-bhakti-vilāsa* 3.47) Prabhupāda was always pure in any situation, because his mind and intelligence were always fixed on Kṛṣṇa, on the order of his *guru mahārāja* and Śrī Caitanya Mahāprabhu.

Even in his dreams and illness he was fixed on Kṛṣṇa and His mission, from the beginning to the end. On the ship to America, he suffered seasickness, vomiting, and two heart attacks, but he dreamed that Lord Kṛṣṇa, in His many forms, was rowing a boat and that He told him that he should not fear but should come along. Thus Śrīla Prabhupāda was reassured of Kṛṣṇa's protection. Later, in New York, Śrīla Prabhupāda told some devotees, "I dreamed that we had a boat, with twenty-five of us on board—twelve *sannyāsīs*, twelve *brahmacārīs*, and me. We went all over the world, and in each port we had *saṅkīrtana*." And toward the end, in Vṛndāvana in 1977, Śrīla Prabhupāda suddenly awoke and told the devotees attending him, "I had a dream. There was a big assembly of drunkards and chanters.

The drunkards were madmen. Some of the drunkards were becoming chanters. But the drunkards would not stop fighting. They were so crazy." Tamal Krishna Goswami asked, "Were you also there?" "Yes, I was standing there also." "Were some of the chanters becoming drunkards?" "No," said Śrīla Prabhupāda. "Chanters cannot fall down. Their names are listed—back to home, back to Godhead. They are in Kṛṣṇa's family."

Yo mad-bhaktaḥ sa me priyaḥ—such a devotee of Mine is very dear to Me. Who could be more dear to Kṛṣṇa than Śrīla Prabhupāda? He surrendered so much, sacrificed so much, served so much, preached so much, gave so much. He did what no one else ever did. He spread Kṛṣṇa consciousness all over the world. He saved people like us. And Lord Kṛṣṇa Himself says,

ya idaṁ paramaṁ guhyaṁ
mad-bhakteṣv abhidhāsyati
bhaktiṁ mayi parāṁ kṛtvā
mām evaiṣyaty asaṁśayaḥ

na ca tasmān manuṣyeṣu
kaścin me priya-kṛttamaḥ
bhavitā na ca me tasmād
anyaḥ priyataro bhuvi

"For one who explains this supreme secret to the devotees, pure devotional service is guaranteed, and at the end he will come back to Me. There is no servant in this world more dear to Me than he, nor will there ever be one more dear." (*Bg* 18.68–69)

Śrīla Prabhupāda is most dear to Kṛṣṇa, and so we surrender to him, as we pray in our *praṇāma-mantra* to him:

nama oṁ viṣṇu-pādāya
kṛṣṇa-preṣṭhāya bhū-tale
śrīmate bhaktivedānta-
svāmin iti nāmine

"I offer my respectful obeisances unto His Divine Grace A.C.

Bhaktivedanta Swami Prabhupāda, who is very dear to Lord Kṛṣṇa on this earth, having taken shelter at His lotus feet." He is very dear to Kṛṣṇa, having taken shelter of Him through *paramparā*, having taken shelter of the lotus feet of his spiritual master, who took shelter of the lotus feet of his spiritual master, and so on, all through the line, all the way back to Kṛṣṇa.

And because Śrīla Prabhupāda is so dear to Kṛṣṇa, his Kṛṣṇa consciousness movement is imbued with great potency. Anyone who sincerely follows Śrīla Prabhupāda, chanting the holy names, following the regulative principles, strictly executing the entire process of devotional service as Śrīla Prabhupāda presented it, will have the potency to attract others to Kṛṣṇa consciousness.

We are seeing it practically. So many people are being attracted. Of course, people are attracted by Śrīla Prabhupāda's books, by the holy names, by the Deities, and by the temples, but these facilities are being maintained and offered to people through Śrīla Prabhupāda's followers. By their potency and mercy, people are being attracted to and engaged in pure devotional service, Kṛṣṇa consciousness. And that potency is coming to them through disciplic succession, through Śrīla Prabhupāda's mercy. It is wonderful.

Thank you for that beautiful question, Gaurāṅga Prabhu. It was the best question anyone could have asked.

Śrīla Prabhupāda—Most Munificent

A talk by Giriraj Swami at Śrīla Prabhupāda's Vyāsa-pūjā celebration in New Dwaraka, Los Angeles, on August 14, 2009.

His Divine Grace A.C. Bhaktivedanta Swami Prabhupāda appeared in this world in Calcutta on September 1, 1896, and left in Vṛndāvana on November 14, 1977. Still, as he wrote of his spiritual master, Śrīla Bhaktisiddhānta Sarasvatī Ṭhākura, in his dedication to *Śrīmad-Bhāgavatam*: "He lives forever by his divine instructions and the follower lives with him." So although from the physical point of view Śrīla Prabhupāda is no longer with us, from the spiritual point of view he is: "He lives forever by his divine instructions." And by following his instructions, we feel his presence—we live with him.

Śrīla Bhaktivinoda Ṭhākura's inscription for the tomb of Haridāsa Ṭhākura in Jagannātha Purī states:

> He reasons ill who tells that Vaiṣṇavas die
> When thou art living still in sound.
> The Vaiṣṇavas die to live, and living try
> To spread the holy name around.

Both Śrīla Prabhupāda's dedication and Bhaktivinoda Ṭhākura's inscription tell us that the spiritual master, the Vaiṣṇava, never dies; he continues to live in sound, in his instructions (*vāṇī*), forever. And by following his instructions, by chanting the holy name, we can fulfill his purpose and live with him.

One verse that especially glorifies Śrīla Prabhupāda's merciful nature and service appears as text 9 in *Śrīmad-Bhāgavatam*, Canto Ten, Chapter Thirty-one: "The *Gopīs'* Songs of Separation." The same verse appears in the fourteenth chapter of *Śrī Caitanya-caritāmṛta's Madhya-līlā*. It is a very beautiful verse in thought and mood.

tava kathāmṛtaṁ tapta-jīvanaṁ
kavibhir īḍitaṁ kalmaṣāpaham
śravaṇa-maṅgalaṁ śrīmad ātataṁ
bhuvi gṛṇanti ye bhūri-dā janāḥ

This verse was sung by the *gopīs* after Kṛṣṇa left them during the prelude to the *rāsa* dance. They were searching the forest of Vṛndāvana for Him, and in their mood of separation they sang this song, or verse, to Him: "The nectar of Your words and the descriptions of Your activities are the life and soul of those suffering in this material world. These narrations, transmitted by learned sages, eradicate one's sinful reactions and bestow good fortune upon whoever hears them. These narrations are broadcast all over the world and are filled with spiritual power. Certainly those who spread the message of Godhead are most munificent."

During the Ratha-yātrā festival Lord Caitanya was in the mood of Śrīmatī Rādhārāṇī when She met Kṛṣṇa at Kurukṣetra and wanted to bring Him back to Vṛndāvana. And when the procession stopped to allow devotees to offer food to Lord Jagannātha, Lord Caitanya, who felt exhausted from His dancing in *saṅkīrtana*, went to a nearby garden to rest. While He was lying on a raised platform, immersed in ecstatic loving feelings, King Pratāparudra entered the garden and, taking permission from the Lord's other associates there, began to massage the Lord's lotus feet and to recite the *gopīs'* songs of separation, which was perfectly suitable for Lord Caitanya's mood.

When Lord Caitanya heard the verse describing the glories of the messages of Godhead and of those who broadcast such messages, He rose, embraced the king, and exclaimed, "*Bhūri-dā! Bhūri-dā!* You are the most munificent! You are the most munificent—because you are giving Me the nectar of *kṛṣṇa-kathā*, which is so glorious."

And that is exactly what Śrīla Prabhupāda did for us—he gave us *kṛṣṇa-kathā*. He gave us many thousands of pages and thousands of hours of *kṛṣṇa-kathā*. He is *bhūri-dā*, the most munificent personality.

Now, to get the full benefit of what Śrīla Prabhupāda came to give us and do for us, and consequently to experience the appreciation and gratitude and love that are naturally due him, we—I—must take advantage of his transcendental gifts, especially *kṛṣṇa-kathā*: first and foremost his books, and also his lectures, morning walks, room conversations, letters—all that he gave us; they are all *kṛṣṇa-kathā*.

Tava kathāmṛtaṁ. The *kathā* that Prabhupāda gave us, and that King Pratāparudra gave Lord Caitanya, is *amṛta*. *Amṛta* means "nectar," literally "that which bestows immortality." (*Mṛta* means "death," or "birth and death," and *amṛta* means "no death.") The demigods drink an *amṛta* that yields a long life of sense enjoyment, but the *amṛta* of *kṛṣṇa-kathā* gives one an eternal life full of bliss and knowledge in the company of Kṛṣṇa and all His associates, including Śrīla Prabhupāda.

Tapta-jīvanaṁ. *Kṛṣṇa-kathā* gives life to those who are aggrieved in the material world. *Tapa* means "pain," "misery," or, more literally, "heat," and thus *tapta* means "pained," "miserable," or "burning." We are all burning in the blazing fire of material existence, suffering the threefold miseries, and the spiritual master is like a raincloud that pours down water to extinguish it. The spiritual master showers the nectar of *kṛṣṇa-kathā* on the parched conditioned souls and thus delivers them from all suffering. It was said of the Six Gosvāmīs, *pāpottāpa-nikṛntanau tanu-bhṛtāṁ govinda-gānāmṛtaiḥ*: "They purified all conditioned souls from the reactions of their sinful activities by pouring upon them transcendental songs about Govinda." (*Ṣaḍ-gosvāmy-aṣṭaka* 3) And it is said of *Śrīmad-Bhāgavatam*, *tāpa-trayonmūlanam*: "It uproots the threefold miseries." (*SB* 1.1.2) Śrīla Prabhupāda has given us *kṛṣṇa-kathā*—*Śrīmad-Bhāgavatam* and the works of the Gosvāmīs—which can deliver us from material miseries and give us new life.

saṁsāra-dāvānala-līḍha-loka-
trāṇāya kāruṇya-ghanāghanatvam
prāptasya kalyāṇa-guṇārṇavasya
vande guroḥ śrī-caraṇāravindam

"The spiritual master is receiving benediction from the ocean of mercy. Just as a cloud pours water on a forest fire to extinguish it, so the spiritual master delivers the materially afflicted world by extinguishing the blazing fire of material existence. I offer my respectful obeisances unto the lotus feet of such a spiritual master." (*Gurv-aṣṭaka* 1)

Tapa also has another meaning—the fire of separation. Śrī Caitanya Mahāprabhu, and Śrīmatī Rādhārāṇī and the other *gopīs*, were burning in the fire of separation from Kṛṣṇa. Talking about Kṛṣṇa, *kṛṣṇa-kathā*, gave them life. Similarly, anyone suffering in separation from Kṛṣṇa or Śrī Caitanya Mahāprabhu or Their associates, or from Śrīla Prabhupāda or his associates, can get solace from *kṛṣṇa-kathā.*

Kavibhiḥ—"great thinkers," "sages," "poets." Śrīla Prabhupāda was a great thinker. Ravīndra Svarūpa Prabhu tells us that as a student of philosophy and religion in the university he had encountered so many philosophical and religious conceptions, but that when he discovered Śrīla Prabhupāda's books and teachings, everything else he had heard and read before was—in clarity, in depth, and in substance—like child's play compared with what Śrīla Prabhupāda gave us. And Śrīla Prabhupāda was also poetic.

Īḍitam—"described." These great thinkers, devotees, and poets, such as Śrīla Prabhupāda, describe Kṛṣṇa.

Kalmaṣāpaham. Kalmaṣa means "sinful reactions," or "material miseries," and *apaham* means "drives away," or "eradicates." Sinful reactions result in material miseries, and *kṛṣṇa-kathā*, chanting and hearing about Kṛṣṇa, brings immediate relief. We have all experienced it. The *Bhakti-rasāmṛta-sindhu* says that from the stage of *sādhana-bhakti* one experiences *kleśaghnī*, the eradication of material miseries. From the very beginning we can experience it. Engaging in *kṛṣṇa-kathā* frees us from sinful reactions and thus enables us to progress in devotional service. As Lord Kṛṣṇa says in the *Bhagavad-gītā* (7.28),

yeṣāṁ tv anta-gataṁ pāpaṁ
janānāṁ puṇya-karmaṇām
te dvandva-moha-nirmuktā
bhajante māṁ dṛḍha-vratāḥ

"Persons who have acted piously in previous lives and in this life and whose sinful actions are completely eradicated are freed from the dualities of delusion, and they engage themselves in My service with determination." Only when we are free from sinful actions and reactions can we take to devotional service with firm determination.

Śrīmat—"filled with spiritual power and opulence." The nectar of *kṛṣṇa-kathā*, according to Śrīla Viśvanātha Cakravartī Ṭhākura, bestows all wealth, up to *prema* (*prema-dhana*), and so, even if we give everything we possess to one who broadcasts (*ātatam*) the messages of Godhead, we will never be able to repay him.

Bhuvi gṛṇanti—"chanted and spread all over the world." This phrase particularly applies to Śrīla Prabhupāda, who left India, journeyed to America, and traveled all over the world to transmit these narrations, to broadcast the message of Kṛṣṇa. No one had ever done that. Śrī Caitanya Mahāprabhu had desired and predicted it, yet even learned scholars in the line of Mahāprabhu and Sarasvatī Ṭhākura could not imagine that it would come to pass. They took Mahāprabhu's statement as a poetic devotional outpouring, not as a literal prediction.

pṛthivīte āche yata nagarādi grāma
sarvatra pracāra haibe mora nāma

"In as many towns and villages as there are on the surface of the earth, My holy name will be preached." (*Caitanya-bhāgavata*, *Antya* 4.126)

Śrīla Bhaktivinoda Ṭhākura made a beginning. He sent copies of his book *Caitanya Mahāprabhu: His Life and Precepts* to some libraries in different parts of the world. And Śrīla Bhaktisiddhānta Sarasvatī Ṭhākura sent some *sannyāsīs* to preach in Europe (though without much effect). But it was Śrīla Prabhupāda who actually traveled and spread the holy name of Kṛṣṇa—*kṛṣṇa-kathā*—all over the world. He personally translated *Śrīmad Bhagavad-gītā*, *Śrīmad-Bhāgavatam*, *Śrī Caitanya-caritāmṛta*, and other Vedic scriptures into English, and he inspired his followers to translate his books into other languages and distribute them everywhere. He also said that if he could live longer he would render more Vedic texts into English, and his followers are continuing his work.

Where would we be now if he hadn't done what he did? We would probably be where we were, or even worse, burning in the blazing fire of material existence, burning in the fire of hellish sinful reactions.

Thus Śrīla Prabhupāda is *bhūri-dā*, the most munificent. Śrīla Rūpa Gosvāmī glorified Lord Caitanya as the most munificent incarnation of Godhead:

namo mahā-vadānyāya
kṛṣṇa-prema-pradāya te
kṛṣṇāya kṛṣṇa-caitanya-
nāmne gaura-tviṣe namaḥ

"Lord Śrī Kṛṣṇa Caitanya is more magnanimous than any other *avatāra*, even more than Kṛṣṇa Himself, because He is bestowing freely what no one else has ever given—pure love of Kṛṣṇa." (Cc *Madhya* 19.53) Personally, Lord Caitanya preached only in India. It was Śrīla Prabhupāda who preached throughout the world, freely distributing *kṛṣṇa-kathā*, *kṛṣṇa-nāma*, and *kṛṣṇa-prasāda*, which bring one to *kṛṣṇa-prema*.

And Śrīla Prabhupāda wanted his followers, the devotees in ISKCON—he specifically mentioned the temple presidents and zonal secretaries—to be munificent, because they are representing Lord Caitanya. We should all be munificent, benevolent. How? By spreading the message of Godhead—distributing transcendental literature and personally speaking about Kṛṣṇa.

Considering the value of what Śrīla Prabhupāda has given us, we can never repay him. Still, we should want to repay him, and act to repay him, by following in his footsteps. As Śrīla Prabhupāda wrote, "If you feel at all indebted to me, then you should preach vigorously like me. That is the proper way to repay me. Of course, no one can repay the debt to the spiritual master, but the spiritual master is very much pleased by such an attitude by the disciple."

Śrīla Prabhupāda is spiritual master—at least *śikṣā-guru*—for all of us, so we must work to repay our debt to him by following in his footsteps and preaching. And to preach, one must also practice; one must have spiritual strength. So we—I—must do both: practice and preach.

At last year's Ratha-yātrā in Los Angeles, soon after the chariots arrived at Venice Beach, I met my dear godbrother Bhārgava Prabhu, and he poured some of the nectar of *kṛṣṇa-kathā* into my ears. The atmosphere at the Ratha-yātrā was surcharged with spiritual potency and emotion and bliss, and he told a story that was most appropriate for the occasion, about the residents of Vṛndāvana going to Kurukṣetra to meet Kṛṣṇa.

Kṛṣṇa Himself was always feeling separation from the residents of Vṛndāvana. In His sleep He would call out the names of the cowherd boys, the cows, and the *gopīs*, and sometimes His pillow would be wet from the tears He had shed.

So, Kṛṣṇa thought that if He went to Kurukṣetra He might be able to meet the residents of Vṛndāvana, because Kurukṣetra, unlike Dvārakā, is not so far from Vṛndāvana. The residents of Vṛndāvana, too, were eager to meet Kṛṣṇa. And so the Vraja-vāsīs journeyed to Kurukṣetra. From the time of His youth, Kṛṣṇa had an understanding with Nanda Mahārāja that no one should ever know about their intimate relationship, because if the demons knew that He had been raised as the son of Nanda in Vraja, they would attack Vraja and do harm to the Vraja-vāsīs—to get at Kṛṣṇa.

When Nanda Mahārāja and the cowherd community reached Kurukṣetra, there were so many people and horses and chariots and elephants and tents everywhere, he couldn't see Kṛṣṇa. But he could smell Him, the divine fragrance of His transcendental body. So he followed the scent to the place from where it was emanating, and then . . . he saw Kṛṣṇa. But was it Kṛṣṇa? He knew Kṛṣṇa as his little cowherd boy. But here was a king, attired in royal garb, with so many princes and warriors, all well dressed and ornamented, offering Him praise and respect and bowing their heads at His feet. Still, Nanda wanted to approach Kṛṣṇa, but remembering their agreement, he restrained himself and retired to the camp allotted to him and the other Vraja-vāsīs.

Later, Kṛṣṇa Himself came, secretly, to meet them all. And He reciprocated their ecstatic loving feelings. It is described that Mother Yaśodā took Kṛṣṇa on her lap and with the tears from her eyes and the milk from her breast, she bathed Him. She performed an *abhiṣeka* of Kṛṣṇa with her love. Yaśodā's body is completely spiritual, composed of *prema*. Her tears are liquid *prema*. Her milk is liquid *prema*. And so she performed a loving *abhiṣeka* for Kṛṣṇa.

Then Kṛṣṇa went out to see the bulls and oxen. They were now all grown up. He went to each of them, one by one. He recalled each one's name and lovingly patted each and every one of them, saying, "Oh, So-and-so, I remember you. I remember when you were just a small bullock, and now you are all grown up, so big and strong." And He affectionately embraced each one.

And I was thinking how merciful Kṛṣṇa is, how kind He is, even to the bulls, to the animals. I remembered Śrīla Prabhupāda's words: "You have seen Kṛṣṇa's picture. He's embracing the calf also, and He's embracing Rādhārāṇī. Not that He's simply attached to Rādhārāṇī and the *gopīs*. He's attached to everyone, every living entity. Kṛṣṇa is the best friend of everyone. So if you want friendship, make friendship with Kṛṣṇa. He'll protect you, and He'll satisfy you in all respects." There is a beautiful picture in which Kṛṣṇa has His arm around a calf. Even if you are an animal (which basically I am), Kṛṣṇa has affection for you, especially if you try to serve Him. "To become an animal of Kṛṣṇa is a great fortune. It is not an ordinary thing. Any associate of Kṛṣṇa—His cowherd boyfriends or calves or cows, or the Vṛndāvana trees, plants, flowers, or water—they are all devotees of Kṛṣṇa. They serve Kṛṣṇa in different capacities. Somebody is serving Kṛṣṇa as an animal. Somebody is serving Kṛṣṇa as a tree, with fruits and flowers, as Yamunā water, or as the beautiful cowherd men and damsels, or as Kṛṣṇa's father and mother. Kṛṣṇa has so many who love Him, and He also loves them." Kṛṣṇa consciousness is so beautiful, and deep.

And then I was thinking about Bhārgava Prabhu—it was not an intellectual idea but a feeling that arose spontaneously in my heart: "You have given me the greatest gift, *kṛṣṇa-kathā*." And that is what Prabhupāda did for us. And that is what we, as his servants and followers, are meant to do for others, and for each other.

"It is called *kṛṣṇa-kathā*, topics about Kṛṣṇa. The topics, or instructions, given by Kṛṣṇa is the *Bhagavad-gītā*, and the topics about Kṛṣṇa, the activities of Kṛṣṇa, is *Śrīmad-Bhāgavatam*. So, some way or other, let us always discuss about Kṛṣṇa. That should be the life of Kṛṣṇa conscious people—to worship Kṛṣṇa in the temple; to sell Kṛṣṇa's books—*Śrīmad-Bhāgavatam*, *Bhagavad-gītā*; to think of Kṛṣṇa—Hare Kṛṣṇa, Hare Kṛṣṇa; to eat *kṛṣṇa-prasāda*; to take all risk for Kṛṣṇa; to do work for

Kṛṣṇa; or, as Arjuna, to fight for Kṛṣṇa. Arjuna did not want to fight, but for Kṛṣṇa's sake he fought. So fight for Kṛṣṇa, work for Kṛṣṇa, think of Kṛṣṇa, eat *kṛṣṇa-prasāda*, talk of Kṛṣṇa, read of Kṛṣṇa. So, Kṛṣṇa, Kṛṣṇa, Kṛṣṇa, Kṛṣṇa, Kṛṣṇa. This is life. This is Kṛṣṇa consciousness. This is a very glorified life." (SP lecture, June 26, 1974)

For *kṛṣṇa-kathā*, for the holy name of Kṛṣṇa, for the beautiful life of Kṛṣṇa consciousness, and for his boundless, causeless mercy, I owe my life to Śrīla Prabhupāda, eternally.

Śrīla Prabhupāda *ki jaya!*

8

Kṛṣṇa and His Devotees

The Mystery of Lord Kṛṣṇa's Birth

Many residents of Mathurā believe that Lord Kṛṣṇa appeared in Mathurā, but the residents of Vṛndāvana know that He was born in Vraja, in Gokula. Yet somehow *Śrīmad-Bhāgavatam* states that Lord Kṛṣṇa appeared in the prison house of Kaṁsa in Mathurā as the son of Vasudeva and Devakī and thereafter was carried by Vasudeva to Gokula to be taken as their son by Nanda and Yaśodā, in exchange for Yaśodā's newborn daughter, Yogamāyā. How to solve this mystery?

Let us turn to *Śrīmad-Bhāgavatam* and look more closely. At the beginning of Canto Ten, Chapter Five, we find *nandas tv ātmaja utpanne jātāhlādo mahā-manāḥ*: "When Lord Śrī Kṛṣṇa appeared as his son, Nanda Mahārāja was overwhelmed with jubilation." And *āhūya viprān veda-jñān snātaḥ śucir alaṅkṛtaḥ/ vācayitvā svastyayanaṁ jāta-karmātmajasya vai*: "Then Nanda Mahārāja arranged to have the Vedic birth ceremony [*jāta-karma*] celebrated for his newborn child." (*SB* 10.5.1–2)

"The *jāta-karma* ceremony can take place when the umbilical cord, connecting the child and the placenta, is cut. However, since Kṛṣṇa was brought by Vasudeva to the house of Nanda Mahārāja, where was the chance for this to happen? Here Śrīla Viśvanātha Cakravartī Ṭhākura and other authorities cite evidence from various *śāstras* that Kṛṣṇa actually took birth as the son of Yaśodā before the birth of Yogamāyā, who is therefore described as the Lord's younger sister." (*SB* 10.5.1–2 purport)

Yogamāyā is described as *adṛśyatānujā viṣṇoḥ*, "the younger sister of Lord Viṣṇu." (*SB* 10.4.9) As Yogamāyā was born from Yaśodā in Vraja, so Lord Kṛṣṇa must have been too. Therefore Śrīla Prabhupāda comments that "When Viṣṇu, or Kṛṣṇa, took birth from Devakī in Mathurā, He must have simultaneously taken birth from Yaśodā in Vraja also. Otherwise how could Yogamāyā have been *anujā,* the Lord's younger sister?"

Śrīla Prabhupāda writes further: "Śrīla Viśvanātha Cakravartī Ṭhākura discusses that Kṛṣṇa appeared simultaneously as the son of Devakī and as the son of Yaśodā, along with the spiritual energy Yogamāyā. As the son of Devakī, He first appeared as Viṣṇu, and because Vasudeva was not in the position of pure affection for Kṛṣṇa, Vasudeva worshiped his son as Lord Viṣṇu. Yaśodā, however, pleased her son Kṛṣṇa without understanding His Godhood. This is the difference between Kṛṣṇa as the son of Yaśodā and as the son of Devakī. This is explained by Viśvanātha Cakravartī Ṭhākura on the authority of *Harivaṁśa.*" (*SB* 10.3.47 purport)

The Viṣṇu who appeared in Mathurā is Vāsudeva Kṛṣṇa, fully grown with four hands and long hair and so many ornaments and symbols of Viṣṇu. The Kṛṣṇa who took birth in Vraja is the original Kṛṣṇa with two hands. When Vasudeva and Devakī prayed to Viṣṇu as the Supreme Personality of Godhead to become like a human baby, the original Kṛṣṇa immediately came to Mathurā from Gokula and absorbed the four-handed Vāsudeva into Himself. Later, when Kaṁsa tried to kill Yogamāyā, she slipped upward, assumed the form of the goddess Durgā, and clearly told him, "The Supreme Personality of Godhead, who has been your enemy from the very beginning and will certainly kill you, has already taken His birth somewhere else." (*SB* 10.4.12)

Further evidence that Kṛṣṇa took birth in Vraja comes later in the Tenth Canto in the "Songs of the *Gopīs,*" where Śukadeva Gosvāmī completely forgets himself. Śukadeva Gosvāmī wanted to encourage Mahārāja Parīkṣit that Kṛṣṇa was the son of Vasudeva, because Vasudeva was Kuntī's brother and Kuntī was Arjuna's mother and Parīkṣit's great-grandmother. Thus, to please Mahārāja Parīkṣit, Śukadeva Gosvāmī tried to suppress the fact that Kṛṣṇa actually took birth as the son of Yaśodā in

Vraja. But in the ecstasy of the *gopīs* in separation from Kṛṣṇa, he forgot himself and cried, *jayati te 'dhikaṁ janmanā vrajaḥ*: "O beloved Kṛṣṇa, Your birth in the land of Vraja has made it exceedingly glorious, and thus Indirā, the goddess of fortune, always resides here. It is only for Your sake that we, Your devoted servants, maintain our lives. We have been searching everywhere for You, so please show Yourself to us." (*SB* 10.31.1) Thus the truth came out. By closely studying the texts of *Śrīmad-Bhāgavatam* under the guidance of Śrīla Prabhupāda and other *ācāryas*, the mystery is solved.

Lord Brahmā, the first *guru* in the disciplic succession, confirms what the other authorities have stated. In his prayers to Lord Kṛṣṇa he addresses Him as the son of the king of the cowherds (*paśupāṅgajāya*), the son of Mahārāja Nanda. "O son of the king of the cowherds, Your transcendental body is dark blue like a new cloud, Your garment is brilliant like lightning, and the beauty of Your face is enhanced by Your *guñjā* earrings and the peacock feather on Your head." (*SB* 10.14.1)

Similarly, Śrī Caitanya Mahāprabhu, in His *Śikṣāṣṭaka* (5), also addresses Kṛṣṇa as the son of Mahārāja Nanda. He refers to Kṛṣṇa as *nanda-tanuja*, literally, born (*ja*) from the body (*tanu*) of Nanda, as He prays, "O My Lord, O son of Mahārāja Nanda [Kṛṣṇa], I am Your eternal servant."

At the end of the last chapter of the Tenth Canto, Śukadeva Gosvāmī refers to Kṛṣṇa as *devakī-janma-vādaḥ*, "known as the son of Devakī." In *Kṛṣṇa*, Śrīla Prabhupāda explains, "The devotees understand that actually Kṛṣṇa was the son of Mother Yaśodā. Although Kṛṣṇa first of all appeared as the son of Devakī, He immediately transferred Himself to the lap of Mother Yaśodā, and His childhood pastimes were blissfully enjoyed by Mother Yaśodā and Nanda Mahārāja. This fact was also admitted by Vasudeva himself when he met Nanda Mahārāja and Yaśodā at Kurukṣetra. He admitted that Kṛṣṇa and Balarāma were actually the sons of Mother Yaśodā and Nanda Mahārāja." Kṛṣṇa is *devakī-janma-vādaḥ* because although He is *known* as the son of Devakī, actually He is not. Factually, He is the son of Mother Yaśodā—or, He is the all-pervading Supersoul, the Supreme Personality of Godhead, who has no mother or father.

In any case, we should never think that Lord Kṛṣṇa was conceived or born like an ordinary human being. He is always transcendental and supreme, and He manifests Himself by His internal potency. Because He wanted to appear like a cowherd boy, His internal potency arranged His apparent birth in Vraja. Otherwise the Lord is unborn and eternal, with no beginning and no end. But just as Brahmā is described as the father of Varāhadeva since Lord Kṛṣṇa appeared as Varāha from the nostril of Lord Brahmā, so Nanda and Yaśodā are known to be the father and mother of Kṛṣṇa when He appears in His original form in Vraja.

In conclusion, we cite one verse from the *Bhakti-rasāmṛta-sindhu*:

kṛṣṇasya pūrṇatamatā
vyaktābhūd gokulāntare
pūrṇatā pūrṇataratā
dvārakā-mathurādiṣu

"Lord Kṛṣṇa is perfect in Dvārakā, more perfect in Mathurā, and most perfect in Vṛndāvana." (*Brs* 2.1.223) Thus we prefer to worship Kṛṣṇa in Vṛndāvana, from beginning to end.

Perfect Question, Perfect Answer

At the opening of a new center of the International Society for Krishna Consciousness in Pune, India, Giriraj Swami addressed a well-attended gathering at the city's main hall, Nehru Memorial. In the audience was Lt. General T. S. Oberoi, in charge of the Southern Command of the Indian Army. (The Southern Command is the largest command in India and covers eight states.) After hearing Giriraj Swami speak, General Oberoi rose and humbly asked a question:

General Oberoi: Your Holiness, I know you are short of time, but may I ask you a question?

Giriraj Swami: Oh, yes.

General Oberoi: There has been a personal conflict in my mind as to what is the aim for which we are born, what is the aim of our life. It certainly could not be the aim to amass some wealth and ultimately die, or to make a building and then die, or to marry and procreate and then die.

For our minor activities in life we have the aims set first, before we get going to achieve them. When we train our people in the army, whatever they have to do we first tell them what is the aim. And once they are clear what is the aim, then we decide what means we have to adopt to achieve that. And invariably we don't go wrong.

Now here it is—my whole life is going to waste, to my mind; I am still not very clear what is the aim of my life. A lot of people have been benefited by this great movement [ISKCON], by chanting, but I still feel that this is all the means to the end. But only once you are very clear what the aim is can you decide whether chanting is the only answer. Would you kindly, Your Holiness, enlighten us about the aim of life so that thereafter we can be very, very clear as to what we have got to do to achieve that aim?

GIRIRAJ SWAMI: Your question is glorious, because it deals with the Absolute Truth and is therefore beneficial for everyone. This same question was asked by Śrīla Sanātana Gosvāmī to Śrī Caitanya Mahāprabhu. Sanātana Gosvāmī had been a very highly placed government servant—prime minister to the Nawab Hussain Shah—but he resigned from his government service to join the mission of Śrī Caitanya Mahāprabhu.

When Sanātana Gosvāmī met Lord Caitanya at Prayag (Allahabad), he said to Him, "My Lord, people praise me that I am a very great man, a very learned scholar, but actually I am a great fool. And I'm such a fool that when they say I am learned, I believe them, even though I do not know even who I am or what is the purpose of my life. So can you please enlighten me as to my actual identity and the ultimate goal of life?" In reply, Lord Caitanya explained that the living entity is the eternal servant of Lord Śrī Kṛṣṇa (*jīvera 'svarūpa' haya-kṛṣṇera 'nitya-dāsa'*) and that the ultimate goal of life is to develop love for Kṛṣṇa (*premā pum-artho mahān*).

As spiritual souls, we are part and parcel of God. And the natural function of the part is to serve the whole. The hand is part of the body, so its natural function is to serve the body. If the hand is not serving the body, it is diseased or dead. In the same way, our natural function is to serve God. And if we are not serving Him, it is to be understood that we are in a diseased condition, that we are spiritually dead. By constitution, we must serve God.

Now, how to serve God? If we understand we are eternal servants of God, or Kṛṣṇa, we have to act in our constitutional position. In other words, in addition to theoretical understanding, we have to engage in the practical activity of serving Kṛṣṇa. So how to serve Kṛṣṇa?

Lord Caitanya has instructed that the highest standard of

service to the Lord is that of the *gopīs* of Vṛndāvana. How is that? Once Lord Kṛṣṇa said that He had a headache and that the only thing that could cure Him would be dust from the feet of His devotee. So His messenger went and announced that Kṛṣṇa had a headache and that He could be cured only by the dust from His devotee's feet. He approached many, but everyone said, "Oh, if the dust from my feet touches the head of the Lord, it will be a great offense. I will go to hell. I'm not going to give dust from my feet for the Lord's head." So the messenger became very discouraged. But Kṛṣṇa advised him, "Now you go to Vṛndāvana and see what happens there."

The messenger went to Vṛndāvana, and immediately all the *gopīs* surrounded him. "Oh, you've come from Lord Kṛṣṇa! How is our Lord? Please tell us, how is He doing?"

The messenger replied, "The Lord has a headache."

"Oh, no! The Lord has a headache. Oh, no! What can we do?"

"The only thing that will cure Him is the dust from His devotee's feet."

Immediately they replied, "Oh, yes, yes! Take it, take it all. Take as much as you want. Take everything."

The messenger said, "Don't you know that you could go to hell for this?"

"We don't care if we go to hell, as long as Kṛṣṇa's headache is cured."

This is love—pure, selfless love of God. And this should be the aim of life. And, as recommended in scripture and by great authorities like Caitanya Mahāprabhu, this love can be achieved simply by sincerely chanting the holy names of the Lord: Hare Kṛṣṇa, Hare Kṛṣṇa, Kṛṣṇa Kṛṣṇa, Hare Hare/ Hare Rāma, Hare Rāma, Rāma Rāma, Hare Hare.

General Oberoi: I thank you, Your Holiness. You have answered my question.

The Mercy of the Devotee

bhajanty abhajato ye vai
karuṇāḥ pitarau yathā
dharmo nirapavādo 'tra
sauhṛdaṁ ca su-madhyamāḥ

"My dear slender-waisted *gopīs*, some people are genuinely merciful or, like parents, naturally affectionate. Such persons, who devotedly serve even those who fail to reciprocate with them, are following the true, faultless path of religion, and they are the true well-wishers." (*SB* 10.32.18)

On the full-moon night of the *śarat* season, Kṛṣṇa played His flute and called the *gopīs* to meet Him. He received them nicely and began to reciprocate with them. Then suddenly He disappeared, and they became mad in separation. They began to address the trees and creepers, "Have you seen Kṛṣṇa? Where is He?" In their transcendental delirium they began to play like Kṛṣṇa and enact His pastimes. Thus they wandered all over the Vṛndāvana forest in search of Him, but still they could not find Him. Finally they decided to return to the bank of the Yamunā where first they had met, and there, in *saṅkīrtana*, to sing out and cry for His mercy.

When Krsna heard the songs of the *gopīs*, His heart melted, and He returned to them. They felt as if their lives had returned to their bodies. But even though they were ecstatic to see Kṛṣṇa again, they also harbored some anger toward Him, thinking that although they had left everything to serve and please Him, He had not reciprocated. Being as intelligent and tactful as they were, however, they did not accuse Him directly. Rather, they wanted Him to admit His fault with His own words. So they asked, "Some people reciprocate the affection only of those who are affectionate toward them, while others show affection even to those who are indifferent or inimical. And yet others will not show affection toward anyone. Dear Kṛṣṇa, please properly explain this matter to us." (*SB* 10.32.16)

Kṛṣṇa replied, "So-called friends who show affection for each other only to benefit themselves are actually selfish. They have no true friendship, nor are they following the true principles of religion. Indeed, if they did not expect benefit for themselves, they would not reciprocate." (*SB* 10.32.17)

In the next verse, quoted at the beginning, Lord Kṛṣṇa mentions two categories of persons who serve others whether the beneficiaries of their service reciprocate or not: those who are merciful and those who are affectionate like parents. And who are in the category of merciful? The devotees of the Lord—and they are the best.

In *varṇāśrama-dharma* fathers and mothers should raise their children without any self-interest. If they serve their children without any expectation of return, they follow the true path of religion. Yet even this performance of *dharma* cannot compare with the mercy of pure devotees.

Parents are affectionate with their children due to their natural relation. And sometimes elders shower affection on children who are not their own, as if they *were* their own. But Vaiṣṇavas are always merciful, even to those to whom they are not related—more merciful and affectionate than even one's own parents. A mother or father may have some self-interest in mind for the future, but the *guru* has no self-interest at all.

Prahlāda Mahārāja is a perfect example of a merciful Vaiṣṇava. He did not want anything from Kṛṣṇa, nor did he want anything from anyone else. He wanted only to help others, to bring them to Kṛṣṇa. When Lord Nṛsiṁhadeva asked Prahlāda to accept some benediction, Prahlāda refused. And even though Hiraṇyakaśipu had tried to kill him, Prahlāda prayed for his deliverance (as well as for the deliverance of all living entities). Thus, although devotees and parents are mentioned together here, the quality of the devotee's love is more exalted.

Whether one loves the *guru* or Vaiṣṇava or not, the *guru* or Vaiṣṇava will love him or her. Of course, such a *guru* or Vaiṣṇava must be qualified and advanced in Kṛṣṇa consciousness. A Vaiṣṇava is happy in the happiness of others, and sorry in the sorrow of others. If his disciple is unhappy, he also feels unhappy. If his disciple is happy, he feels happy.

A father or mother might kill a son or daughter. (We sometimes see such instances reported in the news.) But no *guru* or Vaiṣṇava will do so. Even if someone tries to kill or harm a Vaiṣṇava—of course, the Vaiṣṇava cannot actually be harmed, because he is a pure devotee, protected by Kṛṣṇa—still he will try to give that person *bhakti*. Jagāi and Mādhāi wanted to kill Nityānanda Prabhu, but He gave them *kṛṣṇa-prema*. A prostitute came to denigrate Haridāsa Ṭhākura, but he gave her *kṛṣṇa-prema*. The *guru* is always most merciful.

The *guru* will always be merciful to his disciple, even if the disciple tries to kill him. The disciple is ignorant, but the *guru* knows that the soul is eternal. Vālmīki wanted to kill Nārada, but Nārada said, "Stop!" and he stopped. He was struck with wonder that "I have killed so many persons in the past, and no one could stop me, but just by his word, 'Stop!' I was stopped." Thus Vālmīki developed faith in Nārada, and Nārada instructed him to chant *mara mara mara*, *rama rama rama*, and he delivered him. Although Vālmīki wanted to kill Nārada, still Nārada gave him mercy.

The *guru* will never reject a disciple because the disciple is sinful. Even if the disciple is offensive, when the *guru* sees that the disciple has rendered so much service, he will not leave him. He is so kind. He will not leave any sincere disciple, even if the disciple falls down into sinful activities. Rather, he will come back to him in the next life, or life after life, for hundreds of lives, until the disciple is delivered. We see in the *Bṛhad-bhāgavatāmṛta* how the *guru* of Gopa Kumāra came to him again and again over thousands and millions of years.

Sometimes the reciprocation is not seen. For example, a father may leave his children at home with their mother to go to a distant place to earn money. Every month he sends money for the maintenance of the children, but the children do not see that. They see only that their mother is taking care of them, feeding them, dressing them, sending them to school, and buying schoolbooks and other things. The father's reciprocation is not seen.

Similarly, one may not see the reciprocation of the *guru*. The *guru* may seem very strict and grave, as if he does not love the disciples or students. But actually he loves them more than anyone, and he is serving them and reciprocating with them as no one else can.

Sometimes also the motives of the person may not be seen. For example, a father and mother apparently serve their children even though the children do not serve them, but the parents may be thinking that in the future, in their old age, their children will serve them and take care of them.

Now, one may think that in a similar way the *guru* trains his disciples so that in the future they will continue his mission. But what is his mission? Only to bring the fallen souls to Kṛṣṇa and to please the higher authorities. So in fact the *guru* has no personal self-interest.

In this world, even the purest relationships between parents and children, husbands and wives, and brothers and sisters are tinged with self-interest. Even if they do not want anything else, family members may want affection. Because we have our material senses and mind, we have some self-interest.

In principle, the relationship between *guru* and disciple is pure. But if the disciple and *guru* are not sufficiently pure or advanced in Kṛṣṇa consciousness, there may be some self-interest. Only pure devotees detached from *māyā* can be without self-interest. And the sincere servants of such pure devotees will try to act without self-interest. They will observe their own activities and motives and try to be free from personal interest.

The *gopīs* have no self-interest. They do not want anything from Kṛṣṇa.

āśliṣya vā pāda-ratāṁ pinaṣṭu mām
adarṣanān marma-hatāṁ karotu vā
yathā tathā vā vidadhātu lampaṭo
mat-prāṇa-nāthas tu sa eva nāparaḥ

"Let Kṛṣṇa tightly embrace this maidservant, who has fallen at His lotus feet, or let Him trample Me or break My heart by never being visible to Me. He . . . can do whatever He likes, but He is still the worshipable Lord of My heart." (*Śikṣāṣṭaka* 8)

Thus Kṛṣṇa addresses the *gopīs* as *su-madhyama*. *Su* means "excellent," or "fine," and *madhyama* means "middle," or "waist." By addressing them "My dear slender-waisted *gopīs*," He is also telling them, "Your middle question is the best, and you yourselves are the best example of selfless, pure love. Even though I cannot reciprocate, still you love and serve Me."

Thus Kṛṣṇa concludes:

na pāraye 'haṁ niravadya-saṁyujāṁ
sva-sādhu-kṛtyaṁ vibudhāyuṣāpi vaḥ
yā mābhajan durjara-geha-śṛnkhalāḥ
saṁvṛścya tad vaḥ pratiyātu sādhunā

"I am not able to repay My debt for your spotless service, even within a lifetime of Brahmā. Your connection with Me is beyond reproach. You have worshiped Me, cutting off all domestic ties, which are difficult to break. Therefore please let your own glorious deeds be your compensation." (*SB* 10.32.22)

Kṛṣṇa admitted that he could not reciprocate the *gopīs*' love for Him. But He wanted to experience that love. And so He appeared again, in the present age, as Śrī Kṛṣṇa Caitanya, Gaurahari, with the mood and golden complexion of the *gopīs*, to further glorify them and try to repay His debt to them—and extend their mercy to all of us.

The Glories of Govardhan Hill, The Best Servant of Lord Hari

hantāyam adrir abalā hari-dāsa-varyo
yad rāma-kṛṣṇa-caraṇa-sparaśa-pramodaḥ
mānaṁ tanoti saha-go-gaṇayos tayor yat
pānīya-sūyavasa-kandara-kandamūlaiḥ

"Of all the devotees, this Govardhana Hill is the best! O my friends, this hill supplies Kṛṣṇa and Balarāma, as well as Their calves, cows, and cowherd friends, with all kinds of necessities—water for drinking, very soft grass, caves, fruits, flowers, and vegetables. In this way the hill offers respect to the Lord. Being touched by the lotus feet of Kṛṣṇa and Balarāma, Govardhana Hill appears very jubilant."

—*Śrīmad-Bhāgavatam* 10.21.18

In *Śrīmad-Bhāgavatam*, Śukadeva Gosvāmī describes the activities of Kṛṣṇa and Balarāma throughout the seasons. He describes Their pastimes in the summer season, in the rainy season, and, in the present verse, in autumn. Whenever Kṛṣṇa and Balarāma entered the forest, the *gopīs*, the cowherd girls, would think of Kṛṣṇa's pastimes and glorify them. Although the *gopīs* were at home discussing among themselves, because of transcendental vision and deep attachment for Kṛṣṇa they would speak as if they were with Kṛṣṇa in the forest or at Govardhana Hill.

In this verse the *gopīs* speak with great joy. *Hanta* is an expression of joy. They say, *ayam adrir*: "this hill." If something is very near, we say "this." Although the *gopīs* were far from Govardhana Hill, they felt as if they were nearby. So they say, *ayam adrir*, "this hill," *hari-dāsa-varyo*, is "the best among the servants of Hari, or Kṛṣṇa."

We are also trying to become servants of Lord Hari. And how to serve Hari nicely can be learned from Govardhana Hill.

In *Śrīmad-Bhāgavatam*, Tenth Canto, other devotees have been called *hari-dāsa,* servants of Hari. Mahārāja Yudhiṣṭhira is described as *hari-dāsa* because he performed the *rājasūya* sacrifice to glorify Lord Kṛṣṇa. Many sages and saintly persons, and many kings and other world leaders, came, not just to see Lord Kṛṣṇa but also to see Mahārāja Yudhiṣṭhira and the Pāṇḍavas. Because of the Pāṇḍavas' love for Kṛṣṇa, Kṛṣṇa regularly used to visit their home. Devotees are prepared to go to any length to meet Kṛṣṇa, but the Lord Himself used to come to visit the Pāṇḍavas. And He used to act as their friend, their master, their servant, and their advisor in so many ways.

So Mahārāja Yudhiṣṭhira is called *hari-dāsa.* And not only he and his brothers served Lord Kṛṣṇa, but their wife, their mother, and all of their citizens were fully engaged in the service of the Lord. So Lord Kṛṣṇa was very pleased with them, and Śukadeva Gosvāmī, in ecstasy, appreciating Mahārāja Yudhiṣṭhira and the Pāṇḍavas, speaks of them as *hari-dāsa.*

Another *hari-dāsa* mentioned in the Tenth Canto is Uddhava. Uddhava was the cousin of Lord Kṛṣṇa and very near and dear to Him. Among all the associates of Kṛṣṇa in Dvārakā, Uddhava was the constant companion of the Lord, discussing with Him, even advising Him, and serving Him always. Uddhava was so close to Kṛṣṇa and so qualified that when Kṛṣṇa thought of delivering a message to Vṛndāvana, He sent Uddhava as His representative. Thus Uddhava stayed in Vṛndāvana for several months, reminding its residents of Kṛṣṇa and His pastimes. So Śukadeva Gosvāmī also called Uddhava *hari-dāsa.* And there are many other *hari-dāsas*, such as Nārada.

Still, Govardhana Hill is called *hari-dāsa-varyo*, the best of the servants of the Lord. Why is he considered the best? *Rāma-kṛṣṇa-caraṇa-sparaśa-pramodaḥ. Pramodaḥ* means "jubilant, exceedingly joyful." When a servant engages in the service of the master, the servant should feel joy. And by his service the master should feel joy. Both should feel joy. When the servant sees that the master is feeling joy, the servant's joy increases. And when the master sees that the servant is feeling joy, the master's joy increases. So there is competition between the master and the servant, each trying to give more pleasure to the other. And by giving pleasure to the other, each feels more pleasure himself.

If a servant does not feel joy but rather complains—"Oh, I have been serving my master, but I have had no time to take *prasāda*; I feel so hungry. And I have had no time to get sufficient rest; I feel so tired"—he is not the best servant of his master. The best servant of any master will feel joy in any condition—like Govardhana Hill.

Sometimes the question is raised, How could the whole of Vraja fit under Govardhana Hill when Govardhana Hill is only part of Vraja? The *ācāryas*, previous spiritual masters, have answered that Govardhana Hill felt so much ecstasy in being lifted by Kṛṣṇa that he expanded in size. And what was his service then? He had to shelter the Vraja-vāsīs from the fierce winds, thunderbolts, and torrential rain and hail sent by Indra. But he never felt any distress—"Oh, I am being attacked by hail, rain, thunderbolts, and fierce winds." No. He was jubilant because of being touched by Kṛṣṇa's little finger and being engaged in service to Kṛṣṇa and Kṛṣṇa's devotees. In every condition he felt jubilant to be engaged in their service, especially being touched by the lotus feet of Balarāma and Kṛṣṇa (*rāma-kṛṣṇa-carana-sparaśa*), or Rādhā and Kṛṣṇa.

Govardhana Hill is also the best servant of Lord Hari because he gives his whole body for the service of Hari and His devotees. They walk all over his body. If anyone—even our master—were to walk on our body, we might not feel jubilant.

But Govardhana Hill, offering his own body for the service of the Lord, as a platform on which the Lord could enjoy pastimes with His devotees, felt jubilant. And Govardhana Hill would offer respects (*mānaṁ tanoti*) not only to Kṛṣṇa but to the cows and calves and cowherd boys (*saha-go-gaṇayos tayor*). *Go* means "cows and calves," and *gaṇayos* means "cowherd boys" or all those connected with the cows, including the *gopīs*. In other words, Govardhana Hill didn't want to serve only Kṛṣṇa, or only Kṛṣṇa and Balarāma. He wanted to serve Them along with Their devotees—not only the cowherd boys and girls but even the cows and calves. He wanted to serve them all.

We should learn from Govardhana Hill that we can please the Lord better by serving the Lord's devotees than by trying to serve the Lord directly. In his book *Kṛṣṇa*, Śrīla Prabhupāda comments on this verse. He says that Govardhana Hill knew the secret of how to please the Lord by pleasing His most beloved associates. Govardhana Hill gave his body and everything else for the service of not only the Lord personally but of the Lord's servants as well. That is how he gave them respect.

How did Govardhana Hill serve the Lord and His servants? *Pānīya*—by supplying fresh drinking water, especially from his waterfalls. And Kṛṣṇa and the cowherd boys and calves would also wash their hands and feet in Govardhana's water, as well as drink it. *Sūyavasa*: "very soft grass." Some of the grasses from Govardhana were used to perform sacrifices, and other grasses, especially soft, fragrant grasses, were used to feed the cows so they would be strong and healthy and give nice milk. *Kandara*: "caves." Sometimes, when it was very hot, Kṛṣṇa and Balarāma, or Kṛṣṇa and the *gopīs*, would take shelter in Govardhana's caves and feel cool. And if it was too cold, they would take shelter in the caves to feel warm. *Kanda-mūlaiḥ*: "by roots." The cows and the boys would eat roots from the hill, as well as fruits, vegetables, flowers, and other items. And when Kṛṣṇa and Balarāma walked on Govardhana, he would melt in ecstatic love and his stones would become soft like butter, giving pleasure to the feet of the Lords. And Govardhana would create natural thrones where Kṛṣṇa would sit and enjoy pastimes.

How did Govardhana show his joy? His tall grasses were his bodily hairs standing up in ecstasy, the water trickling through his stones was his ecstatic perspiration, and his gushing waterfalls were his tears of love. Everything of Govardhana is eternal, full of knowledge, and full of bliss.

Although Kṛṣṇa once revealed that He Himself is Govardhana Hill, here we see the *gopīs* appreciating Govardhana as the best of Kṛṣṇa's servants, not as Kṛṣṇa. Why? The *gopīs* are in the mood of separation. They want to meet and serve Kṛṣṇa. They have not yet directly met Him, but by seeing Him or hearing about Him they have become attached to Him. So the *gopīs* are thinking, "One can fulfill one's desires only by the mercy of great souls. Who are great souls? The servants of Lord Hari. And Govardhana Hill is the best of them. So we should go to Govardhana, and by his mercy all our desires will be fulfilled; we will be able to meet and serve Kṛṣṇa."

Because the *gopīs* were under the protection of their elders and other relatives, they had no chance to meet Kṛṣṇa. So they thought, "We will tell our elders that we want to go to Mānasī-gaṅgā to bathe and then take audience of Harideva." Śrī Harideva, Kṛṣṇa in the form of Lord Nārāyaṇa, is the presiding Deity of Govardhana Hill. But actually the mercy one can get from *hari-dāsa*, the Lord's servant, is greater than the mercy one can get from Harideva, the Lord. So on the pretext of going to Govardhana Hill to worship Harideva, they went to get the mercy of Govardhana himself, the best of Hari's servants, to be able to meet Kṛṣṇa.

All scriptures advise that we should serve great souls and get their mercy. From the First Canto of *Śrīmad-Bhāgavatam* (*syān mahat-sevayā*) to the Fifth Canto (*mahat-sevāṁ dvāram āhur vimuktes*) and throughout, as well as from other scriptures and authorities, we know that by serving great souls—pure devotees—we can get the greatest mercy and the greatest benefit. And of all the devotees, Govardhana Hill is the best. So if we go to Govardhana and get his mercy, we will get the greatest mercy that anyone can get, and our desire to meet and serve Rādhā and Kṛṣṇa will be fulfilled.

Now, devotees have asked which statement is correct—that Govardhana is Kṛṣṇa's devotee, or that he is Kṛṣṇa directly. Actually, both are correct. During the Govardhana-pūjā, Kṛṣṇa expanded Himself into a huge form and declared, "I am Govardhana Hill." So in fact, He is Govardhana Hill. But the *gopīs* worshiped Govardhana Hill as the best devotee of Kṛṣṇa, *hari-dāsa-varyo.* So both ways of seeing are valid. But I think the mercy we can get from the devotee of Kṛṣṇa is more than the mercy we can get from Kṛṣṇa directly. By following the *gopīs* we can benefit more.

In a similar way, we see that Gaura, Kṛṣṇa Caitanya, is also Kṛṣṇa, but that as Kṛṣṇa He did not give *prema*, love of Godhead, as He did as Gaura. As Gaurahari He was more merciful, because He was in the mood of Hari's servant. If we aspire to serve Hari's servant, we can benefit more than if we try to serve Hari directly. Gaurahari aspired to be *gopī-bhartuḥ pada-kamalayor dāsa-dāsānudāsaḥ*—a servant of the servant of the servant of the lotus feet of Śrī Kṛṣṇa, the maintainer of the *gopīs*. And approaching Govardhana Hill, His ambition was fulfilled. *Śrī Caitanya-caritāmṛta* (*Antya* 14.104–111) describes:

> When Śrī Caitanya Mahāprabhu saw all the Vaiṣṇavas, He returned to partial external consciousness and spoke to Svarūpa Dāmodara. Śrī Caitanya Mahāprabhu said, "Who has brought Me here from Govardhana Hill? I was seeing Lord Kṛṣṇa's pastimes, but now I cannot

> see them. Today I went from here to Govardhana Hill to find out if Kṛṣṇa was tending His cows there. I saw Lord Kṛṣṇa climbing Govardhana Hill and playing His flute, surrounded by grazing cows. Hearing the vibration of Kṛṣṇa's flute, Śrīmatī Rādhārāṇī and all Her *gopī* friends came there to meet Him. They were all very nicely dressed. When Kṛṣṇa and Śrīmatī Rādhārāṇī entered a cave together, the other *gopīs* asked Me to pick some flowers.
>
> "Just then, all of you made a tumultuous sound and carried Me from there to this place. Why have you brought Me here, causing Me unnecessary pain? I had a chance to see Kṛṣṇa's pastimes, but I could not see them."

If we approach Govardhana Hill following in the line of Śrī Caitanya Mahāprabhu, we may also get the mercy to become a servant of the servant of the best of Lord Hari's servants. And so we pray to Govardhana, "Please fulfill our desires."

Conclusion

Conclusion: Watering the Seed

By the mercy of the spiritual master and Kṛṣṇa, one gets the seed of devotional service, and by their mercy the seed grows into a full-fledged creeper that carries the disciple to Kṛṣṇa and the spiritual world:

upajiyā bāḍe latā 'brahmāṇḍa' bhedi' yāya
'virajā,' 'brahma-loka' bhedi' 'para-vyoma' pāya

"As one waters the *bhakti-latā-bīja*, the seed sprouts, and the creeper gradually increases to the point where it penetrates the walls of this universe and goes beyond the Virajā River between the spiritual world and the material world. It attains *brahma-loka*, the Brahman effulgence, and, penetrating through that stratum, it reaches the spiritual sky and the spiritual planet Goloka Vṛndāvana." (Cc *Madhya* 19.153)

The mercy of the spiritual master carries the disciple from the material world to the spiritual world where he (or she), under the eternal guidance of the spiritual master, attains direct loving service to Śrī Śrī Rādhā-Kṛṣṇa and Their associates in Śrī Vṛndāvana.

Thus we glorify the spiritual master:

nāma-śreṣṭhaṁ manum api śacī-putram atra svarūpaṁ
rūpaṁ tasyāgrajam uru-purīṁ māthurīṁ goṣṭhavāṭīm
rādhā-kuṇḍaṁ giri-varam aho rādhikā-mādhavāśāṁ
prāpto yasya prathita-kṛpayā śrī-guruṁ taṁ nato 'smi

"I bow down to the beautiful lotus feet of my spiritual master, by whose causeless mercy I have obtained the supreme holy name, the divine *mantra*, the service of the son of Śacīmātā, the association of Śrīla Svarūpa Dāmodara Gosvāmī, Rūpa Gosvāmī, and his older brother Sanātana Gosvāmī, the supreme abode of Mathurā, the blissful abode of Vṛndāvana, the divine Rādhā-kuṇḍa and Govardhana Hill, and the desire within my heart for the loving service of Śrī Rādhikā and Mādhava in Vṛndāvana." (Raghunātha dāsa Gosvāmī, *Muktā-carita*)

And even if we have not yet attained what the spiritual master has come to give, still we have hope that some day we may.

All glories to Śrīla Prabhupāda!

Epilogue

On Separation from Śrīla Prabhupāda

We will never be separated from Śrīla Prabhupāda if we sincerely desire to have his association. He is ready and waiting. Any time we turn to him, he is there—to guide us and help us. Mainly he is there to give us instruction in service—and to chastise us if we disobey. But we should never go away.

We always have that choice, but leaving him would be the greatest loss, complete disaster. It is better to accept chastisement and try to improve, difficult as it may seem, and win his favor again, rather than try to run and hide, avoiding or, still worse, trying to forget.

Of course, Śrīla Prabhupāda loves us even when he chastises us. In fact, his chastisement is proof that he loves us, cares for us, and wants us to improve and become good devotees of Kṛṣṇa.

And if we follow his instructions, he is very pleased, very easily pleased, and he reciprocally blesses us, encouraging us and giving us further direction.

We should never become puffed up or complacent, however, thinking that because Śrīla Prabhupāda is reciprocating with us he is favoring us or that we are perfect. Far from it. Śrīla Prabhupāda is helping us out of his causeless mercy. We have no other qualification whatsoever. Our only hope is Śrīla Prabhupāda's causeless mercy—that's all. So if we become proud, thinking that we are special or Śrīla Prabhupāda's favorite, Śrīla Prabhupāda is not pleased. He may by his mercy arrange some difficulty to humble us, so we come crawling back to his shelter.

Overall, Śrīla Prabhupāda is a perfect person. He is wonderful. And as we approach him, he reciprocates. And he is very personal—even humorous at times—as well as very kind and compassionate. If we make mistakes, he forgives us. He is always ready to forgive and give us another chance to serve him. And when we follow his instructions, he is pleased. He reciprocates by giving us more service.

So my advice to everyone—and this advice is directed more toward my mind than toward anyone else—is to always remember Śrīla Prabhupāda and never forget him. He is always there. He is our father, our best friend, and our very life.

Appendixes

Glossary

Abhimanyu 1. The heroic son of Arjuna and Subhadrā.
2. The shadow of Kṛṣṇa in *vraja-līlā* who serves as the cowherd husband of Śrīmatī Rādhārāṇī.

Absolute Truth The ultimate source of all that exists.

ācārya One who teaches by personal example. *Ācāryas* in the pure Vaiṣṇava line instruct people and initiate them into the Supreme Lord's devotional service.

A.C. Bhaktivedanta Swami Prabhupāda The founder-*ācārya* of ISKCON and foremost preacher of Kṛṣṇa consciousness in the Western world.

Advaita Ācārya An incarnation of Lord Mahā-viṣṇu, who appeared as one of the Pañca-tattva. See *Pañca-tattva.*

Ajāmila A *brāhmaṇa* whose attraction to a prostitute led him into sinful life but who was saved on his deathbed by helplessly crying for his son Nārāyaṇa, thus unintentionally chanting the Lord's holy name.

Ajita The Supreme Lord who is unconquerable.

akiñcanā One who has no material possessions or attachments.

Ambarīṣa A saintly Vaiṣṇava king famous for using all his resources and bodily activities in devotional service to the Supreme Lord. Angered by a minor accidental fault of the king's, the sage Durvāsā tried to kill him, but Lord Viṣṇu sent the Sudarśana disc to attack Durvāsā, who finally had to beg the king's forgiveness.

ānanda Bliss, happiness.

anātha "Without a fitting master"; one who is not protected.

anujā "Born after." Can refer to a younger sister or brother.

ārati A standard ceremony of worship with offerings of lamps, fans, incense, flowers, water, and other items, similar to the custom of welcoming a guest into one's home, especially at night (*ā-rātrikam*).

arcanaṁ The process of Deity worship.

Ardha-kumbha-melā "Half Kumbha-melā"; a spiritual fair held at Prayāga six years after each full Kumbha-melā. It is smaller than the full *melā* yet attended by millions of people. See *Kumbha-melā.*

Arjuna The third of the five Pāṇḍava brothers, an intimate friend and devotee of Kṛṣṇa, and a great warrior. Kṛṣṇa spoke the *Bhagavad-gītā* to him just before the Battle of Kurukṣetra, which he was instrumental in winning, with Kṛṣṇa as his chariot driver.

āsana 1. Seat, throne.
2. Posture assumed in *yoga* practice.

āśrama 1. The hermitage of a sage or teacher.
2. In the *varṇāśrama* social system, the four spiritual orders of life: *brahmacārī* (celibate student), *gṛhastha* (householder), *vānaprastha* (retired), and *sannyāsa* (renounced).

aṣṭa-kālīya-līlā Kṛṣṇa's eightfold daily pastimes.

aṣṭāṅga-yoga The eightfold system of mystic *yoga* practice taught by the sage Patañjali in his *Yoga-sūtras*, ultimately meant for realizing the Lord in the heart, the Paramātmā feature of Godhead.

asura A demon, one who opposes the demigods and service to the Lord.

ātmā The individual spirit soul, an eternal fragment of the Supreme Personality of Godhead.

ātma-nivedanam The devotional process of offering Kṛṣṇa everything, including one's body, mind, intelligence, and whatever one possesses.

avatāra "One who descends," a manifestation of the Supreme Lord in the material world.

bābājī A renounced person fully dedicated to hearing and chanting about Kṛṣṇa and residing in Vraja, Gauḍa-maṇḍala, or any other holy place. *Bābājīs* are beyond the *varnāśrama* system.

Balarāma (Baladeva, Balabhadra) Kṛṣṇa's first plenary expansion, who appears in *kṛṣṇa-līlā* as Kṛṣṇa's elder brother, the son of Vasudeva and Rohiṇī.

Bali King of the Daityas (demons), son of Virocana, and grandson of the great Vaiṣṇava Prahlāda. When Lord Vāmana tricked Bali into donating three paces of land and then with two steps covered the universe, Bali achieved perfection by surrendering his very self to the Lord.

Bhagavad-gītā "The Song of God," the book in which the Supreme Lord, Kṛṣṇa, explains the science of *yoga*, giving essential teachings on progressive spiritual life and pure devotion to God, spoken five thousand years ago to His friend Arjuna moments before the great battle at Kurukṣetra. Vyāsadeva included the *Bhagavad-gītā* in the *Bhīṣma-parva* section of the *Mahābhārata*.

bhāgavata A person or narration related to Bhagavān, especially a devotee of the Lord, or the scripture *Śrīmad-Bhāgavatam*.

bhāgavata-dharma The ultimate system of self-realization, which teaches pure devotion to the Supreme Lord; the religious principles enunciated by the Lord; the eternal function of the living being, devotional service to the Supreme Lord.

bhāgavata-śravaṇa Hearing *Śrīmad-Bhāgavatam.*

bhajana 1. Loving devotional service to the Supreme Lord. 2. A devotional song in glorification of the Lord.

bhakta A devotee of the Supreme Lord.

bhakti Devotional service to the Supreme Lord. *Bhakti* in practice is the prime means of achieving spiritual success, and perfected *bhakti,* pure love of God, is the ultimate goal of life.

bhakti-latā-bīja The seed of devotional service.

Bhakti-rasāmṛta-sindhu Literally, "The Ocean of the Pure Nectar of Devotional Service," Rūpa Gosvāmī's textbook on the principles and cultivation of devotional service (*bhakti*), both in practice and in perfection.

Bhaktisiddhānta Sarasvatī Ṭhākura An *ācārya* in the Brahma-Madhva-Gauḍīya Vaiṣṇava *sampradāya,* the founder-*ācārya* of the Gauḍīya-maṭha, and the spiritual master of His Divine Grace A.C. Bhaktivedanta Swami Prabhupāda.

Bhaktivinoda Ṭhākura An *ācārya* in the Brahma-Madhva-Gauḍīya Vaiṣṇava *sampradāya,* the spiritual master of Gaurakiśora dāsa Bābājī, and the father and first spiritual instructor of Bhaktisiddhānta Sarasvatī Ṭhākura.

bhakti-yoga The spiritual process of linking to the Supreme Lord through pure devotional service.

Bhārata-varṣa The planet earth, named after Bharata the son of Ṛṣabhadeva. In a more restricted sense, greater India.

bhāva-bhakti The stage of devotional service after *sādhana-bhakti* and before *prema-bhakti*; the preliminary stage of love of Godhead.

Bhīṣma (-deva) The son of Śāntanu and Gaṅgā. He is one of the Twelve Mahājanas, great authorities on Vedic knowledge. As the elder of the Kuru warriors, he led Duryodhana's forces in battle until he was felled by the arrows of Arjuna. He passed away gloriously at his own chosen moment in the presence of Kṛṣṇa.

bhoga Material sense enjoyment; or, food before it has been offered to the Deity.

bhoga-tyāga Position of alternating sense enjoyment and renunciation.

bhukti Material enjoyment.

bhūri-dā Most munificent.

bīja Seed.

Brahmā The first finite living being in the material creation. He was born from the lotus growing from the navel of Garbhodakaśāyī Viṣṇu. At the beginning of creation, and again at the start of each day of his life, Brahmā engineers the appearance of all the species and the planets on which they reside. He is the first teacher of the *Vedas* and the final material authority to whom the demigods resort when belabored by their opponents.

brahmacārī In the *varṇāśrama* system, a celibate student in the first phase of spiritual life, receiving education at the ashram of a spiritual master.

Brahman 1. The impersonal, all-pervasive aspect of the Supreme Truth.
2. The transcendental sound of the *Vedas* (*śabda-brahman*).

brāhmaṇa (brahmin) A member of the intellectual class, which consists mainly of teachers and priests and is one of the four occupational divisions in the *varṇāśrama* social system.

Brahma-sampradāya One of the four authorized lines of devotees of the Lord, descending directly from the Supreme Lord through Brahmā.

Bṛhad-bhāgavatāmṛta A book written by Sanātana Gosvāmī that deals with the subject of devotees, devotional service, and Kṛṣṇa. It presents the essence of the message of *Śrīmad-Bhāgavatam*.

Brijbāsīs See *Vraja-vāsīs*.

Buddha An empowered incarnation of Kṛṣṇa whose mission was to stop the misuse of the *Vedas*, especially with regard to the performance of animal sacrifices, by promoting the principle of nonviolence (*ahiṁsā*).

Caitanya-bhāgavata A detailed account of the life and precepts of Lord Caitanya, by Vṛndāvana dāsa Ṭhākura.

Caitanya-caritāmṛta A major work on Caitanya Mahāprabhu's life and teachings, by Kṛṣṇadāsa Kavirāja Gosvāmī.

Caitanya Mahāprabhu The original Supreme Personality of Godhead, Kṛṣṇa, acting in the guise of His own devotee. He advented Himself in 1486 at Māyāpur, West Bengal, and introduced *saṅkīrtana*, the congregational chanting of the holy names, as the *yuga-dharma* for the present age. He propounded the sublime philosophy of *acintya-bhedābheda-tattva*, the inconceivable simultaneous oneness and difference between the Lord and His energies, and taught the pure worship of Rādhā and Kṛṣṇa.

Cāṇakya Paṇḍita A prominent *brāhmaṇa* advisor to King Candragupta, famous for his aphorisms on politics and morality.

caṇḍāla A member of the most degraded class of men, an outcaste.

chāṭāi Palm frond.

Dāmodara Kṛṣṇa, who was "bound at the waist (*udara*) with rope (*dāma*)" by Mother Yaśodā as a punishment for stealing butter.

daṇḍa 1. A rod.

2. The sixtieth part of a twenty-four hour period. According to Vedic calculation, the whole day and night is divided into sixty parts, called *daṇḍas*.

daṇḍavat Prostrated obeisances.

darīs Large carpets of coarse cotton fabric.

dāsya (-bhāva, -rasa) The mellow of servitude, one of the five direct devotional relationships with the Supreme Lord.

deity An authorized worshipable form of God or of a demigod or other devotee. The Lord and His devotees manifest themselves in such forms, which may be made of stone, wood, metal, earth, paint or ink, sand (drawn upon the ground), or jewels, or conceived of in the mind.

demigods Pious finite living beings endowed with the intelligence and influence necessary to administrate the material universe on behalf of the Supreme Lord. Lesser demigods reside in Svarga, and their king is Indra. They govern under the direction of higher demigods, who reside on higher planets.

Devakī The wife of Vasudeva and mother of Kṛṣṇa in Mathurā.

dhāma A domain where the Supreme Lord personally resides and enjoys eternal pastimes with His loving devotees.

dharma Religious principles, or, more properly, an individual's duty; also, the inseparable and distinctive nature of a thing, like the heat of fire or the sweetness of sugar or, in the case of the living entity, the innate desire and capacity to serve.

dhoti A long cloth, traditionally worn by Indian men, that covers the lower half of the body.

Dhruva A son of Uttānapāda, grandson of Svāyambhuva Manu, and great-grandson of Lord Brahmā. Insulted by his stepmother, Dhruva left home at the age of five, and after six months of severe austerities he achieved perfection. Lord Vāsudeva (Viṣṇu) gave Dhruva his own spiritual planet, called Dhruvaloka, or the polestar, at the top of the universe.

duḥkha Grief, sorrow.

Durgā Lord Śiva's eternal consort. She has many names and forms and joins Lord Śiva in his incarnations. She is the "superintendant of the prison house" of the material world.

Duryodhana The eldest son of Dhṛtarāṣṭra and chief rival of the Pāṇḍavas. He made many attempts to cheat the Pāṇḍavas of their right to the Kuru throne. After defying the good advice of Bhīṣma, Droṇa, and Kṛṣṇa he perished with his ninety-nine brothers in the Battle of Kurukṣetra.

Dvaipāyana Vyāsa The empowered compiler of the *Vedas*. A different *vyāsa*, "editor," appears at the end of each Dvāpara age, when understanding of the *Vedas* becomes helplessly confused. The current Vyāsa, Kṛṣṇa Dvaipāyana, is an incarnation of the Supreme Lord. The *Vedānta-sūtra* and *Mahābhārata* are his personal compositions, and the culmination of his literary effort is *Śrīmad-Bhāgavatam*.

Dvāpara (-yuga) The third of four repeating ages (*yugas*) of universal time. During its 864,000 years, the mode of passion becomes dominant, and temple worship is the recommended process for God realization. The latest Dvāpara-yuga ended about five thousand years ago, after the departure of Lord Kṛṣṇa.

Dvārakā The eternal abode in which Kṛṣṇa fully displays the royal opulence of God. While on earth, Kṛṣṇa resettled the entire population of Mathurā in the city of Dvārakā, which He manifested on the ocean, near the coast of the Ānarta province (Gujarat).

Ekādaśī The spiritually auspicious eleventh day after the full moon and the new moon, meant for increasing one's devotion to Lord Hari, Kṛṣṇa, by fasting from at least grains and beans and increasing one's devotional activities, especially the chanting of the Hare Kṛṣṇa *mahā-mantra*.

Gaṇeśa The first son of Lord Śiva and Pārvatī. He has the head of an elephant and removes obstacles for those who worship him.

Gaṅgā (-devī) The Ganges, the great sacred river that flows from the peaks of the Himalayas to the Bay of Bengal. Due to contact with the toe of Lord Viṣṇu, the supreme pure, she purifies and delivers from sin anyone who comes in contact with her waters.

Ganges See *Gaṅgā*.

Garbhodaka Ocean The body of water that fills the bottom part of each material universe.

Garbhodakaśāyī Viṣṇu The second of the three Puruṣas.

Garuḍa Purāṇa One of the eighteen major *Purāṇas*, which deals prominently with death and the transmigration of the soul.

Gauḍīya Maṭha The Kṛṣṇa conscious institution founded by Bhaktisiddhānta Sarasvatī Ṭhākura.

Gauḍīya-sampradāya A branch of the Brahma-Madhva-sampradāya founded by Śrī Caitanya Mahāprabhu for inundating the world with pure devotion to Rādhā and Kṛṣṇa.

Gauḍīya Vaiṣṇavas Followers of Lord Caitanya.

Gaurahari Śrī Caitanya Mahāprabhu, the Golden Avatāra, the combined form of Rādhā and Kṛṣṇa.

Gaurakiśora dāsa Bābājī The spiritual master of Bhaktisiddhānta Sarasvatī Ṭhākura.

Gaurāṅga Lord Caitanya, who has a golden (*gaura*) body (*aṅga*—limbs).

Gaura-Nitāi Lord Caitanya (Gaura) and Lord Nityānanda (Nitāi).

Gaura-pūrṇimā The appearance day of Lord Caitanya.

Giridhārī Kṛṣṇa, the lifter of Govardhana Hill.

Gītā See *Bhagavad-gītā*.

Gītā Jayantī The celebration of the appearance of the *Bhagavad-gītā*.

Godhead The Absolute Truth, the Supreme Reality, progressively realized initially as the impersonal, all-pervasive oneness; more fully as the Supersoul within the heart of every living being; and ultimately as the all-opulent Supreme Person.

Gokula The place (*kula*) of cows (*go*). The first home of the infants Kṛṣṇa and Balarāma in Vraja, before Nanda's cowherds moved to Nanda-grāma. It is situated in the Mahāvana forest, on the eastern shore of the Yamunā, seven miles south of Mathurā City. The name Gokula is also sometimes used to distinguish Kṛṣṇa's abode on earth from Goloka in the spiritual world.

Goloka The planet (*loka*) of cows (*go*). The eternal abode of the Supreme Lord in His original form of Kṛṣṇa. It is situated above all the other Vaikuṇṭha planets and has three sections: Vṛndāvana, Mathurā, and Dvārakā. There is also a heavenly Goloka in the material world.

Gopa Kumāra The hero of *Śrī Bṛhad-bhāgavatāmṛta*.

Gopāla Bhaṭṭa Gosvāmī One of the Six Gosvāmīs of Vṛndāvana, who assisted Sanātana Gosvāmī in his writing.

gopīs Cowherd girls or women, especially Kṛṣṇa's young girlfriends in Vraja, who are His most intimate devotees.

gosvāmī One who controls his mind and senses. When capitalized, it may be a title of one in the renounced order of life or it may refer specifically to any of the Six Gosvāmīs of Vṛndāvana.

Govardhana A large hill situated fifteen miles west of Mathurā City. Kṛṣṇa lifted it and for seven days held it aloft as a huge umbrella to protect the residents of Vraja from a devastating storm caused by the jealous Indra. Also, the main village alongside the hill.

Govardhana-pūjā The worship of Govardhana Hill, inaugurated by Kṛṣṇa to replace the Vraja-vāsīs' yearly ritual sacrifice to Indra, which now includes offering small mountains of food and circumambulating the hill or its replica.

Govinda Kṛṣṇa, the Lord who gives pleasure to the cows, the earth, and everyone's senses.

Govinda-līlāmṛta An esoteric book by Śrīla Kṛṣṇadāsa Kavirāja Gosvāmī.

gṛhastha A member of the household order of life, the second stage in the *varṇāśrama* system.

gulābjāmuns Golden ghee-fried milk balls soaked in sugar syrup.

guṇas The three modes, or controlling principles, of material creation—*sattva* (goodness), *rajas* (passion), and *tamas* (ignorance).

guru A teacher or spiritual master.

guru-dakṣiṇā A disciple's gift to his spiritual master.

gurukula "The *guru's* family"; a teacher's ashram or school where traditional education is given.

Guru Mahārāja Form of address for one's spiritual master.

Gurv-aṣṭaka A prayer of eight verses by Viśvanātha Cakravartī Ṭhākura in glorification of the spiritual master.

haṁsa Swan.

Hanumān Lord Rāmacandra's faithful eternal servant, who has the body of a *kimpuruṣa*, a humanlike monkey. The son of Añjanā, he was minister to Sugrīva in the monkey kingdom of Kiṣkindha.

Hare Kṛṣṇa mantra A sixteen-word prayer composed of the names Hare, Kṛṣṇa, and Rāma—Hare Kṛṣṇa, Hare Kṛṣṇa, Kṛṣṇa Kṛṣṇa, Hare Hare/ Hare Rāma, Hare Rāma, Rāma Rāma, Hare Hare. *Hare*, the personal form of God's own happiness, His eternal consort, Śrīmatī Rādhārāṇī; *Kṛṣṇa*, "the all-attractive one"; and *Rāma*, "the all-pleasing one," are names of God. The purport of the prayer is "My dear Rādhārāṇī and Kṛṣṇa, please engage me in Your devotional service." The *Vedas* recommend the chanting of the Hare Kṛṣṇa *mantra* as the easiest and most sublime method for awakening one's dormant love of God. These names have been particularly recommended as the great chant for deliverance in this age.

Hari The Supreme Lord, Kṛṣṇa, or Viṣṇu, who takes away His devotees' material attachments and miseries.

hari-dāsa "Kṛṣṇa's servant," an epithet for anyone who serves Kṛṣṇa.

Haridāsa Ṭhākura A great devotee of Śrī Caitanya Mahāprabhu, he is known as the *nāmācārya*, the master who taught the chanting of the holy names by precept and by his own example.

hari-dāsa-varyaḥ The best among the Lord's servants: Govardhana Hill.

Harideva The Supreme Lord, who removes obstacles to spiritual progress; the Deity of the Supreme Lord Nārāyaṇa who presides at Govardhana Hill.

hari-nāma The holy name of Kṛṣṇa.

Hari-vaṁśa The appendix to the *Mahābhārata*; compiled by Dvaipāyana Vyāsa, it is a summary of Kṛṣṇa's pastimes.

Himalayas The tallest mountains on earth, partially in what is now northern India, described as the residence of sages, demigods, and incarnations such as Lord Śiva, Nara-Nārāyaṇa, and Vyāsadeva.

Hiraṇyakaśipu One of the first great demons in the universe. He and his demonic brother Hiraṇyākṣa were doorkeepers of Vaikuṇṭha but were cursed when they refused entry to the four Kumāra sages. Hiraṇyakaśipu's son Prahlāda was a fully surrendered devotee of Viṣṇu. For persecuting Prahlāda, Hiraṇyakaśipu was killed by Lord Nṛsiṁha.

Hiraṇyākṣa The older brother of Hiraṇyakaśipu. When Hiraṇyākṣa tried to obstruct Lord Varāha from lifting the earth from the depths of the Garbha Ocean, the Lord killed him.

impersonalists A class of transcendentalists who believe that the ultimate reality is impersonal and desire to become one with it.

Indra (Mahendra) The king of the demigods and ruler of Svargaloka. In each *manvantara* there is a different Indra. The name of the current Indra is Purandara.

Īśopaniṣad The briefest and one of the most important of the *Upaniṣads*.

Jagāi and Mādhāi Two debauchees who were converted into Vaiṣṇavas by Nityānanda Prabhu's mercy. In their original identities they are Jaya and Vijaya.

Jagannātha "Lord of the universe," Kṛṣṇa; specifically, an ancient deity of Kṛṣṇa installed along with deities of His brother Balarāma and sister Subhadrā in the holy city of Purī on the coast of Orissa, where He was worshiped by Śrī Caitanya Mahāprabhu.

Jagannātha Purī See *Purī*.

Janmāṣṭamī The celebration of Kṛṣṇa's appearance in this world.

japa Chanting of a *mantra* quietly to oneself.

japa-mālā String of one hundred and eight beads used to chant a *mantra*.

jāta-karma Ritual Vedic birth ceremony in which the umbilical cord is severed.

Jīva Gosvāmī One of the Six Gosvāmīs of Vṛndāvana and the greatest scholar in the Gauḍīya-sampradāya. His most important works are the *Ṣaṭ-sandarbha* and *Gopāla-campū*.

jñāna-yoga The spiritual discipline of cultivating knowledge of pure spirit.

jñānī A practitioner of *jñāna-yoga*, or, more generally, any learned person.

jyotir-liṅga Any of the twelve self-manifested *śiva-liṅgas*.

kadamba *Anthocephalus indicus*, a tree whose fragrant flowers appear as yellow-green balls.

Kali (-yuga) "Quarrel"; the fourth of four repeating ages (*yugas*) of universal time. In each Kali-yuga the world degrades into hypocrisy, dishonesty, and conflict. The present Kali-yuga began 5,000 years ago and will continue for another 427,000 years. Kali is also the name of the ruler of the Age of Quarrel.

Kāliya The many-headed serpent who poisoned a lake within the Yamunā and was then subdued by Kṛṣṇa, who danced on his hoods and then banished him from Vraja.

Kaṁsa The king of Bhoja and son of Ugrasena who usurped the throne of Mathurā. After sending many demons to Vraja to kill Kṛṣṇa and Balarāma, he finally brought the two brothers to Mathurā to be killed in a wrestling tournament, but Kṛṣṇa killed him instead.

karatālas Hand cymbals used in *kīrtana*.

karma Work; material action and its reactions.

karma-yoga The process of achieving God realization by dedicating the fruits of one's work to God.

karmī A fruitive worker; in Vedic culture, one whose aim is to achieve material elevation by acting dutifully, especially by performing Vedic sacrifices.

Kārtika The Vedic month corresponding to October–November, in which Lord Dāmodara is worshiped.

kāruṇikāḥ Merciful.

Kauravas (Kurus) The descendants of the ancient king Kuru. They ruled in north-central India. Five thousand years ago, at the time of the schism between the sons of the two brothers Pāṇḍu and Dhṛtarāṣṭra, which led to a fratricidal war over the throne of Hastināpura, the names Kuru and Kaurava referred specifically to the party of Duryodhana, the son of Dhṛtarāṣṭra.

kīrtana Glorification of the Supreme Lord; narrating or singing the names and glories of the Supreme Personality of Godhead, the primary devotional practice in the present Age of Kali.

kṛpaṇa A miser, one who wastes his life by not striving for spiritual realization.

Kṛṣṇa The original Supreme Personality of Godhead, who enjoys as a youthful cowherd with His family and friends in Vṛndāvana and later as a heroic prince in Mathurā and Dvārakā.

kṛṣṇa-bhakti Devotion to Kṛṣṇa.

Kṛṣṇa consciousness Awareness of one's eternal relationship with the Supreme Personality of Godhead; the process that enables one to return to the spiritual world; Śrīla Prabhupāda's condensed rendering of Rūpa Gosvāmī's Sanskrit phrase *kṛṣṇa-bhakti-rasa-bhāvitā matiḥ*, "to be absorbed in the mellows of executing devotional service to Kṛṣṇa."

kṛṣṇa-kathā Discussion of Kṛṣṇa.

kṛṣṇa-līlā Kṛṣṇa's pastimes.

kṛṣṇa-prasāda See *prasāda* and *mahā-prasāda*.

kṛṣṇa-prema Pure love for Kṛṣṇa, which is the perfection of life.

kṣatriya A member of the second of the four occupational classes in the *varṇāśrama* social system. The *kṣatriyas* are the political and military leaders of society. They are expected to be heroic, charitable, selflessly dedicated to the welfare of all citizens, submissive to the spiritual authority of the *brāhmaṇas*, and ready to use force to stop wrongdoing.

Kumbhakarṇa One of Rāvaṇa's brothers, a mighty demon with an insatiable appetite, who slept six months of the year. When Rāvaṇa needed help to meet the attack of Lord Rāmacandra's army, Kumbhakarṇa was awakened with great difficulty, and ultimately killed by Lord Rāma.

Kumbha-melā A spiritual fair (*melā*) held every twelve years at a place where millions of years ago drops from the pot (*kumbha*) of nectar churned by the demigods and demons fell. From all over India, millions of pilgrims and saintly persons seeking spiritual upliftment gather at the Trivenī—the confluence of the three holy rivers Ganges, Yamunā, and Sarasvatī—at Prayāga, near the modern city of Allahabad. Taking bath at the Trivenī at the astrologically auspicious time assures the worshiper liberation from the cycle of birth and death. The other three Kumbha-melās take place at Haridwar, Nasik, and Ujjain.

kuṇḍa A lake or pond; often refers to one of the sacred ponds in Vṛndāvana.

Kuntī (Pṛthā) One of King Pāṇḍu's two wives. With the help of various demigods, she became the mother of Karṇa, Yudhiṣṭhira, Bhīma, and Arjuna.

kurtā A long loose-fitting collarless Indian-style shirt.

Kurukṣetra "The holy field of the Kurus," where in ancient times the members of that dynasty performed sacrifices. Lord Kṛṣṇa spoke the *Bhagavad-gītā* to Arjuna there, just moments before the start of the great battle.

lakh One hundred thousand.

Lalitā (-devī) One of Śrīmatī Rādhārāṇī's principal direct expansions and most intimate friends. She is Rādhārāṇī's chief companion and, being slightly older than Rādhā, Her advisor on appropriate behavior.

Laṅkā The demon Rāvaṇa's island kingdom (or, also, his capital), often identified with the modern country of Sri Lanka. Rāvaṇa's kingdom was destroyed by Lord Rāmacandra's army.

līlā "Pastimes," the eternal activities of the Supreme Lord in loving reciprocation with His devotees. Unlike the affairs of materially conditioned souls, the Lord's *līlās* are not restricted by the laws of nature or impelled by the reactions of past deeds.

loka Planet.

Mādhāi See *Jagāi*.

Madhva (-ācārya) The founding *ācārya* of the modern-day Vaiṣṇava *sampradāya* originally started by Lord Brahmā. He appeared in the thirteenth century as a Karnataka *brāhmaṇa*, taught a strictly theistic version of *Vedānta* philosophy, vigorously opposed the *Advaita-vāda* of Śaṅkarācārya, and established the worship of Śrī Kṛṣṇa at Uḍupī.

mādhurya (-bhāva, -rasa) The mellow of devotional service to Kṛṣṇa in conjugal love, one of the five primary relationships with Kṛṣṇa.

mahājana A "great person," one who understands the Absolute Truth and acts accordingly; especially when capitalized, any one of the twelve great self-realized souls, authorized agents of the Lord, whose duty is to preach and exemplify the principles of devotional service for the benefit of the people.

mahā-mantra The great chant for deliverance: Hare Kṛṣṇa, Hare Kṛṣṇa, Kṛṣṇa Kṛṣṇa, Hare Hare/ Hare Rāma, Hare Rāma, Rāma Rāma, Hare Hare.

Mahāprabhu Supreme master of all masters; refers to Lord Caitanya.

mahā-prasāda The sanctified remnants of food offered directly to the Supreme Lord and left by Him for the benefit of His devotees.

Mahārāja "Great ruler," a term of address for kings, renounced holy men, and *brāhmaṇas*.

Mahā-viṣṇu The first of the three Puruṣas. He lies in the Causal Ocean on the bed of Ananta Śeṣa and glances at His personified material energy, Māyā, to initiate the creation.

mahotsava A great festival.

Mākhana-cora Kṛṣṇa, the butter thief.

Mānasī-gaṅgā A sacred lake situated at the midpoint of Govardhana Hill. Kṛṣṇa created it from His mind and filled it with the waters of the Gaṅgā and other holy lakes and rivers.

maṅgala-ārati In Deity worship, the first *ārati* of the day, performed an hour and a half before sunrise.

mantra "That which delivers the mind," a sacred invocation chanted to purify the mind and fulfill various aspirations.

Manus The original progenitors and lawgivers of the human race. In each day of Brahmā there are fourteen Manus.

manvantara The period of a Manu's reign, lasting 306,720,000 years.

Mathurā (-dhāma, -maṇḍala, -purī) The eternal abode in which Kṛṣṇa manifests Himself as the Lord of the Yādavas. During His descent to earth, Kṛṣṇa reclaimed Mathurā for the Yādavas by killing Kaṁsa and installing Ugrasena on the throne. Kṛṣṇa resided in Mathurā for thirty-three years before relocating the Yādavas to Dvārakā.

mathurā-vāsa "Residing in Mathurā"—one of the five most potent forms of devotional service.

māṭi Dirt, earth (sand), or clay.

Māyā The Supreme Lord's inferior, material energy; she keeps the conditioned souls in countless varieties of illusion.

Māyāvāda The impersonal philosophy of "oneness" that holds that the Absolute Truth, one without a second, is formless and changeless and that whatever has name and form is an illusion imposed on that Truth.

Māyāpur A village in West Bengal, India, where Lord Caitanya appeared.

Māyāvādī A proponent of the impersonal Māyāvāda philosophy.

mlecchas Uncivilized humans, generally meat-eaters, who are outside the Vedic social system.

mokṣa (mukti) Liberation from the cycle of birth and death.

mūḍhā Fool, rascal.

Muktā-carita A book by Raghunātha dāsa Gosvāmī.

mukti See *mokṣa*.

Mura The five-headed demon employed by Narakāsura to guard his capital, Prāgjyotiṣa-pura (which exists today as Tejpur in Assam). When Kṛṣṇa invaded the city, He killed Mura and then Naraka.

Murāri Kṛṣṇa, the enemy of the demon Mura.

nāmābhāsa The "reflection of the Lord's names." Refers to chanting done without offense but also without love. *Nāmābhāsa* earns one immediate freedom from sinful reactions and liberation from material existence. Synonyms for *ābhāsa* include "glimpse," "hint," "semblance," and "shadow."

nāma-kīrtana The chanting of the holy name.

Nanda Mahārāja The king of the cowherds of Vraja. He and his wife Yaśodā, who are the greatest of devotees in the mood of parents, raised Kṛṣṇa from His infancy until He left Vraja for Mathurā.

Nārada (-muni) One of the principal associates of Lord Nārāyaṇa. He travels throughout the spiritual and material worlds glorifying the Lord and preaching pure devotional service, and he reveals confidential information to various parties to advance the Supreme Lord's pastimes.

Nārāyaṇa Viṣṇu; the Personality of Godhead as the Lord of Vaikuṇṭha, the infinitely opulent spiritual world.

Narottama dāsa Ṭhākura A renowned sixteenth-century Vaiṣṇava spiritual master in the disciplic succession from Śrī Caitanya Mahāprabhu, most famous for his many devotional songs. He was the initiated disciple of Lokanātha Gosvāmī and studied under Jīva Gosvāmī and preached widely throughout India.

Navadvīpa (-dhāma) Lord Caitanya Mahāprabhu's eternal abode, nondifferent from Kṛṣṇa's Vṛndāvana abode. On earth, Navadvīpa is located in the district of Nadia, West Bengal.

Nawab Hussain Shah Officially known as Ālāuddīna Saiyada Husena Sāha Seripha Makkā, he ruled Bengal for twenty-three years, from 1420 to 1443 Śakā Era (1498 to 1521 CE).

Nectar of Devotion Śrīla Prabhupāda's summary study of Rūpa Gosvāmī's *Bhakti-rasāmṛta-sindhu*.

Nectar of Instruction Śrīla Prabhupāda's translation, with elaborate purports, of Rūpa Gosvāmī's *Upadeśāmṛta*.

nirākāra Formless.

Nityānanda The principal associate of Lord Caitanya, He is the incarnation of Lord Balarāma.

Nṛsiṁha (-deva) The pastime incarnation of the Supreme Lord Viṣṇu as half-man half-lion. He appeared in order to deliver the saintly child Prahlāda from the persecutions of his demonic father, Hiraṇyakaśipu. When Hiraṇyakaśipu demanded of Prahlāda, "If your god is everywhere, is he also in this pillar?" Lord Nṛsiṁha burst out of the pillar and ripped Hiraṇyakaśipu apart.

Padma Purāṇa One of the eighteen major *Purāṇas*, which consists of a conversation between Lord Śiva and his wife Pārvati.

pakorā A bite-size chunk of vegetable dipped in spicy batter and deep-fried in ghee or oil.

paṇḍāl "Tent"; often refers to religious programs and lectures held under large tents.

Pāṇḍavas The five sons of Pāṇḍu. The three older Pāṇḍavas—Yudhiṣṭhira, Bhīma, and Arjuna—were born to Pāṇḍu's wife Kuntī through the agency of the three demigods Yamarāja, Vāyu, and Indra. The other two sons, Nakula and Sahadeva, were born of Pāṇḍu's other wife, Mādrī, through the agency of the Aśvinī-kumāras.

paṇḍita A scholar learned in Vedic literature, not only academically but also by dint of spiritual realization. The term is also loosely applied to any type of scholar.

parakīya (-bhāva, -rasa) The mellow of the *gopīs'* paramour relationship with Kṛṣṇa, a subdivision of *mādhurya (-bhāva, -rasa)*.

paramahaṁsa "Perfect swan," a completely pure devotee of the Supreme Lord, beyond any influence of material illusion.

Paramātmā The Supersoul, the expansion of the Supreme Lord in the heart, who accompanies every conditioned soul as indwelling witness and guide.

paramparā Literally, "one after the other"; an authorized Vaiṣṇava disciplic succession; more ordinarily, a lineage passing down a tradition.

Paraśurāma An empowered incarnation of Lord Kṛṣṇa. He appeared as a *brāhmaṇa* but had the qualities of a warrior. When Paraśurāma's father was killed by the wicked king Kārtavīrya, Paraśurāma vowed to exterminate all the degraded *kṣatriyas* on earth, and he fulfilled that vow twenty-one times, destroying twenty-one consecutive generations of lawless members of the ruling class.

parikramā 1. Circumambulation of a sacred area, site, deity, or saintly person.
2. A journey, usually by foot, to various sites of pilgrimage.

Parīkṣit The son of Abhimanyu who inherited the Kuru throne from Yudhiṣṭhira. Kṛṣṇa personally saved him in his mother's womb, and thus the child was named Parīkṣit, because throughout his life he kept searching (*parīkṣeta*) for the person who had protected him.

Prabodhānanda Sarasvatī A Vaiṣṇava author and devotee of Śrī Caitanya Mahāprabhu.

Prabhu "Master." Used as a form of address or added to a devotee's name to show respect.

Prabhupāda "One at whose feet (*pāda*) are many devotees (*prabhus*)," an honorific title used to designate or address an *ācārya*.

Prabhupāda (Śrīla) See (as used in this book) A.C. *Bhaktivedanta Swami Prabhupāda.*

Prahlāda One of the greatest devotees of Lord Viṣṇu. As the five-year-old son of the mighty demon Hiraṇyakaśipu, he dared to openly worship the Personality of Godhead and preach His glories. Hiraṇyakaśipu tried many ways to kill the boy but failed to harm him. Finally, Lord Viṣṇu appeared as Lord Nṛsiṁha, killed Hiraṇyakaśipu, and enthroned Prahlāda as king of the demons.

praṇāma-mantra An offering of respect conveyed by a short verbal expression praising the qualities and achievements of the honored person.

prasāda (prasādam) The sanctified remnants of food or other items that have been offered to the Supreme Lord. By accepting Kṛṣṇa's *prasāda*, one can rapidly become purified and achieve pure love of God.

prema Pure ecstatic love of God.

Pṛthu An empowered incarnation of the Supreme Lord, who appeared as an ideal king and brought forth the resources of the earth.

pūjā Formal worship of the Supreme Lord, a demigod, or a respected person.

pūjārī A devotee who performs direct worship of a deity.

Purāṇas Eighteen major and eighteen minor Vedic texts recounting histories from the earth and other planets, compiled five thousand years ago by Dvaipāyana Vyāsa.

Purī (Jagannātha Purī, Nīlācala, Nīlādri) A holy city in Orissa, on the Bay of Bengal, where Lord Jagannātha resides.

Puruṣa The Supreme Lord in a Viṣṇu expansion for the creation of the material world.

puṣpa-samādhi A memorial in which the flowers worn by a departed spiritual master or saintly devotee are enshrined and worshiped.

Pūtanā An infanticidal witch who entered Vraja disguised as a beautiful woman and offered the child Kṛṣṇa her poisonous breast milk, which He sucked out along with her life. Thus killed by Kṛṣṇa, Pūtanā was elevated to Kṛṣṇa's eternal service in the mood of a mother.

Rādhā (-rāṇī, Rādhikā) The personification of Kṛṣṇa's original pleasure potency, from whom all His internal energies expand. She is His eternal consort in Vṛndāvana and the most exalted and beloved of His devotees.

Rādhā-kuṇḍa The bathing place of Śrīmatī Rādhārāṇī; a sacred pond near Govardhana Hill created by Rādhārāṇī and Her *gopī* companions. It is the supreme holy place of Vraja, especially worshipable for Gauḍīya Vaiṣṇavas. The seven major Gauḍīya Vaiṣṇava temples of Vṛndāvana also exist there, as well as *bhajana-kutīras* of many Gauḍīya Vaiṣṇava *ācāryas*. Rādhā-kuṇḍa is the site of the most intimate loving affairs of Śrī Śrī Rādhā-Kṛṣṇa, and her waters are considered nondifferent from Rādhārāṇī Herself and bestow love of Godhead.

Rādhā-Rādhānātha 1. Rādhā and Kṛṣṇa, the Lord of Śrīmatī Rādhārāṇī.
2. The Rādhā-Kṛṣṇa Deities in the ISKCON temple in Chatsworth, Durban, South Africa.

Rādhā-Rāsabihārī 1. Rādhā and Kṛṣṇa, the enjoyer of the *rāsa* dance.
2. The Rādhā-Kṛṣṇa Deities at Hare Krishna Land, Juhu, Mumbai, India.

Rādhāṣṭamī The festival celebrating Rādhārāṇī's appearance day.

Raghunātha Bhaṭṭa Gosvāmī One of the Six Gosvāmīs of Vṛndāvana, especially well-known for sweetly singing the *Bhāgavatam* and never hearing or speaking about worldly topics or criticism of Vaiṣṇavas.

Raghunātha dāsa Gosvāmī One of the Six Gosvāmīs of Vṛndāvana, born around 1494 CE in Bengal. His forefathers were all Vaiṣṇavas and very rich men. Raghunātha dāsa was a family man, but he had no attachment to his estate or wife and tried many times to run away from home. He finally managed to escape his father's vigilance and in 1517 CE went to Jagannātha Purī to meet Śrī Caitanya Mahāprabhu. He resided for most of his life at Rādhā-kuṇḍa and wrote three books, *Stava-mālā* (or *Stavāvalī*), *Dāna-carita*, and *Muktā-carita*. His only concern was to engage in the service of the Lord, and he gradually reduced his eating and sleeping to almost nil. The *Gaura-gaṇoddeśa-dīpikā* (186) states that Raghunātha dāsa Gosvāmī was formerly the *gopī* named Rasa-mañjarī and that sometimes it is said that he was Rati-mañjarī.

rajo-guṇa The mode of passion, one of the three modes of material nature, which leads to ambition and fruitive activity.

Rāma (-candra) Incarnation of the Supreme Lord as a perfect, righteous king, born as the son of Daśaratha and Kauśalya. Rāma is also a name of Lord Kṛṣṇa, meaning "the source of all pleasure," and a name of Lord Balarāma and of Lord Paraśurāma.

Rāmānanda Rāya An intimate associate of Śrī Caitanya Mahāprabhu in His later pastimes.

Rāmānuja (-ācārya) The founding—and most prominent—*ācārya* of the Śrī- (Lakṣmī-) sampradāya, one of the four Vaiṣṇava *sampradāyas* in Kali-yuga.

rasa Transcendental taste, or mellow; the boundless pleasure enjoyed in one of the five primary relationships with Kṛṣṇa: reverence, servanthood, friendship, parental affection, and conjugal love.

rāsa (-līlā) Kṛṣṇa's divine dance with the young *gopīs*, the grand celebration of their conjugal love.

rasagullā A Bengali sweet consisting of balls of fresh curd cooked and soaked in sugar syrup.

Ratha-yātrā The yearly festival in Purī during which Lord Jagannātha travels on His cart from the Nīlācala temple to the Guṇḍicā temple, which represents Vṛndāvana. His brother Balarāma and sister Subhadrā accompany Him on their respective carts. Lord Caitanya would observe this Guṇḍicā-yātrā with great festivity. Ratha-yātrā festivals are now held throughout the world.

Rati-mañjarī A maidservant of Śrīmatī Rādhārāṇī who assists Rūpa-mañjarī.

Rāvaṇa The demonic king of Laṇkā who conquered the universe and abducted the wife of Lord Rāma, who then invaded his kingdom and killed him.

Rūpa Gosvāmī One of the Six Gosvāmīs of Vṛndāvana and the prime authority on the science of *rasa*, loving exchanges with God, which he expounded in his *Bhakti-rasāmṛta-sindhu* and *Ujjvala-nīlamaṇi*. He was also an eminent playwright and poet. Many Gauḍīya Vaiṣṇavas consider themselves *rūpānugas*, followers of Rūpa Gosvāmī.

Rūpa-mañjarī Rūpa Gosvāmī's form as a *gopī-mañjarī*, the leader of the maidservants of Śrī Rādhā.

Śacī (-devī, -mātā) The mother of Lord Caitanya Mahāprabhu and wife of Jagannātha Miśra of Navadvīpa.

sac-cid-ānanda "Eternal existence, knowledge, and bliss," the constitutional nature of the Supreme Lord and of the finite living beings. The Supreme Lord's *sac-cid-ānanda* nature is always manifest, whereas that of the *jīvas* is covered by material illusion when they turn away from the Lord.

Ṣaḍ-gosvāmy-aṣṭaka A prayer of eight verses by Śrīnivāsa Ācārya in glorification of the Six Gosvāmīs of Vṛndāvana.

sādhana-bhakti Devotional service in practice, performed with the senses, by which ecstatic love for the Supreme Lord is awakened.

sādhu A saintly person.

sādhu-saṅga The association of saintly persons, especially more advanced devotees.

Śaivites Devotees of Lord Śiva.

sakhya (-bhāva, -rasa) The mellow of devotional service to Kṛṣṇa in friendship, one of five primary relationships with Kṛṣṇa.

sakhyam One of the nine processes of devotional service, "becoming the friend." Also, see *sakhya*.

samādhi 1. Fully matured meditation, the last of the eight steps of the *yoga* system taught by Patañjali. A perfected devotee of the Supreme Lord also achieves *samādhi*.

2. The tomb where the body of a spiritually advanced soul is laid after his departure from this world.

sampradāya A disciplic succession of spiritual masters, along with the followers in that tradition, through which spiritual knowledge is transmitted; a school of thought.

Sanātana Gosvāmī One of the Six Gosvāmīs of Vṛndāvana, the older brother and *śikṣā-guru* of Rūpa Gosvāmī and author of *Śrī Bṛhad-bhāgavatāmṛta*.

sanātha "With a fitting master"; one who is protected.

Śaṅkarācārya The most influential teacher of Māyāvāda philosophy. According to the *Padma Purāṇa*, he is an incarnation of Lord Śiva sent to earth in Kali-yuga by Kṛṣṇa to bewilder the atheists by distorting the teachings of *Vedānta*.

saṅkīrtana Congregational chanting of the names and glories of Kṛṣṇa—the *yuga-dharma*, or prime means for spiritual success, in the Age of Kali.

sannyāsa The renounced order of life, the final stage in the *varṇāśrama* system.

sannyāsī A man in the renounced order. *Sannyāsīs* take a vow of lifelong celibacy.

Sanskrit The oldest language in the world; the language of the *Vedas*.

śaraṇāgati 1. Surrender.
2. *capitalized* A set of poems composed by Bhaktivinoda Ṭhākura.

śāstra Revealed scripture; an authorized textbook on any subject.

sat Eternal, unlimited existence.

sattva-guṇa The mode of goodness, one of the three modes of material nature, characterized by knowledge, purity, peace.

śikhā A tuft of hair at the back of the head, marking one as a devotee of Kṛṣṇa.

śikṣā-guru Instructing spiritual master.

Śikṣāṣṭaka Eight (*aṣṭa*) verses composed by Śrī Caitanya Mahāprabhu, glorifying the Lord's holy names and instructing (*śikṣā*) the reader how to chant them and advance in Kṛṣṇa consciousness.

Śiva A special expansion of the Supreme Lord, who is uniquely neither God nor *jīva*, but "almost God." He is God (Viṣṇu) in contact with the material nature. He energizes the material creation and, as the presiding deity of the mode of ignorance, controls the forces of destruction.

śiva-liṅga A rounded stone symbolizing Lord Śiva's creative potency, often worshiped by Śaivites.

Śiva Purāṇa One of the eighteen major *Purāṇas*.

Six Gosvāmīs Direct followers of Śrī Caitanya Mahāprabhu who systematically presented His teachings and excavated holy places in Vṛndāvana.

śloka A Sanskrit verse.

śraddhā Faith.

śravaṇa (śravaṇam) The primary devotional practice of hearing the glories of the Supreme Lord.

Śrī A name for Lakṣmī, the goddess of fortune, the eternal consort of the Supreme Lord Nārāyaṇa. Also, a term of respect used before the names of Deities, revered texts, respectable persons, and sacred objects.

Śrīdhara Svāmī The author of the earliest extant Vaiṣṇava commentaries on the *Bhagavad-gītā* and *Śrīmad-Bhāgavatam*. He taught pure Vaiṣṇava philosophy and worshiped Lord Nṛsiṁhadeva. Lord Caitanya declared that anyone who wants to write a commentary on *Śrīmad-Bhāgavatam* must follow Śrīdhara Svāmī's.

Śrī-guru-vandanā A song from *Prema-bhakti-candrikā* by Śrīla Narottama dāsa Ṭhākura.

Śrīla "Endowed by the goddess of fortune," a respectful title used by Gauḍīya Vaiṣṇavas for their spiritual masters.

Śrīmad-Bhāgavatam The "beautiful story of the Personality of Godhead," also known as the *amala-purāṇa*, the completely pure, "spotless *Purāṇa*," which teaches unalloyed devotional service to Kṛṣṇa, the original Supreme Personality of Godhead.

Śrīmān "Having the favors of the goddess of fortune," an honorific title preceding the name of a respected male. It also means "very beautiful."

Śrīmatī The female form of the title Śrīmān.

Sudāmā (-Vipra) A schoolmate of Kṛṣṇa's who later, being impelled by his wife's entreaties, visited Kṛṣṇa in Dvārakā to ask for aid. When he returned home without having asked, he found his poor hut transformed into a palace.

śūdra A member of the laborer class, the fourth of the four occupational classes in the *varṇāśrama* social system.

Śukadeva Gosvāmī A great renounced sage, son of Dvaipāyana Vyāsa. He heard *Śrīmad-Bhāgavatam* from his father and later repeated it to Mahārāja Parīkṣit.

Supersoul Paramātmā, an expansion of the Supreme Lord that pervades the universe and dwells in the heart of every living entity.

Supreme Personality of Godhead The Supreme Lord Kṛṣṇa (and His direct expansions).

Sutala (-loka) Among the seven subterranean heavens, the third closest to the earth. Bali Mahārāja lives there, with Vāmana as the guard at his gate.

svāmī (swami) One who controls his senses; title of one in the renounced order of life.

Svarga (-loka) The heavenly domain (above Bhuvarloka) of Indra, king of the demigods.

Śyāmasundara A name of Kṛṣṇa meaning "blackish" (*śyāma*) and "beautiful" (*sundara*).

tamo-guṇa The mode of darkness, or ignorance—one of the three modes of material nature. It causes delusion, foolishness, and inertia.

tapasya Austerity; voluntary acceptance of some material trouble for progress in spiritual life.

tilaka Sacred clay markings placed on the forehead and other parts of the body to designate one as a follower of Viṣṇu, Rāma, Śiva, Vedic culture, etc.

titikṣavaḥ Tolerant.

transcendental Above the modes of material nature.

Tṛṇāvarta A demon friend of Kaṁsa's who assumed the form of a whirlwind and entered Vraja to kill Kṛṣṇa but instead was killed by Him.

tulasī The sacred plant most dear to Kṛṣṇa. *Tulasī* is an expansion of the *gopī* Vṛndā. Without the leaves of the *tulasī* plant, offerings of food and worship to Lord Viṣṇu are incomplete.

tyāga Renunciation.

Uddhava One of Kṛṣṇa's closest friends, His most confidential advisor in Mathurā and Dvārakā.

Upadeśāmṛta A practical guide to the development of Kṛṣṇa consciousness composed by Rūpa Gosvāmī. It was translated into English and commented upon by Śrīla Prabhupāda in *The Nectar of Instruction.*

Upaniṣads The philosophical chapters of the *Vedas*, organized into one hundred and eight books. They are also called *Vedānta*, meaning "the culmination of Vedic knowledge," and were explained by Dvaipāyana Vyāsa in his *Vedānta-sūtra.*

uttama-adhikārī A first-class devotee who is expert in knowledge of Vedic literature and has full faith in the Supreme Lord.

vaḍa Savory fried dumplings.

Vaikuṇṭha (-loka) "The place free from anxiety"; the kingdom of God, full of all opulences and unlimited by time and space.

vairāgya Detachment.

Vaiṣṇava (Vaiṣṇavite) A devotee of the Supreme Lord Viṣṇu. Since Kṛṣṇa and Viṣṇu are different aspects of the same Supreme Person, devotees of Kṛṣṇa are also Vaiṣṇavas.

vaiśya A member of the third among the four occupational divisions of the *varṇāśrama* social system. *Vaiśyas* are farmers, bankers, and businessmen.

Vālmīki The sage who composed the *Rāmāyaṇa.* At first a vicious criminal, Vālmīki became purified by unintentionally chanting the name Rāma.

Vāmana (-deva) Lord Viṣṇu's form as a young *brāhmaṇa* boy, one of the *daśa-avatāras*, ten famous incarnations of the Lord. After begging three steps of land from Bali Mahārāja, Vāmanadeva covered the entire universe with His first two steps, and for the third step Bali offered his own head. Pleased with Bali's surrender, Lord Vāmana offered to become the guard at Bali's door.

vānaprastha Retired life, the third stage in the *varṇāśrama* social system, in which a man, sometimes together with his wife, gives up the *gṛhastha-āśrama* and visits holy places of pilgrimage or resides in a forest or holy place; a person in the *vānaprastha-āśrama.*

vandanaṁ The devotional process of offering prayers and obeisance to the Lord.

Varāha (-deva) Lord Viṣṇu's incarnation as a huge boar, who killed the demon Hiraṇyākṣa and lifted the earth from the depths of the Garbhodaka Ocean.

varṇāśrama (-dharma) The Vedic social system, consisting of four occupational divisions (*varṇas*) and four spiritual stages (*āśramas*).

Varuṇa The demigod who presides over water and the oceans.

Vasudeva Kṛṣṇa's father in Mathurā and Dvārakā.

Vāsudeva Kṛṣṇa, the son of Vasudeva. Vāsudeva is also the name of Kṛṣṇa's first expansion outside Gokula, and of the first of the quadruple expansions in Vaikuṇṭha.

vātsalya (-bhāva, -rasa) The mood of parental affection toward Kṛṣṇa, one of the five primary relationships with Him.

Vedānta-sūtra A concise systematic explanation of the *Upaniṣads*, written by Dvaipāyana Vyāsa and commented upon by the impersonalist Śaṇkara and by great Vaiṣṇava *ācāryas* such as Rāmānuja, Madhva, and Baladeva Vidyābhūṣana.

Vedas The original revealed scriptures, eternal like the Supreme Lord, and thus authorless. Because in Kali-yuga the *Vedas* are difficult to understand or even study, the *Purāṇas* and epic histories, especially *Śrīmad-Bhāgavatam*, are essential for gaining access to their teachings.

Vedic Pertaining to the *Vedas* or, more broadly, following or derived from their authority.

vigraha "Form." Often refers to a temple deity (*arcā-vigraha*).

Virajā River The river that divides the material world from the spiritual world.

viṣaya Materialistic activities.

Viṣṇu The Supreme Lord in His opulent feature as the Lord of Vaikuṇṭha, who expands into countless forms and incarnations.

Viṣṇudūtas The messengers of Lord Viṣṇu, similar to Him in appearance, who protect devotees within the world and take perfected devotees to Vaikuṇṭha at the time of death.

viṣṇu-tattvas The Supreme Personality of Godhead and His direct expansions.

Viśvanātha Cakravartī A prominent seventeenth-century Gauḍīya Vaiṣṇava *ācārya* in the line of Narottama dāsa Ṭhākura, and a *śikṣā-guru* of Baladeva Vidyābhūṣaṇa. He wrote commentaries on the *Bhagavad-gītā* and *Śrīmad-Bhāgavatam* and on books by important followers of Śrī Caitanya Mahāprabhu.

Vraja (-bhūmi, -dhāma) The eternal place of Kṛṣṇa's pastimes with the cowherds, manifest on earth in the district of Mathurā.

Vraja-vāsīs The residents of Vṛndāvana.

Vṛkāsura A demonic worshiper of Śiva who tried to kill him but was ultimately killed by Lord Kṛṣṇa.

Vṛndāvana Kṛṣṇa's most beloved forest in Vraja-bhūmi, where He enjoys pastimes with the cowherd boys and the young *gopīs*; also, the entirety of Vraja.

Vyāsa (-deva) See *Dvaipāyana Vyāsa*.

vyāsāsana "The seat of Vyāsa," a special seat reserved for the spiritual master, the representative of Vyāsadeva.

Wardha A town near Nagpur in the Indian state of Maharashtra.

Yama (-rāja) The judge of sinful persons at death.

Yamunā The holiest of rivers, flowing through Vraja-bhūmi, and in which Kṛṣṇa enjoyed many youthful pastimes. The Yamunā personified is also known as Kālindī, who after Kṛṣṇa established His capital at Dvārakā became one of His eight principal queens.

Yāmunācārya Also known as Ālabandāru, he was born as a king and later became a great *ācārya* in the Śrī-sampradāya and the spiritual master of Rāmānujācārya.

Yaśodā (Yaśodāmayī) Kṛṣṇa's mother in Vraja. She raised Him from infancy until He moved to Mathurā. She is the most exalted of Kṛṣṇa's devotees in *vātsalya-rasa*.

yoga "Yoking," a spiritual process for linking oneself with the Supreme. There are various kinds of *yoga*, including *karma-yoga* (the offering of the fruits of one's work for the pleasure of the Supreme), *jñāna-yoga* (the cultivation of spiritual knowledge of the soul and Supersoul), *aṣṭāṅga-yoga* (the eightfold process of meditation taught by Patañjali), and *bhakti-yoga* (pure devotional service to the Personality of Godhead).

Yogamāyā Kṛṣṇa's spiritual illusory energy. Under her influence, Kṛṣṇa and His associates forget that He is God and enjoy humanlike pastimes. When Kṛṣṇa descends to earth, Yogamāyā appears as His sister Subhadrā and as Paurṇamāsī. Her partial expansion is Mahāmāyā, the material illusory energy.

Yogeśvara The supreme master of *yoga*, Kṛṣṇa.

yogī A practitioner of *yoga*.

Yudhiṣṭhira The eldest of the five Pāṇḍavas, the sons of Pāṇḍu. At Pāṇḍu's request he was begotten in Pāṇḍu's wife Kuntī by Yamarāja, the maintainer of religious principles. Thus Yudhiṣṭhira strictly performed religious duties all his life and could never say anything untrue. He was installed as emperor of the world at the end of the Battle of Kurukṣetra.

yuga-dharma The recommended spiritual process, or *dharma*, for each age.

yukta-vairāgya Befitting renunciation, in which one appropriately uses material sense objects in the service of the Supreme Lord, Kṛṣṇa.

Sanskrit Pronunciation Guide

Throughout the centuries, the Sanskrit language has been written in a variety of alphabets. The mode of writing most widely used throughout India, however, is called *devanāgarī*, which means, literally, the writing used in "the cities of the demigods." The *devanāgarī* alphabet consists of forty-eight characters: thirteen vowels and thirty-five consonants. Ancient Sanskrit grammarians arranged this alphabet according to practical linguistic principles, and this order has been accepted by all Western scholars. The system of transliteration used in this book conforms to a system that scholars have accepted to indicate the pronunciation of each Sanskrit sound.

VOWELS

a	ā	i	ī	u	ū	ṛ
ṝ	ḷ	ai	o	au		

CONSONANTS

Gutturals:	**ka**	**kha**	**ga**	**gha**	**ṅa**
Palatals:	**ca**	**cha**	**ja**	**jha**	**ña**
Cerebrals:	**ṭa**	**ṭha**	**ḍa**	**ḍha**	**ṇa**
Dentals:	**ta**	**tha**	**da**	**dha**	**na**
Labials:	**pa**	**pha**	**ba**	**bha**	**ma**
Semivowels:	**ya**	**ra**	**la**	**va**	
Sibilants:	**śa**	**ṣa**	**sa**		
Aspirate:	**ha**	Anusvara: **- ṁ**	Visarga: **ḥ**		

NUMERALS

0	1	2	3	4	5	6	7	8	9

The vowels are written as follows after a consonant:

ā	i	ī	u	ū	ṛ	ṝ	e	ai	o	au

For example:	**ka**	**kā**	**ki**	**kī**	**ku**	**kū**
kṛ	**kṝ**	**kḷ**	**ke**	**kai**	**ko**	**kau**

Generally two or more consonants in conjunction are written together in a special form, as for example: **kṣa tra**. The vowel **"a"** is implied after a consonant with no vowel symbol. The symbol *virāma* indicates that there is no final vowel.

THE VOWELS ARE PRONOUNCED AS FOLLOWS:

a — as in but
ā — as in far but held twice as long as **a**
i — as in pin
ī — as in pique but held twice as long as **i**
u — as in push
ū — as in rule but held twice as long as **u**
ṛ — as in rim
ṝ — as in reed but held twice as long as **r**
ḷ — as in happily
e — as in they
ai — as in aisle
o — as in go
au — as in how

THE CONSONANTS ARE PRONOUNCED AS FOLLOWS:

Gutturals
(pronounced from the throat)
k — as in kite
kh — as in Eckhart
g — as in give
gh — as in dig-hard
ṅ — as in sing
ñ — as in canyon

Palatals
(pronounced with the middle of the tongue against the palate)
c — as in chair
ch — as in staunch-heart
j — as in joy
jh — as in hedgehog

Cerebrals
(pronounced with the tip of the tongue against the roof of the mouth)
ṭ — as in tub
ṭh — as in light-heart
ḍ — as in dove
ḍh — as in red-hot
ṇ — as in sing

Dentals
(pronounced like the cerebrals but with the tongue against the teeth)
t — as in tub
h — as in light-heart
d — as in dove
dh — as in red-hot
n — as in nut

Labials
(pronounced with the lips)
p — as in pine
ph — as in up-hill

Semivowels
y — as in yes
r — as in run
l — as in light

b — as in **b**ird
bh — as in ru**b-h**ard
m — as in **m**other
v — as in vine, except when preceded in the same syllable by a consonant, then as in swan

Sibilants
ś — as in the German word *sprechen*
ṣ — as in shine
s — as in sun

Aspirate
h — as in home

Anusvara
ṁ — a resonant nasal sound as in the French word *bon*

Visarga
ḥ — a final h-sound: aḥ is pronounced like aha; iḥ like ihi.

There is no strong accentuation of syllables in Sanskrit, or pausing between words in a line, only a flowing of short and long syllables (the long twice as long as the short). A long syllable is one whose vowel is long (**ā, ī, ū, ṝ, e, ai, o, au**) or whose short vowel is followed by more than one consonant. The letters **ḥ** and **ṁ** count as consonants. Aspirated consonants (consonants followed by an **h**) count as single consonants.

Abbreviations

Books of His Divine Grace A.C. Bhaktivedanta Swami Prabhupāda:

Bg—Bhagavad-gītā
Cc *Ādi—Śrī Caitanya-caritāmṛta Ādi-līlā*
Cc *Madhya—Śrī Caitanya-caritāmṛta Madhya-līlā*
Cc *Antya—Śrī Caitanya-caritāmṛta Antya-līlā*
NOI—The Nectar of Instruction
SB—Śrīmad-Bhāgavatam

Other works:

Brs—Bhakti-rasāmṛta-sindhu by Śrīla Rūpa Gosvāmī
Bs—Bhakti-sandarbha by Śrīla Jīva Gosvāmī
Cb—Caitanya-bhāgavata by Śrīla Vṛndāvana dāsa Ṭhākura

General Index

A

B

G

H

on book distribution, 170, 253
on brotherhood, 72
on business, 238–239
on chanting Hare Kṛṣṇa, 65, 241, 243–244
on chanting sixteen rounds, 23–25, 243–244
on collecting, 233–234
on cultivating important people, 201
on dancing in *kīrtana*, 238
on dealing with big men, 38
on decor for restaurant, 239
on difficulties at Hare Krishna Land, 134
on disciples' affection for him, 256
on eagerness, 187
on enthusiasm, 177
on falldown of leaders, 205
on foreign devotees, 238
on getting life members, 215–216
on getting what he wants, 227
on Giriraj's simplicity, 41
on *gurukula* education, 234–235
on Hare Krishna Land, 237
on his books in universities, 197
on his contribution, 22
on his disciples, 119
on his money in New York, 87
on his reason for going to America, 138
on his style of preaching, 202
on holidays, 187
on hospitals, 84
on increasing book distribution, 174
on *kīrtana*, 135
on Kṛṣṇa's mercy, 214
on liking everybody, 37
on making movies, 201
on management and managing, 199, 249, 254
on managing or preaching, 201
on marriage, 197
on message of the *Gītā*, 250–253
on misrepresentation of the *Gītā*, 18–19, 250–253
on new girls, 249
on not leaving ISKCON, 202
on people's own ideas of spiritual life 17
on pleasing Kṛṣṇa, 217
on politicians, 241
on prayer for health, 46
on preaching the *Bhagavad-gītā*, 18, 250–253
on protection, 60
on rejecting disciples, 94
on remaining a *sādhu*, 129
on remembering, 240
on satiation, 107
on selling tickets, 233
on sex attraction, 241
on sex desire, 197
on spontaneous Vaiṣṇavism, 216–217
on surrender, 23–24
on sweetballs, 108
on the behavior of an educated man, 153
on the holy name, 107
on the Juhu land struggle, 225
on the main medium for

The Author

Giriraj Swami was born Glenn Phillip Teton, the only son of a respected Chicago lawyer. In March of 1969, while studying at Brandeis University in Boston, he met His Divine Grace A.C. Bhaktivedanta Swami Prabhupāda, the founder-*ācārya* of the International Society for Krishna Consciousness, and considered that he learned more from Śrīla Prabhupāda in five minutes than he had learned in his twenty years of academic education. After graduating from Brandeis *cum laude*, Glenn took formal initiation from Śrīla Prabhupāda and was given the spiritual name "Giriraj das." Giriraj quickly became a leading member of the Boston center. He was then given the opportunity to go to India with Śrīla Prabhupāda and helped establish his mission there.

In 1972, after Giriraj had toured India with Śrīla Prabhupāda, Prabhupāda appointed him president of ISKCON Bombay and trustee of the Bhaktivedanta Book Trust. Since then, he has made many significant contributions to Śrīla Prabhupāda's mission, most notably overseeing all aspects of the development of Hare Krishna Land in Juhu, Bombay. He was instrumental in the development of the Bhaktivedanta Ashram in Govardhana and more recently led the development of the Kirtan Ashram for renounced women, the Bhaktivedanta Hospice, and the Vrindavan Institute of Palliative Care, all in Vṛndāvana, India. Through all his efforts, Giriraj Swami has become known for the austerities he has accepted, for his loyalty and dedication to Śrīla Prabhupāda's mission, and for his ability to raise funds and cultivate important members of society.

In the year following Śrīla Prabhupāda's departure in 1977, Giriraj das was awarded the renounced order of life and appointed president of ISKCON's board of trustees in India. In 1982 he was made a member of ISKCON's Governing Body Commission, the ultimate managing authority for the movement, and went on to oversee the Society's activities in Bombay, Mauritius, South Africa, Spain, Portugal, Sri Lanka, and Pakistan.

Giriraj Swami has toured extensively throughout India and many other countries, carrying knowledge of Kṛṣṇa and helping to develop Śrīla Prabhupāda's mission. He has also taught at the Vaiṣṇava Institute for Higher Education in Vṛndāvana and now gives presentations at *japa* retreats and workshops for the Bhagavat Life educational foundation.

Although for the past ten years health considerations have limited his international travels, Giriraj Swami has taken this as an opportunity to focus more on one of Śrīla Prabhupāda's personal instructions: to write. Now based in Southern California, he is a frequent contributor to *Back to Godhead* magazine and is working on several publications, including books about his search for a spiritual master and his early days in the Boston temple, his travels with Śrīla Prabhupāda in India from 1970 to 1972, and Śrīla Prabhupāda's monumental efforts in Bombay.